AF830684

Understanding Financial Crises

Incorporating a broad range of economic approaches, *Understanding Financial Crises* explores the merits of various arguments and theories which have been used to explain the causes of financial crises.

The book explores eight of these different explanations: underconsumption, debt accumulation, financialization, income inequality, financial fragility, tendency of rate of profit to fall, human behavior, and global imbalances. The introduction provides a brief overview of each argument along with a comparison of their relative merits. Each chapter then introduces one of the arguments, explores a historical case, and focuses on the insights that can be gleaned into the global crisis in 2007–2008. The book draws on insights from various schools of thought including post-Keynesian economics, Marxist economics, behavioral economics, neoclassical economics, and more, to provide a pluralist overview of the causes of economic crises in general and the Great Recession in particular.

This book marks a significant contribution to the literature on economic and financial crises, political economy and heterodox economics. It is well suited to academicians, practitioners, and financial analysts working within the relevant fields.

Ensar Yılmaz is a professor at Yıldız Technical University, Istanbul, Turkey, where he teaches in the Department of Economics. He is the author of several articles in the subjects of macroeconomics, financial regulation, income distribution and game theory.

Routledge Frontiers of Political Economy

The Political Economy of Prosperity
Successful Societies and Productive Cultures
Peter Murphy

Macroeconomic Measurement Versus Macroeconomic Theory
Merijn Knibbe

Hayek's Market Republicanism
The Limits of Liberty
Sean Irving

The End of Individualism and the Economy
Emerging Paradigms of Connection and Community
Ann E. Davis

Profit, Accumulation and Crisis in Capitalism
Long-term Trends in UK, US, Japan and China, 1855–2018
Minqi Li

Global Imbalances and Financial Capitalism
Stock-Flow-Consistent Modelling
Jacques Mazier

Markets, Community, and Just Infrastructures
Nancy Neiman

The Informal Economy
Measures, Causes, and Consequences
Ceyhun Elgin

Understanding Financial Crises
Ensar Yılmaz

For more information about this series, please visit:
www.routledge.com/books/series/SE0345

Understanding Financial Crises

Ensar Yılmaz

Routledge
Taylor & Francis Group
LONDON AND NEW YORK

First published 2021
by Routledge
2 Park Square, Milton Park, Abingdon, Oxon OX14 4RN

and by Routledge
52 Vanderbilt Avenue, New York, NY 10017

Routledge is an imprint of the Taylor & Francis Group, an informa business

© 2021 Ensar Yılmaz

The right of Ensar Yılmaz to be identified as author of this work has been asserted by him in accordance with sections 77 and 78 of the Copyright, Designs and Patents Act 1988.

All rights reserved. No part of this book may be reprinted or reproduced or utilised in any form or by any electronic, mechanical, or other means, now known or hereafter invented, including photocopying and recording, or in any information storage or retrieval system, without permission in writing from the publishers.

Trademark notice: Product or corporate names may be trademarks or registered trademarks, and are used only for identification and explanation without intent to infringe.

British Library Cataloguing-in-Publication Data
A catalogue record for this book is available from the British Library

Library of Congress Cataloging-in-Publication Data
Names: Yılmaz, Ensar, 1970– author.
Title: Understanding financial crises / Ensar Yılmaz.
Description: Abingdon, Oxon; New York, NY: Routledge, 2020. |
Series: Routledge frontiers of political economy |
Includes bibliographical references and index.
Identifiers: LCCN 2020012120 (print) | LCCN 2020012121 (ebook)
Subjects: LCSH: Financial crises.
Classification: LCC HB3722 .Y55 2020 (print) |
LCC HB3722 (ebook) | DDC 338.5/42–dc23
LC record available at https://lccn.loc.gov/2020012120
LC ebook record available at https://lccn.loc.gov/2020012121

ISBN: 978-0-367-48067-7 (hbk)
ISBN: 978-1-003-03782-8 (ebk)

Typeset in Bembo
by Newgen Publishing UK

Ji diya min a hezkirî re
(To my beloved mother)

Contents

Figures

Tables

Acknowledgment

This book has had a long gestation, and along the way I have accumulated more intellectual debts than I can remember. I started working on the book during the Fall 2016 semester at Yildiz Technical University. My colleagues and students there thus offered me helpful comments and suggestions, all of which I take very seriously, much of which I accepted, and some of which actually got incorporated into the final draft. Here I would like to acknowledge their valuable suggestions.

For his generous readings and critical feedback on earlier drafts of this volume, I would like to thank Ercan Eren. I would like to thank Zeynep Kaplan for her valuable help. And I would like to thank Ibrahim Engin Kılıç for his tireless support as a research assistant during the early phases of his graduate career.

Finally I would like to thank my family for their love, support and encouragement. Each member of my family has played a particularly important role in keeping me on track.

Introduction

Financial crises are a prevalent phenomenon in history. Even during times when market mechanisms did not exist in the complete sense, financial crises occurred, although not very often. For example, the "Tulip Mania" in 1637 in the Netherlands was a speculative bubble on prices of bulbs, which can be regarded as assets. When the prices of bulbs collapsed, those buying them with debt went bankrupt. From the late 18th century on, when modern capitalism in England began to develop, financial crises became an unavoidable element of capitalist economies. Starting in the 19th century, scholars developed economic theories to understand financial crises.

A financial crisis destroys the normal functions of economic systems, thereby damaging the efficiency of the economy. Despite continuous attempts to prevent crises, they persistently continue to happen regardless of time and space. A capitalist economy eventually recovers from crisis and repeats itself in the future. As Leon Trotsky once noted, *capitalism lives by crises and booms, just as a human being lives by inhaling and exhaling. First there is a boom in industry, then a stoppage, next a crisis, followed by a stoppage in the crisis, then an improvement, another boom, another stoppage, and so on . . . The fact that capitalism continues to oscillate cyclically . . . merely signifies that capitalism is not yet dead, that we are not dealing with a corpse.*

The crises can be regarded as a litmus test for the performance of economics because understanding crises can help us understand the main mechanisms of economies in a broader sense. The crises are a kind of a stress test for economic theory. If an economic theory cannot predict a crisis or cannot see the main problematic issues in the economies that can lead to drastic ruptures, it implies that it does not understand even the normal functioning of an economy. In other words, failings to understand crises generate failings to understand non-crisis times because they are not accidental failings. Failings that might not be so apparent or that can be covered by a residual error term that is "too small to matter" can in fact be a big matter that should be considered. That is, the small matter can be likened to a small crack in the foundation. Hence theoretical frameworks employed to analyze economic systems should pass the test of economic crises as they elaborate their normal functioning.

Most mainstream economists have ignored the systemic character of crises, presenting them as a "black swan" phenomenon, i.e., as a rare and completely unpredictable but massive event. But, in recent years, many economists, even some mainstream economists, have regarded the crises a "white swan" phenomenon instead of black swan one, that is, they think of crises as the outcome of an ordinary, recurring, and predictable process. In recent years, the regularity of crises has been emphasized by countless studies such as in the book *This Time Is Different: Eight Centuries of Financial Folly* by Carmen Reinhart and Kenneth Rogoff.

Since 1980, the world has experienced six significant financial crises: the Latin American debt crisis of the early 1980s; the Japanese crisis of the 1990s; the Tequila crisis of 1994, whose center was Mexico, affecting other Latin American countries; the East Asian crisis of 1997–1998; the global financial crisis of 2007–2008; and the Eurozone financial crisis of 2010–2013. And additionally there have been many national crises such as the 2001 crisis in Argentina, the crises in Turkey in 1994 and 2001, and in a more extensive region, the Scandinavian crisis of the early 1990s. It is estimated that there were 47 banking crises between 1970 and 2000.

In all these crises, even if they have their unique individual features—the nature of the shock, the object of speculation and the form of credit expansion, they have some enduring common features. In a phrase: the more something changes, the more it remains the same. Details proliferate but structure abides.

Most frightening is that the crises seem to have become bigger and more globally devastating over time. The last two—the global and Eurozone financial crises—struck the core of the world economic system, affecting economies that generate not much less than half of global economic product. The emerging and developing countries managed the consequences relatively well. But that story is not over: It may well turn out that the ways in which these economies responded to the crisis, particularly fiscal and credit expansion, have brought substantial longer-term fragilities.

It is widely known that there are deep differences between various crisis theories. Nevertheless they share several common points. Firstly, in almost all crisis theories, the crisis comes up after an unsustainable boom stage. During the boom stage, either financial or non-financial (mainly real estate) asset prices go up or overproduction due to high investment can occur. Or both financial and production (investment) can affect each other during the boom stage in the way that Austrian economists and Minsky integrate them. Secondly, in all crisis theories there are feedbacks that deepen and determine their direction. They can be classified as objective and subjective feedbacks. While the former defines more structural factors such as the changes in asset and product prices, interest rates, income and wealth, etc., the latter is more about behavioral responses of economic agents triggered by changes in expectations. Thirdly, in all models of financial crises, there are triggering mechanisms that start the booms. They can be credit expansion, capital flows, income inequalities, falling profits, behavioral biases, deregulative policies or technological or financial innovations, etc. Fourthly, crisis theories recognize implicitly or explicitly that financial agents respond immediately to changes in the economy. They are very flexibly adjusted to economic and political factors. An elastic financial system creates sufficient endogenous credit to feed expansion or contraction.

The crisis of Global Recession in 2007–2008 clearly discredited the neoclassical school of economics. It placed a lot of criticisms on this paradigm because its analytic tools appeared to be not enough to analyze the crises described above. In fact, the neoclassical paradigm recognizes the existence of business cycles, which, as its proponents claim, mainly arises from the transitory imbalances between demand and supply for some reason. But they focus on exogenous disturbances rather than their endogenous dynamics. This view starts with William Stanley Jevons, who argued that sun spots determined business cycles in the economy due to their cyclical effects on agriculture, and spillover effects to profitability of other businesses. Leon Walras also regarded crises as temporary disturbances in which prices cannot set the equilibrium between supply and demand.

In a similar framework to these authors, neoclassical economists have subsequently developed theories regarding business cycles. According to these theories, cycles are not crises but small fluctuations. Due to the self-regulation mechanisms of markets, their effects are transitory. The cycles mainly originate from external factors. Hence they do not come out of endogenous mechanisms of capitalistic production. This is succinctly elaborated in "real business cycle theories". Their main argument is that business cycles are a result of optimal adjustment to external changes, especially technological shocks. Hence an economic cycle is random and has a pattern of fluctuations around a trend.

However, it must be mentioned that neoclassical economics has failed. It has a lot of weaknesses that prevent it from understanding the economy as a whole; not only crises. Among them, the most critical weakness is its obsession with the notion of equilibrium. This obstructs sight of the real dynamics of economies. It does not want to see the critical role of credit and debt in the market economies. It rejects the power and class divisions in many aspects of economic relations. The role of finance in shaping incentives is not considered, and furthermore distances finance from economics. The concerns of income and wealth inequalities are not being incorporated into neoclassical analysis. Additionally, the proponents of neoclassical paradigm resist benefiting from perspectives presented by behavioral economics, ignoring behavioral biases and their aggravating effects during crises. Lastly they reduce uncertainty to estimable risk. This is a critical weakness that places a barrier on understanding the open-system character of the dynamics of capitalism.

Economic thinking has produced a large variety of crisis theories which explain financial crises and their effects on economic development. These theories are based on different paradigms. The aim of this book is to introduce and discuss different theories which attempt to explain financial crises and which are considered to be important in their respective fields. In this sense, I try to cover all the important streams of thinking, and present their key arguments and their relevance for understanding the relevant crises.

Who or what is to blame in crises? What is causa remota? What is causa proxima? I see that when dealing with theoretical views on crises, causa proxima and causa remota frequently change place among theories. Causa remota of one theory sometimes becomes causa proxima of another theory. Hence differentiating causa remota from causa proxima can be hard. Different reasonings emphasize different causes depending on their emphasis on remote and proximate causes. In this book it will be seen that causes presented by different theories can be regarded as closely connected to each other but they focus on what they want to emphasize.

In this book what I also want to show is that all theories are based on a narrative that is trying to convince us. But I do not believe that there can be a general theoretical approach for understanding all crises, whether it is built up using axioms or through the formal process of inductive logic. The approach for determining the cause of the extinction crisis for dinosaurs will not carry over to create a theory that also works for passenger pigeons. Like financial crises, every extinction can be explained ex post, and many could be predicted based on the propagation and cascade of events, but they do not follow some general theory, and starting with axioms is not going to get you where you want to go.

Therefore all the economic theories in this book capture some fraction of reality. In this sense they complement each other most of the time even if they compete with each other. As mentioned above, the proximate cause of a theory can be the remota cause of another theory. Or the cause of a crisis stressed by a theory can loom in one crisis much more greatly but can recede in another crisis. The degree of explanatory effectiveness can vary with respect to crises. I hope this book helps this perspective.

Meanwhile here I have to mention that the chapters in this book are not just allocated to seemingly non-orthodox paradigms. My objective is simply to help understand financial crises without excluding any paradigm specifically. But it is clear that the mainstream arguments mostly appear in the book in the form of being criticized. This is because, to me, they could not succeed in a satisfactory manner when looking at their performance in understanding the crises in the past.

The book consists of eight chapters, each of which is based on arguments of a category of crisis theory. The title of each chapter is based on the main argument of the theory in question. They are mainly underconsumption, overindebtedness, income inequality, financialization, financial fragility, falling rate of profits, human behavior, and global imbalances. The relations between these arguments are frequently discussed throughout the book. This helps us to see the links between the various crisis theories. The empirical relevance of the arguments of the crisis theories elaborated in this book is widely discussed in the context of the global crisis in 2007–2008, in addition to other crises from the past.

In the first chapter of the book, I study the roles of notions such as underconsumption and its related concepts overproduction and disproportionality on economic crises in their historical and analytical contexts. Additionally, their empirical relevance particularly to the global crisis in 2007–2008 is also debated there.

Underconsumption theories have played an important part in crisis debates. From this perspective, income distribution is mainly seen as the source of underconsumption. This is unsustainable in the long run due to consumption patterns of the poor and the rich. In a similar context, I also incorporate Keynes's insufficient demand approach to the underconsumption debate. In fact, he redefined the problem in terms of aggregate demand, rather than underconsumption. In Keynes's view, the reason for crises was lack of demand, but he did not reason in the way theories of underconsumption did. He argued that investment expenditure in this sense plays a critical role.

It appears that income distribution seems critical in determining degree and patterns of consumption. However, I focus on their relevance to crises in separate chapters in this book (underconsumption in Chapter 1 and income inequality in Chapter 4). This is because there are several other dimensions of underconsumption and income inequality related to crises, but independent of each other, having their own dynamics. Furthermore, overproduction and disproportionality approaches that are covered in Chapter 1, despite their connection with underconsumption, have different explanations for crises than underconsumptionists, which are not directly related to income inequality.

In Chapter 2, I search for the importance of debt accumulation in the emergence of crises, especially in the global crisis in 2007–2008. In fact, since the global financial crisis of 2007–2008, scholars have increased their interest in the relationship between debt and economic activities. They mainly argue that debt, "domestic or sovereign" or "private or public", can be critical not only at the occurrence of crises, but also in their duration and severity.

The frequency of debt crises has increased across the world since the deregulation of lending and global financial flows in the late 1970s. More people and countries have become more dependent on debt over time. The financial crisis that began in 2007–2008 was especially a crisis in debt markets. Despite the fast recovery in stock markets, the problems in debt markets still continue more or less. Therefore in order to understand the global crisis and other relatively minor crises, we should focus on debt markets more.

Historically there has almost been no economic crisis in which there has been no debt. Hence the causal relationship between debt and financial crises has always been more critical. The accumulation of debt may evolve with one cause or another. I focus on the roles of the probable causes such as inequality, global imbalances, and behavioral biases on overindebtedness in the different chapters of the book. However, due to the complexity of debt accumulation and its critical role in causing and deepening crises, I wanted to focus on the issue of debt in particular in a separate chapter. Its dynamics and effects require more scrutiny.

In Chapter 3, I firstly analyze financialization and its link with crises. Then I focus on the connections between financialization, neoliberal policies and crises. It is widely recognized that financialization has been becoming the overwhelming force behind economic activities. This means that economies, particularly those of advanced countries, pass from one stage to another, where the gravity of economic activity shifts from production to finance. In line with this, there have been dramatic changes in financial institutions and products in the last decades.

However, financialization is not by itself an isolated development in the economy. It has affected and been affected by some important trends in economies. In recent years, the linkages between financialization, inequality, and overindebtedness have been deepening further and have more implications at the aggregate level.

Some views treat the financial sphere as a "superstructure" wholly dependent upon a "material base" in the real economy. However, this view may not be enough to understand the dynamics of capitalism. Financialization has also been influential in restructuring capitalist relations and changing the conduct of economic agents in several ways. That is, it is not only a passive response but also a constructive power. It is clear that extensive development of finance and financial motives have been critical in the evolution of neoliberalism. All these issues and their relevance to crises in the last decades will be covered in this chapter.

Chapter 4 aims to discuss theoretical and empirical dimensions of the relationship between increasing inequality and occurrence of crises. In this way, I focus on the main arguments of the mainstream theories and non-mainstream theories on the links between income inequalities and crises and their validity in the context of the crises in history, and in particular the global crisis in 2007–2008.

For a long time, many economists have disregarded the macroeconomic implications of inequality. But a striking yet overlooked similarity between the two major economic crises over the past century, the Great Depression in 1929 and the Great Recession in 2007–2008, which is increased inequality preceding these two crises, motivates researchers further to search whether there is a sound connection between inequalities and crises. In this sense, even some mainstream economists have questioned the assumptions used in mainstream economics and have acknowledged that income inequality can trigger crises. Rajan (2010) was one of the first economists that put forward a theoretical link between inequality and the global crisis in 2007–2008. And it is also quite recently that academic attention has been drawn to the simultaneous rise in both income and wealth inequalities in parallel to increasing financialization and overindebtedness during the period where neoliberal policies have been followed.

Hence, there can be various causal or correlative relationships in the context of crises between variables such as rising inequalities, excess leverage of poor households, increasing role of financialization, and neoliberal policies. But it is hard to isolate them. In this sense, all these factors are discussed in a more integrative manner in this chapter.

In Chapter 5, I discuss Minsky's financial instability hypothesis. It is widely regarded that the global crisis in 2007–2008 is a Minskian crisis. It has been thought that the processes identified by Minsky's financial instability hypothesis explain what happened along the route toward this global crisis. Hence no economist has been referred to as much as Hyman Minsky concerning the financial crisis of 2007–2008. Many economists have referred to the crisis as a "Minsky moment", questioning whether the US has become a "Ponzi nation".

Minsky constructs his theoretical framework on a dynamic economic process. This perspective is totally distinct from the mainstream approach using equilibrium notions that regard the economic problem as one of establishing efficient market allocations. Process issues are disregarded in this equilibrium perspective. In Minsky's view, the potentiality of instability is always present in modern financial capitalism. Thus the economic system is prone to financial crises.

The financial instability hypothesis is a theory of crises, in which the real and the financial sides of the economy interact and lead to a cyclical sequence of events. Hence due to focusing more on the connection between real and finance, Minsky's views differentiate from the points elaborated by the arguments of financialization, which mainly emphasize financial structures and motives (discussed extensively in Chapter 3). Meanwhile, from some respects, behavioral biases in Minsky's views also resemble the arguments of behavioral economics. In this sense, his emphasis on the role of changing psychology and expectations in financing behavior (switch from hedge to speculative or from speculative to Ponzi finance) becomes important. Hence behavioral biases discussed in Chapter 7 can also help readers understand Minsky's arguments more.

In Chapter 6, I study the Marxian hypotheses regarding falling rate of profits and their empirical validity to explain economic crises. Marxian theories of crisis have a long history and they have been debated in many places and diverse contexts. The recent crisis in 2007–2008 has renewed the Marxian debate on crisis theory.

In fact, Marx and Marxists mostly consider crisis at the level of an abstract model of capitalism in which there can be some inherent tendencies such as underconsumption, falling rate of profit, overproduction, disproportionality among different production departments, or profit squeeze. However, it is extremely hard to use empirical studies to search for the validity of these hypotheses due to measurement issues, diverse definitions, and several counteracting tendencies in a dynamic economic structure.

This chapter mainly focuses on Marxian structural approaches containing tendency of the rate of profit to fall, profit squeeze, and social structure of accumulation. Their main common argument is that economic crises can be analyzed in the context of structural trends such as profitability and capital accumulation despite diverging from each other in some points. The tendency of the rate of profit to fall hypothesis is the most common perspective among them, on which we focus most in this chapter.

Chapter 7 focuses on how human psychology can be a contributing factor to the financial crises using methodology of behavioral economics. It is generally accepted that a bubble is an episode in which irrational thinking or behavioral biases cause the price of an asset to rise to a level that is higher than it would be in the absence of the biases or the irrationality.

Particularly along with the global crisis in 2007–2008, many scholars recognized the importance of behavioral biases as a contributing factor to the crisis. Furthermore, they focused more on historic episodes of destabilizing speculation. They draw attention to the point that the phrases used in the literature during the previous crises can help us see the importance of psychology: exuberance, greed, financial frenzies, fear, feverish speculation, overconfidence, and herding etc. All these expressions have been widely used across space and time during the times of crises. And they imply the behavioral components of crises regardless of country and period. However, mainstream economics interprets such actions as irrational and defines them as anomalies even though these sorts of actions are persistent and continuously verified by observations.

In this chapter we also discuss how behavioral perspective can be important for understanding overindebtedness, people's response to income inequalities and actions of financial actors in the context of crises. However, this perspective alone may not be enough to understand crises without taking the structures that facilitate the emergence of behavioral biases, which are analyzed in diverse chapters in this book.

In the last chapter of the book, the issue of global imbalances is discussed in the context of crises. Global imbalances were being debated frequently before the global crisis in 2007–2008. Since then, they have been still on the agenda of economists and practitioners. The term global imbalances is mainly used to describe the external imbalances of large economies that lead to disruptions to the global economy, and even deep crises.

Historically, there has been always an accumulation of current account surpluses for countries that have been technologically advanced or had valuable commodities. This is regarded as normal or a good imbalance. However, in recent years, the gap between surplus and deficit countries has been widening sizably and becoming detrimental to the world economy. It is clear that excessive global imbalances can turn into a global threat due to not having self-correction mechanisms to truncate these tendencies.

Global imbalances are, in fact, a very complicated issue, associated with many other issues such as underconsumption, overproduction, income inequality, financialization and liberalism. In this final chapter, we look at their global implications as well. For example, underconsumption and overproduction manifest at the global scale, that is, in terms of global imbalances. Thus, the unbalanced structure in consumption (low saving) of the US was partially related to another type of structural imbalance in consumption (high saving) in China. And both countries were—in fact still are—quite bad in their income distributions. This also affected global imbalances further. We discuss these issues as well in this chapter.

1 Underconsumption, overproduction, and disproportionality

1.1 Introduction

As of the beginning of the 19th century crises started to appear more often. This caused scholars to think more about their causes. They asserted various theoretical explanations for this. One of these theoretical explanations was underconsumption that was mainly defined as a natural consequence of capitalist relations. In fact there are two versions of this theory that have developed over time. One of them is a more traditional one, represented by Thomas Robert Malthus, Jean Charles Sismondi and Karl Marx; the other is a more recent and modern one that was elaborated by John Maynard Keynes.

Underconsumption theories played an important part in economic policy debates. In the face of an abundance of unused factors of production on the one hand, and poverty and unsatisfied needs on the other, the intuitive appeal of these arguments explains their popular success. These arguments date back to the early 19th century when Malthus and Sismondi explained crises as a disequilibrium between supply and demand for consumption goods. They focus on the effects of savings. High savings reduce the demand for consumption and increase production capacities and future supply.

From this point of view, income distribution is seen as the source of underconsumption. The share of capitalists' income in national income grows over time. The production of consumption goods financed by their savings is not consumed by the income of the masses, which cannot increase enough. Sismondi expressed the trend of this development but did not promote the regularity of this to a great extent. Hence until the English economist John A. Hobson, there was no in real sense an "underconsumption theory" that emphasized regularity of underconsumption. So Hobson was one of the first of the modern scholars to pioneer the idea of underconsumption. He pointed out that the incomes of the rich in modern societies rise more rapidly than their expenditures, which naturally generates greater saving, hence resulting in underconsumption. Hobson was not a Marxist, but his influence on later Marxist writers was so great that he cannot be disregarded in studies of Marxist theories. However, contemporary underconsumption theory is much more closely identified with John Maynard Keynes, who put forward similar arguments and defined the problem as lack of effective demand. He mainly believed that the government can fix this problem by fiscal expansion.

Even though underconsumption theory is emphasized frequently in the literature, another important theory related to underconsumption arguments is overproduction theory. We can find traces of this view in Marx as well. Marx insisted that the emergence of crises is not directly related to insufficient consumption, but it is more about the expansion of capital. He argues that inbuilt tendencies in capitalism such as improvements in technology, rising levels of productivity, and harsh competition among capitalists persistently increase the amount of production in the economy. This leads to overproduction, which is a rise of production of commodities relative to the market for those commodities. In other words, overproduction is production of commodities in excess of what can be sold at a profit. This imbalance of production and consumption underlies the tendency to crisis.

Another theory related to both underconsumption and overproduction is disproportionality theory. Disproportionality theory mainly asserts that disproportional growth rates between two different departments of production are the main cause behind disruptions in the economy. While one of these departments is the sector that produces factors of production called Department I, producing machinery and capital goods, another is the sector that produces consumption goods called Department II. If the production of one of these departments exceeds the other, this likely leads to a crisis. The disproportionality theory was mainly proposed by Mikhail Tugan-Baranov, who criticized the underconsumptionist view on the basis of Marx's reproduction process. He argued that disproportionalities were the most critical cause in the economy even though they were not necessarily to lead to crises. He drew attention to themes of the ignorance of capitalists about future developments in the markets and the amplifying effects of credit expansion on disproportionalities.

In this chapter we delve into these three related theories explaining economic crises. Each theory will be argued theoretically and empirically. Hopefully this will help us understand their relevance to crises in general.

1.2 Underconsumption theory from a historical perspective

The classical economists of the 19th century investigated the phases of economies which, they thought, tend toward their normal or natural states. Hence business cycles were not the main concern of classical economic theory. Malthus (1766–1834) was the first to admit that crises might arise from conditions inherent in the capitalistic system. According to him, production depended on the continuation of effective demand. He elaborated that the value of commodities produced was always more than the total payments made to the labor who produced them. Hence the demand for laborers is not big enough to maintain a smooth production process. Additional demand source would be required. Even capitalists could not meet this demand because they saved more than they spent. Malthus argued that this additional demand could come from what was called unproductive consumption. The sources of unproductive consumption were servants, statesmen, soldiers, lawyers, physicians, and so on.

The implications of Malthus's explanations were taken up and elaborated by Jean Charles Sismondi (1773–1842). Sismondi was the first one to present a systematic approach to business cycles. He considered the main weaknesses of the economic system which classical economists generally overlooked. His arguments formed an important point of departure for later socialist thought.

Sismondi noticed some contradictions of industrial capitalism; hence he diverged from economic liberalism (at the beginning he was a liberal). The expansion of industrial capitalism, he argued, led to further production but it simultaneously aggravated the conditions of the masses. Along with increasing sophistication in machinery and productivity of labor, the number of the unemployed increased drastically. This created a downward pressure on wages. Sismondi argued that as capitalism increased industrial production too much, it eventually ended up with the constraints of effective demand determined by the masses who got poorer over time. Hence this contradiction of capitalism would generate "general gluts", namely economic crises described as an overproduction of commodities in general.

Sismondi's ideas of political economy arose from his efforts to explain why underconsumption was the main cause of crises. Sismondi defined four distinct conditions for the occurrence of crises. Firstly, knowledge about the conditions in the market is imperfect. The nature of the market is really unknown to the producer. The producer's knowledge on tastes, purchasing power, and quantities demanded is limited. With this limited information, he determines his production quantity and price. A high price in relation to production costs induces greater production to increase profits. But he does not know the production levels of other producers. Hence there is always a possibility of overproduction of certain commodities due to underconsumption.

Secondly, Sismondi regarded the unequal distribution of income as a contributing factor to crises. While workers' incomes are constantly depressed to the level of subsistence, the purchasing power accumulates into the hands of the rich. Thus, the capitalists take away the surplus value produced by the labor; the part remaining to the workers is not enough to meet total production. Furthermore, the competition between workers to get a job pushes their wages downward as well. This also contributes to underconsumption. Thirdly, the previous year's income level determines the purchasing power available to purchase consumer goods; any increase in production in the current year will lead to a surplus of commodities. This mainly arises from the fact the last year's income level is less than the value of the goods produced in the present year. This implies underconsumption. Lastly, Sismondi asserts that the capitalists' motivation of further production fundamentally guides the capitalist system. Hence investment decisions may not be constrained by consumers' needs. This leads to higher accumulation of capital stock, which eventually causes overcapacity and overproduction thereby resulting in a crisis.

Sismondi had some suggestions to eliminate the negative effects of an economic crisis. For this, he focused on governmental regulations to manage the level of overall production and to regulate the inventions that would lead to larger production. In line with this, the state should intervene in industry and support the return of independent artisans. And income inequalities should be eliminated. Since income inequalities originated from the separation of wage-earners from property, the state should provide property to workers that could help them to produce in the long-run. But until then Sismondi suggested that the government could protect workers against the hazards of unemployment, illness, and old age.

Even though the efforts by Sismondi to explain economic crisis were ignored by the classical economists, a German economist, Johann Rodbertus (1805–1875), drew attention to the views of Sismondi on business cycles. Rodbertus explained crises with the developments in income distribution that deteriorated in disfavor of wage-earners. Despite workers' purchasing power declining, capitalists, without taking this fact into account, would continue to expand production. But much of the income created would go to those who saved more, hence underconsumption eventually would occur. Rodbertus, like Sismondi, also did suggest some remedies to handle the problem of underconsumption. For example, he suggested that means of production should be owned socially and income should be distributed in proportion to the labor of each. The only way to achieve this was to form a socialistic state under a benevolent monarchy.

Another important figure who is associated with underconsumption hypothesis is Karl Marx (1818–1883). Marx argued that the fundamental dimensions of capitalism were represented in the theories of Ricardo and Sismondi. He regarded Ricardo as representing the positive side of capitalism, overlooking the demand constraints that capitalism caused but instead focusing on its productive force. But Sismondi, in Marx's view, focused on the negative side of capitalism, drawing attention to the limiting aspect of underconsumption. However, even though there were some thoughts of Marx on the issue of underconsumption, there is an ongoing debate whether Marx was underconsumptionist or not due to the fact that Marx did not elaborate a systematic analysis on the crises of capitalism. We will discuss this issue below in more detail.

Rosa Luxemburg (1871–1919) is also another scholar who is generally grouped with the underconsumptionists. In her book *Accumulation of Capital* (1913), Luxemburg argued that the reproduction of the capitalist system required the realization of surplus value. If it was not provided, the capitalist system would collapse. Similar to Luxemburg, some other Marxian economists such as Karl Kautsky and Rudolf Hilderding, and more recently scholars Michael Sweezy and Michael Baran in the 1950s, also emphasized realization failure of surplus in their explanation of crisis.

We know that Malthus had the view that even though there could be fluctuations due to temporary deficiencies in the demand for goods (general glut), they did not have a regular pattern. On the contrary, Sismondi had assumed some form of regularity in business cycles, but there was not a refined theory of underconsumption until the English economist John A. Hobson (1858–1940). Hobson can be thought of as the first modern scholar to advance the idea of underconsumption systematically. He pointed out that the rich saved more due to the fact that they made less expenditure in proportion to their income. When this new saving was used to buy new capital to expand production, it would increase the supply of goods. This in turn increased the incomes of the investors, whose marginal propensity to save was high. Finally markets would have more goods that could not be sold, because much of the income created had been saved. Hence, in Hobson's view, both underconsumption and oversaving would lead to overinvestment, causing the recurring unemployment of labor and capital. Due to this, he disagreed with the view that more saving would create more accumulation. On the contrary, this would aggravate the problem of underconsumption further.

Hobson's theory was quite different from that of his contemporaries concerning distribution of income. Part of the income received by labor is for maintenance, or subsistence, which enables workers to renew their biological strength and to reproduce their labor supply. Additional income provides for growth in the economy, because workers who receive payments above their subsistence become better educated and healthier. If wages are higher than maintenance (costs of subsistence) and the productive surplus (costs of growth), the remaining part will be an unproductive surplus that does not increase output. Hobson also argued that capital also has two similar costs to labor, namely maintenance and growth costs. The maintenance costs provide for the replacement of depreciated capital. However, an additional profit is required for investment, and hence further accumulation of capital. In other words, more profit than the replacement of depreciated capital is required to bring about saving that will be invested. This growth of capital was called growth cost by Hobson. However, if profit is above the level required for the maintenance and sound growth of capital, it is unproductive.

In Hobson's view, labor just meets its needs (subsistence costs) and does not cover the full costs of growth. The larger amount of surplus value remains in the hands of capitalists, thus they save more. However, their increasing saving also depends on the consumption of workers that creates a demand for the products produced. In this sense, saving and consumption should not diverge from each other. Saving plays a socially useful role here. Some appropriate rate of saving increases both production and consumption at the same time. This provides a sound growth trend consistent with full employment. However, if saving is too high, unemployment then rises. On the contrary, if saving is too low, productive potential is wasted, and the future is sacrificed to the present.

This is mentioned in Mummery and Hobson (1889, p. 373) in the following manner:

> Our purpose is to show ... that an undue exercise of the habit of saving is possible, and that such undue exercise impoverishes the Community,

> throws labourers out of work, drives down wages, and spreads that gloom and prostration through the commercial world which is known as Depression in Trade; that, in short, the effective love of money is the root of all economic evil.

Therefore, in Hobson's view, oversaving and underconsumption create business cycles. In times of economic expansion, prices are generally high; capital investment is high, provided by the increasing bank credits; and the productive potential grows more rapidly than consumption. This leads to a crisis of underconsumption. In this case, prices fall in order to clear the market so that saving and spending once again balance, and then profitable investments slowly return. And then the same market mechanism happens again, resulting in a new crisis. Hence Hobson argues that the critical problem of capitalist production is the recurring tendency of unemployment of labor and capital.

Until the Great Depression in 1929, which was the worst economic crisis that was seen in the history of the developed countries, the underconsumption theories mentioned above had been largely ignored. The Great Depression again drew attention, to some extent, to the underconsumption theories developed by the early classical economists, even though mainstream economists insisted on not considering them seriously. However, these theories were embraced by John Maynard Keynes (1883–1946). He emphasized the role of effective demand in the performance of economies. This perspective was in essence the same as the traditional underconsumption theories, but with its presentation and language largely changed. Although classical underconsumption theory had always been viewed with suspicion by mainstream thought, Keynes's views on underconsumption were regarded as free of these old-fashioned implications. This subject will also be discussed below in more detail under contemporary Keynesian underconsumption theory.

In the 1940s and 1950s, Paul Baran and Paul Sweezy developed the most sophisticated exposition of orthodox Marxist crisis. They constructed a stagnationist theory which was mainly based on Marxist underconsumptionism. This view combined some ideas of Marx and Kalecki, and associated the Keynesian stabilization with militarism, imperialism, and waste expenditures made to absorb increasing surplus, which is why they are also called Keynesian Marxists. However, during the 1960s, the tradition of this thought weakened as new types of crises emerged that could not be fixed by Keynesian consumption measures.

1.3 Underconsumption theories

1.3.1 Marxist underconsumption theory

One of the main characteristics of Marxist theory is its emphasis on economic crisis. In the studies of Marx and Engels, the tendency of the capitalist system toward crisis was always one of their main arguments despite it not being elaborated succinctly in their studies. In his writings, Marx sometimes appears to have related crises to underconsumption, overproduction, disproportionality, and declining rate of profits without ever clearly putting forward one or the other theory.

Some Marxists, from some remarks by Marx in his studies, concluded that Marx developed a reasoning that supported an underconsumption view of crisis. Marx, for example, expressed the following remarks in *Capital III* (1894, Chapter 30):

> The last cause of all real crisis always remains the poverty and restricted consumption of the masses as compared to the tendency of capitalist production to develop the productive forces in such a way, that only the absolute power of consumption of the entire society would be their limit.

Although the debate among Marxists has always continued through citations from Marx, he in fact regarded underconsumption as a persistent state in capitalism and an important factor leading to a crisis given the dynamics of accumulation and the rising organic composition of capital (capital–labor ratio). Engels (1878) states this position very clearly:

> The underconsumption of the masses, the restriction of the consumption of the masses to what is necessary for their maintenance and reproduction, is not a new phenomenon. It has existed as long as there have been exploiting and exploited classes. . . . The underconsumption of the masses is a necessary condition of all forms of society based on exploitation, consequently also of the capitalist form; but it is the capitalist form of production which first gives rise to crises. The underconsumption of the masses is therefore also a prerequisite condition for crises, and plays in them a role which has long been recognized. But it tells us just as little why crises exist today as why they did not exist before.
>
> (Anti-Duhring, Part III: Socialism, III. Production)

According to Marx, purchases and sales, and supply and demand under capitalism are independent from each other. This situation bears the possibility for crisis to occur. In the case of the pure exchange of commodities, the equilibrium between production and consumption, and sales and purchases is reasonable at first glance. This is because the one selling his/her product is also the one who is to purchase a commodity produced. In this case, any consumption deficiency will not occur. Thus as argued by Say and Ricardo, those sales and purchases are in equilibrium and those production and consumption match. Therefore general overproduction and hence crisis will not occur. This is called Say's law[1]. However, as claimed by Marx, this simple argument is totally senseless under capitalistic production. Therefore, Say's law reduces the economic exchange to exchange of products, which in turn removes the possibility of a crisis.

However, in some cases the equilibrium between purchases and sales disappears. For example, people sometimes hold money in their hands after selling their commodities in the market instead of making expenditure on another commodity. Hence this commodity will not be bought and money will be saved instead of buying the commodity. This possibility always exists and is not just a random occurrence. Furthermore it can occur on a larger scale.

Marx (1867, pp. 208–209) mentions this as follows:

> Nothing could be more foolish than the dogma that because every sale is a purchase, and every purchase a sale, the circulation of commodities necessarily implies an equilibrium between sales and purchases ... But no one directly needs to purchase because he has just sold. Circulation bursts through all the temporal, spatial and personal barriers imposed by the direct exchange of products, and it does this by splitting up the direct identity present in this case between the exchange of one's own product and the acquisition of someone else's into the two antithetical segments of sale and purchase. To say that these mutually independent and antithetical processes form an internal unity is to say also that their internal unity moves forward through external antitheses.

In addition to the argument of independence between demand and supply, there are two other sound arguments behind underconsumption theory developed later by Marxists. These are the centrality of capitalist investment and the existence of workers under other capital. We will now explain them.

(i) The centrality of capitalist investment

In the capitalist system, a stable demand can be generated. However there is no guarantee for this. There are two separate processes in capitalist reproduction. While one is the generation of surplus value from production, the other is the realization of surplus value from consumption. There is no automatic mechanism to balance these two separate processes because the capitalist reproduction is not centrally planned. Hence what is created as surplus value is not necessarily realized; thus lack of effective demand can come out as a serious problem in the capitalist system.

Underconsumption theory generally emphasizes the spending decisions of consumers or workers as the source of aggregate demand. However, this approach has an important flaw because the important component of aggregate demand is disregarded. This is capitalist expenditure. According to Marxists, in fact spending decisions of workers derive from this capitalist expenditure.

This means that aggregate demand is mainly capitalist demand. There are three components of this capitalist expenditure: (1) consumption expenditure (2) expenditure made for workers (wages) and (3) expenditure for purchasing means of production (investment). The second expenditure, namely expenditure made for workers by the capitalists as wages for their working in the production process, is used for consumption by the workers. This has two important consequences. First, consumption derives from the capitalist decisions about how much wage is given to workers and how many workers are employed. This view points out that the disruptions in effective demand are mainly associated with the expenditure by capitalists rather than the expenditure by workers. Second, consumption expenditure by capitalists can help realization of the surplus value (first expenditure above) but it is not enough for this. Therefore the third expenditure, namely expenditure for purchasing means of production (investment), becomes critical here.

In order to understand this better, we can use the rationale behind the circuit of capital. This is symbolically defined as $M-C-C'-M'$. This circuit's starting point is for the firm to make a capital expenditure of M, thus, the firm starts with a certain level of money M to buy commodities represented by C (labor and non-labor inputs). The factors of production are placed into production. After production is finalized, the firm obtains the finished commodity C' and sells it to get the money M'. Notice that the starting money of the capitalist was M and the end point of the production money is now M'. If $M' > M$, this means that surplus value is generated and realized, thus production by the firm makes sense.

This process in fact contains a critique of Say's law. It can help us to distinguish differences between types of transactions from a class perspective. The capitalist starts with a purchase and ends up with a sale, that is, $M-C-M'$. The important component of this purchase is labor power. The capitalist pays this as wages, which is the income of workers who use them to purchase their means of subsistence. Thus, the worker starts with selling his labor power and ends up with purchasing his means of subsistence, that is, $C-M-C'$.

This important difference in starting points between a capitalist and a worker is very important to show the priority of decisions. In comparison to capitalists, it is clear that the working class is less likely to stop buying their means of subsistence, which are necessary to survive. These purchases, however, are quite different with the capitalist class because they spend only a minor part of their income for such kinds of needs. Their larger expenditure is on investment that furthers more production to grab more surplus value. And this is not related to the satisfaction of any human need. Hence, if expectations of profitability become pessimistic, their expenditure on investment can fall sharply. If this spreads all over the economy, overproduction can occur, that is, aggregate supply is going to be larger than aggregate demand. This implies a crisis.

(ii) Workers under other capital

Underconsumption can also emerge in a case in which capitalists prefer the increase in wages of other capitalists rather than increasing the wages of their own workers. This is because this situation expands the market without suffering an increase in production cost. While the worker is the seller of a commodity (his labor power), he is the buyer of a commodity produced in the market. The labor is paid as wages after he sells his labor. This is the source of demand for the products of capitalists in the market. However the capitalists want to restrict their cost by pressing down wages, which in turn lowers the demand for the whole market.

Marx argued that capitalists are aware that the workers of other capitalists are purchasers of their own products, hence there is an externality which they cannot control directly. The increase in consumption (increasing wages) appears to be beneficial. However, they cannot manage this directly. This becomes visible especially during crises. In order to get out of the crisis, wages should be raised, but the question is the wages of workers of which capitalists. For each individual capitalist, increasing the wages of their own workers reduces their profits, and will worsen their economic welfare.

In capitalists' view, consumption of all the workers represents the whole demand. All the capitalists (producers of consumption goods directly and producers of production goods indirectly) are concerned with the expansion of the whole market because it is related to the market of their products. At the first glance, there is a conflict relationship between the capitalist and his own workers but due to the interconnectedness of capitalists this relationship may not that conflictual. However, the problem here is who is to move first, thus who is to raise wages of his workers first. Marx expresses this as follows:

> Actually, the relation of one capitalist to the workers of another capitalist is none of our concern here. It only shows every capitalist's illusion, but alters nothing in the relation of capital in general to labor. Every capitalist knows this about his worker, that he does not relate to him as producer to consumer, and [he therefore] wishes to restrict his consumption, i.e. his ability to exchange, his wage, as much as possible. Of course he would like the workers of other capitalists to be the greatest consumers possible of his own commodity. But this is just how the illusion arises—true for the individual capitalist as distinct from all the others—that apart from his workers the whole remaining working class confronts him as consumer and participant in exchange, as money-spender, and not as worker.
>
> (Marx, 1857, p. 420)

To summarize, each capitalist tends to think of the other workers not working in their firms just as customers. Hence they want these workers' wages to rise because this increases the demand for their own commodities rather than increasing wages of their own. In fact, this is a state of prisoner's dilemma[2]. Each capitalist prefers the other capitalists to increase the wages of their workers and in the end nobody does this. Consequently the required demand for each capitalist or firm will not be enough to sustain their businesses due to underconsumption.

1.3.2 Keynesian underconsumption theory

In the 1930s the developed capitalist countries experienced what was the greatest crisis until then. To many scholars at the time, the occurrence of the Great Depression indicated the problem of the lack of demand as pointed out by theories of underconsumption that were developed by the early classical economists of the 19th century. However, even this crisis did not make the attention of modern mainstream economic theory shift to these kinds of explanations. It was Keynes, following the Great Depression, who pointed out the significance of the aggregate demand on the level of economic activity. Although in Keynes's views there were to a certain extent similarities with theories of underconsumption, he totally changed and modernized the characteristics of the problem.

Keynes, in his book *The General Theory*, redefined the insufficient demand problem in a more technical sense. In this way, he aimed to avoid the political and ideological debates associated with theories of underconsumption. In other words, he, by redefining the problem in terms of aggregate demand, distanced himself from theories of the classical underconsumptionists and socialists. Instead of suggesting the public ownership of factors of production by Marxists, he developed a new remedy to cope with the problems of underconsumption or insufficient aggregate demand. He mainly supported the intervention of the government to counteract the fall in demand by making expenditures to push up the economy. This is simply the use of fiscal policy, which is expressed by the metaphor of the economy as a car driven by the government in the driver's seat and fiscal policy serving as the steering wheel.

In Keynes's view, high unemployment and stagnation in the market economies are usual events that we can face. He mentioned this in this way: *"... the evidence indicates that full, or even approximately full, employment is of rare and short-lived occurrence"*. He also points out, *"it [the economic system] seems capable of remaining in a chronic condition of sub-normal activity for a considerable period ..."* (Keynes, 1936, pp. 249–250).

In fact, Keynes defined this problem as a sort of market failure rather than a deeper systematic problem of capitalism. This market failure, which is a situation in which the allocation of goods and services by a free market is not efficient, can be solved using appropriate policy instruments. Furthermore in Keynes's view, some decentralized decisions or coordination problems can aggravate the economy. This situation is described by the remarks in the General Theory (pp. 210–211):

> An act of individual saving mean—so to speak—a decision not to have dinner today. But it does not necessitate a decision to have dinner or to buy a pair of boots a week hence or a year hence or to consume any specified thing at any specified date. Thus it depresses the business of preparing today's dinner without stimulating the business of making ready for some future act of consumption. It is not a substitution of

> future consumption-demand for present consumption-demand—it is a net diminution of such demand . . . If saving consisted not merely in abstaining from present consumption but in placing simultaneously a specific order for future consumption, the effect might indeed be different. For in that case the expectation of some future yield from investment would be improved, and the resources released from preparing for present consumption would be turned over to preparing for the future consumption . . .

These kinds of problems that can lead to more severe crises always concerned Keynes. He was afraid of conflictual social changes that would likely endanger the liberal system, resulting in socialism. In Keynes's view, the reason for crises was lack of demand, but he did not reason in the way theories of underconsumption did. He argued that investment expenditure plays a decisive role. According to Keynes, investment expenditure is governed jointly by marginal efficiency of capital (MEC), which is that rate of discount which would equate the price of a fixed capital asset with its present discounted value of expected income and the rate of interest which is also determined jointly by the supply of money and demand for money. In this sense, Keynes defines two important factors affecting the magnitude of a deficiency of effective demand: declining marginal efficiency of capital and increasing demand for money (liquidity preference). They are explained in more detail below.

(i) A fall in the MEC schedule

The fall in the MEC can stem from several reasons, such as capital accumulation, technological progress or an external shock such as the overvaluation of the domestic currency. Keynes argued that especially capital accumulation reduces marginal efficiency of capital (MEC), which is mainly the rate of profit on new investment. Keynes defines this relation as follows: *"If there is an increased investment in any given type of capital during any period of time, the marginal efficiency of that type of capital will diminish as the investment in it is increased . . . "* (Keynes, 1936, p. 136).

Keynes argued that the MEC and net investment are inversely related to each other because of two factors: one is that the return of capital will reduce due to increasing supply of capital (declining marginal productivity) and the other is that the production of capital goods will become more expensive due their increasing production cost. This simply results in the fact that the firms are faced with the cases of both lower selling prices and increasing costs. More investment leads to more production, which in turn lowers the prices of products in the market. Costs increase due to the fact that the higher demand for capital pushes up its price, which enters as cost into the accounts of producers.

The critical question here is how to cope with a general fall in demand. At a given rate of interest, the fall in the MEC schedule will generate a fall in investment, which will in turn, by reducing aggregate expenditure and income, subsequently generate a fall in consumption (through the multiplier). The only way to avoid this result is for the rate of interest to be reduced immediately. Such a fall in interest rate would offset the decline in investment, and can also stimulate consumption. If the sum of these positives is great enough to offset the initial negative effect on investment expenditure, then aggregate demand will again increase.

However, Keynes argued that it is hard to reduce the rate of interest as required. When the interest rate drops, the demand for liquid or monetary assets goes up. Given the stock of money, the interest rate, which balances the desire to hold money with the available money stock, is not free to fall. Furthermore, even if the interest rate is reduced as desired through monetary policy, it may not yield the results as desired due to the response of investment, thus elasticity of investment with respect to interest rate may not be high enough due to a pessimistic environment. Keynes thought of another option to counteract the fall in aggregate demand leading to a chronic unemployment: that is the fall in money wages in response to unemployment. So prices also fall. This in turn increases the real stock of money (M/P =real money stock, where M is money stock and P is price level), resulting in a fall in the rate of interest (this process is called the Keynes effect). However Keynes argued that this case may not also solve the problem because the general deflation environment can aggravate the issues further. Lower wages due to unemployment might not generate full employment because the lower demand along with lower wages will not create additional demand that will increase employment.

According to Keynes, even if employment increases because of decreased wages, higher investment accompanied by higher employment causes a lower MEC and an insufficient incentive to invest. If wages can fall fast, Keynes argued that this method can be partially more effective than the slow fall in wages, but still has ambivalent effect. This is because the fall in wages, even if small, will destroy optimistic expectation of higher wages in the future, which leads to a fall in demand and further unemployment. Hence, Keynes argued that flexibility of wages is not enough to maintain full employment.

Consequently Keynes was aware of the fact that there should be another source of consumption to tackle with the problem of insufficient demand because he knew the importance of consumption and pointed this out as follows: *"in the normal state of modern industrial communities, consumption limits production and not production consumption"*. (Keynes, 1936, p. 368). Therefore, Keynes suggests something else other than increasing investment directly to increase aggregate consumption. He advises increase of government expenditures. Expansionary fiscal policy will counteract the fall in demand in general. Even wasteful spending by the government (such as pyramid building) can increase social welfare.

The implications of Keynes's underconsumption analysis were quickly analyzed by other economists. For example, Pigou (1943) disagreed with Keynes's underemployment equilibrium. He argued that the fall in prices would have wealth effect on money balances to recover aggregate demand (Pigou effect). This view was extended to incorporate nominal wage rigidity as a problem that prevents prices from tending into equilibrium. Hence rigidity in labor markets was pointed out as being a source for the existence of a possible disequilibrium in the general economy, and thus the reason for unemployment. Such an argument (price and wage rigidity) is still the main argument of New Keynesian macroeconomics.

(ii) An increase in liquidity preference

Keynes defines liquidity preference as the demand for money, which determines the rate of interest along with supply of money. The demand for money does not refer to saving or money required for spending on goods and services but the demand for the actual stock of money to hold as liquid balances. Classical economists mainly believe that people hold money for transaction purposes. Keynes added the possibility of demand for money as an asset, i.e., speculative balances. Speculative demand for money changes with respect to varying expectations on returns in security market, and the extent to which individuals prefer holding of money to other financial assets is referred to as liquidity preference.

Keynes's argument here is clear. An increase in the desire to hold liquid money balances to avoid losses in a declining securities market will force the rate of interest upward, hence depressing investment for all given the MEC schedule. The multiplier will lead to a further fall in aggregate demand. Thus an increase in liquidity preference is balanced with an increase in interest rate where the stock of money is given at the time. The fall in aggregate demand is realized through the depressing effect of high interest on investment, thus reducing aggregate demand.

Finally, in contemporary literature, we can also see traces of insufficient demand or underconsumption. Contemporary economists share the views that point out that insufficient demand or underconsumption is influential on the stagnation or emergence of crises. They differ on the main causes of insufficient demand. This can be classified as follows: (i) Insufficient demand occurs due to both low level of personal and investment spending in relation to GDP (Bernanke, 2007). (ii) Insufficient demand mainly arises from wrong macroeconomic management restrictive monetary policy (Romer, 2002). (iii) Insufficient demand stems either from inadequate consumption of workers or from insufficient consumption of financial rentiers (Argitis and Pitelis, 2008). It seems striking that no economist given above implies marginal efficiency of capital as a main cause of economic stagnation pointed out by Keynes theory.

1.3.3 Some empirical trends related to consumption during the global recession

Now in this section we want to see how underconsumption or in less ideological terms, the deficient purchasing power, is visible and can be regarded as a serious cause of the crises observed. For this, let us look at the most proximate crisis, which is the Global Recession that broke out in 2007. Looking at respective

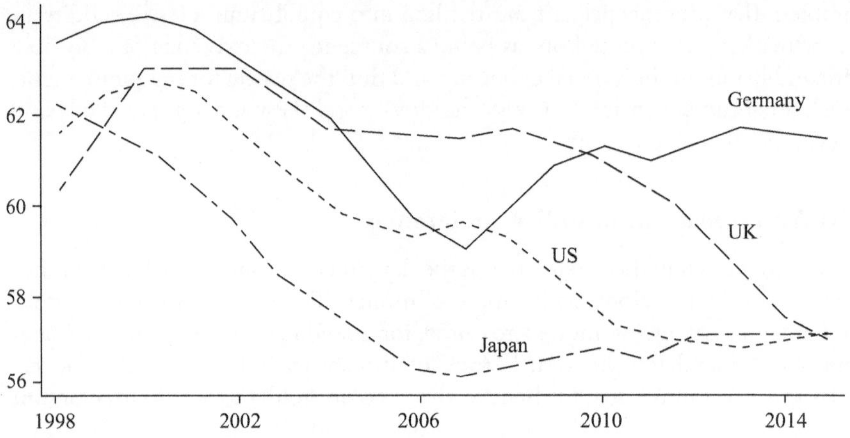

Figure 1.1 Labor share in some advanced countries (%).
Source: Berger and Wolff (2017).

empirical observations about consumption patterns and related variables in the US can help us with this. Some of them are as follows:

(i) A declining share of wages

It is fairly evident that the labor share of income in total national income in many countries and the global scale has been declining. Even though the estimation of labor share is problematic, it is quite clear that there has been a general decline all over the world. This is very clear in some selected advanced countries as seen in Figure 1.1. It seems that decline in the labor share in the US accelerated as of the early 2000s. In the UK, the fall in the labor share has been visible only more recently. It has declined continuously since 1980. The trend in Germany is a little different. It was quite comparable to the decline in the US, the UK, and in Japan until the Global Crisis, but then diverged from them in an upward manner.

The case of the United States is more critical because it is where the Global Recession started. Figure 1.2 shows the main trend in the share of wages in total income for the non-financial corporate sector in the longer period interval, starting in the late 1970s. There is no visible downward trend. This in fact is not consistent with the fact of stagnation of real wages of the majority of wages-earners while labor productivity grew continuously. Furthermore, taking into account only production workers, their real wages increased more slowly than the average. This seeming contradiction mainly stems from the fact that upper wages (including all bonuses, stock-options) increased much faster. This is seen in Figure 1.2. If the highest 5% of wages are excluded, the share of the remaining 95% shows a declining pattern since 1980. Furthermore, if

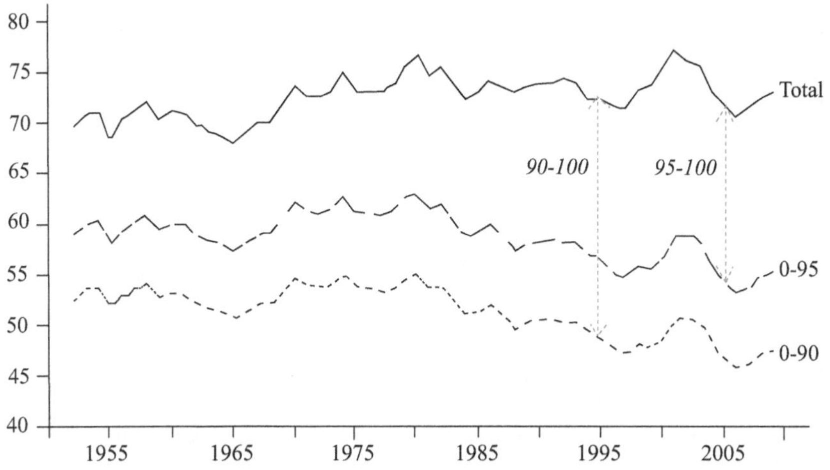

Figure 1.2 Percentage shares of wages in total income: the US non-financial corporate sector.
Source: Duménil and Lévy (2014).

instead of the highest 5%, the highest 10% is excluded, the distance between the two variables is constant as seen in Figure 1.2. Therefore it implies that income is concentrated in the upper 5%, but the income share of the 90–95 fractile did not change too much and the share of the 0–90 declined (Duménil and Lévy, 2014).

Some scholars such as Resnick and Wolff (2010) explained the crisis in 2007–2008 with stagnating wages. According to them, wage growth fails to keep pace with rising productivity since the 1970s. The relative fall or stagnation of wages, according to these authors, can be attributed to four additional factors contributing to the declining wage share: globalization that provides firms with opportunities to relocate their production in the countries with lower wages, new technologies that replace labor, entry of women into employment, and labor immigration. These factors pushed wages downward strongly.

(ii) Rising consumption and declining savings

During the neoliberal decades since the 1980s, saving rates in the US declined dramatically, until almost zero. The saving rate of both the higher income groups and lower income groups declined. The traditional savers also spent during the liberal decades; this especially accelerated until the Global Recession. Thus increasing income inequality did not help reduce the total demand in the economy. On the contrary, there was a great increase in expenditure during this period. While lower income groups experienced underconsumption, the fall in consumption was offset by additional demand by upper income groups. This expenditure pattern is shown in Figure 1.3. In this figure, household

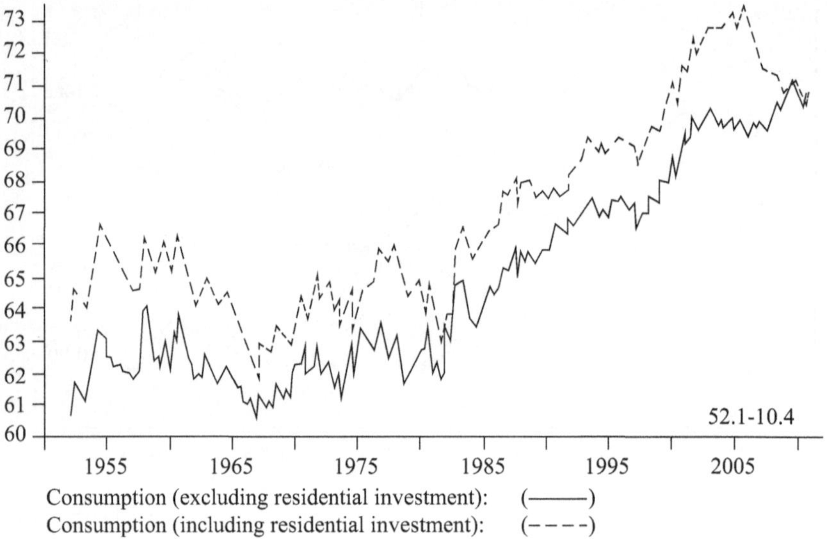

Figure 1.3 Household consumption in the US (% of GDP).
Source: Duménil and Lévy (2014).

consumption and total expenditure including residential are seen. In total, as seen, spendings increased almost 10 percentage points of GDP between 1980 and 2006. Hence there does not seem to be a decline in consumption over the period; thus instead of underconsumption there is an overconsumption supported by the rich groups (Duménil and Lévy, 2014).

This fact is also visible in Figure 1.4. As can be seen, labor productivity increases significantly despite the stagnation in wages (implying decline in labor share). However, consumption pattern is also upward despite the stagnation in wages. Beginning in the late 1970s, especially for the relatively poor groups, debt was the only way to maintain their consumption and thereby bank loans and credit cards were extensively used. Thus wage-earners began to consume beyond their budgets. This ultimately was unsustainable, which will be debated further in the following chapters of this book.

Therefore, in light of this data, some scholars assert that the Great Recession in 2007–2008 seems a crisis related to "excess demand" rather than "insufficient demand". In fact, there was a similar development in the 1920s before the Great Depression. During the 1920s—"the roaring twenties"—the economic boom was related to newly emergent consumption areas, such as how use of electricity induced people to buy electrical appliances and furniture for their houses. Moreover the more affordable cars (Ford's new Model T) were widely purchased by the public. And advertising fueled this consumption frenzy and even caused people to buy more on credit.

Consumption was also induced before the global crisis in 2007–2008 with various policies and developments, some of which can be defined as follows:

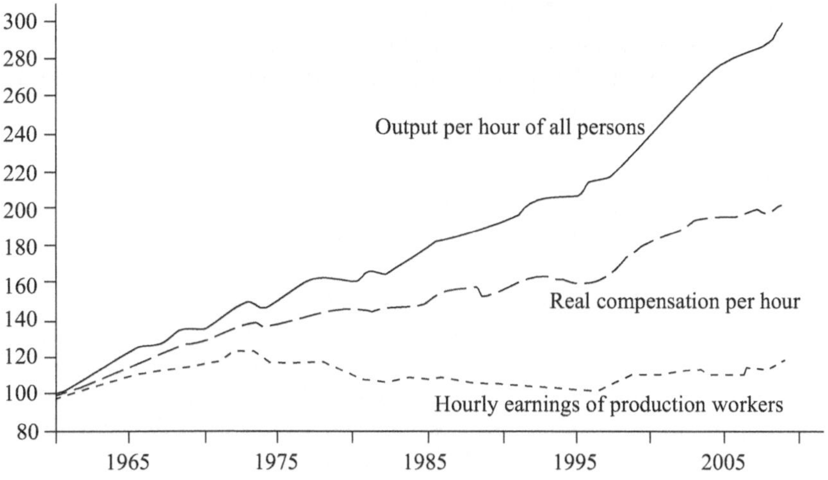

Figure 1.4 Labor productivity, compensations of labor, and ratio of prices (indices, 1960=100), the US business sector.
Sources: Kotz (2009) and Shaikh (2011).

(i) Loose monetary policy, such as reducing interest rates. Especially during the beginning of the 2000s after the dot.com crisis, interest rates declined and this in turn induced consumption through borrowing. So firms and households who wanted loans could obtain money more easily, but this in turn could place them into trouble with excessive borrowing.

(ii) Overdraft consumption, such as installments, shopping by credit card, and subprime mortgages. These payment instruments removed the limits imposed on cash-constrained consumers. Therefore consumption was financed by debt. This fact was valid during both of the great crises (Global Depression and Global Recession). Before the Global Depression, people used to buy even equities by down payments. During the 2000s leading to Global Recession, houses in particular were bought by installments.

(iii) Increasing inequality between the poor and the rich induced a catch-up incentive by the poor in consumption. As discussed in the later chapters of this book, due to the rise in income inequality since the 1980s, the relatively poor segments of society imitated the consumption patterns of the affluent. However, this was not supported by their own income sources because of stagnant wages as shown above. Hence they applied to borrow and this was not sustainable as seen during the Global Recession.

The policies followed above—overdraft consumption, the fall in interest rates, and catch-up incentives—created an impressive impact on aggregate demand over the last decades. Hence the tension between consumption and production was mitigated.

However, we have to mention that people's—especially poor people's—excessive consumption does not mean that they have enough purchasing power.

Due to tight budget constraint, the bottom income groups' demand is far from being satisfied so they see no alternative but credit consumption. It is exactly such borrowing that misled people into excess demand (overconsumption). Thus their demand is excessive relative to their income, which is too low due to big income disparity. However, this borrowing could not be sustained for a long time, so they ended up with defaults. As simple statistics to capture this case, Kumhof and Ranciere (2010) showed that bottom income groups' debt-to-income ratio increased from 62.3% in 1983 to 143.2% in 2008.

Regarding the role of insufficient demand in the emergence of crises, there is also another argument asserting that even though insufficient demand is not a cause of crises, during the hard times of a crisis people lower their consumption, hence effective demand is reduced and the crisis is deepened. This simultaneity, that is, the fall in consumption and the occurrence of crises at the same time, creates a misunderstanding that the fall in consumption is the reason for crises. In fact, during crises, the fall in consumption aggravates the effects and duration of crises but it is not the reason for crises. Hence, to get out of a crisis, we need to urge the actors in the economy to consume more. However, due to pessimistic expectations, it is hard to urge households to consume and firms to invest. As Keynes suggested, the only exit is to resort to the government. Thus, the government can expand public purchase when people consume less, because the poor cannot afford to consume enough and the rich start to save more. Hence the government has to compensate for this and act as "consumer" and "investor". For example, the Roosevelt Administration in the 1930s expanded investment in the construction of infrastructure such as roads, airports, schools, and hospitals. Furthermore, the welfare policies developed by the USA during the Global Depression in the 1930s were effective at increasing demand in the economy (such as the introduction of the social security system in 1935 and the Fair Labor Standards Act in 1938).

During the Global Recession in 2007–2008, in order to stimulate the economy, many countries applied expansionary fiscal policies in response to the recession. These countries increased their fiscal expenditure and reduced taxes to eliminate the stagnation in their economies. In fact all these were fiscal policy applications suggested by Keynesian theory to induce aggregate demand and to compensate for the fall in other expenditures, such as investment and general consumption. For example, firstly in 2008 the US Congress passed the Economic Stimulus Act, a $152-billion stimulus to mitigate the negative impacts of the crisis.

Later the US brought together many stimulus measures under the American Recovery and Reinvestment Act of 2009, a $787-billion bill including expenditures from rebates on taxes to investment. And the European Union also followed similar expansionary policies. It passed a 200-billion euro plan with member countries developing their own national plans. The stimulus plans of member nations amounted to at least 1.2% of GDP (Barrios et al., 2010).

1.4 Overproduction theory

Even though the underconsumption explanation of crises is frequently emphasized, another related but distinctive explanation is overproduction, which provides different perspectives from underconsumption theory.

Marx, in fact, as mentioned above, did not accept the main arguments of the theory of underconsumption; instead he focused on the essential limits of capital in the production process. According to Marx, the term "overproduction" has a potential to be misunderstood because it can create an illusion that the essential needs of everybody were provided. However, even though the most basic needs of the workers are limited, they may not be provided, especially during crises, thus the times of overproduction.

It is generally recognized that producers aim to expand their capital accumulation rather than meeting the needs of consumers. During the earlier stages of capitalist development, capitalists introduced several methods to increase the production of surplus value such as reducing wages, increasing labor productivity and increasing working hours. But there were limits to these policies to extract more surplus value. Hence capitalists applied other methods to overcome these barriers they faced such as developing new production methods to heighten the productivity of labor.

Capitalists try to increase the production of commodities. As long as they overcome the barriers to production, they increase the mass of commodities produced. This motivation to increase the mass of commodities is not the result of meeting the demand of consumers but it is mainly to grab more surplus value. The direct consequence of this is that the expansion of demand falls short of the growth of production.

The extent of competition among capitalists is not limited to the limits of the market. The capitalist does not take the conditions of production, or the extent of the market, as given but rather confronts them as barriers to the production and realization of surplus value. The overproduction of commodities is the result of every capitalist attempting to overcome these barriers, and capitalist competition is no more than the repetitive manifestation of the tendency to overproduction. Competition expresses the threat of extinction which confronts every capitalist, but the capitalist who succeeds in overcoming the barriers is able to realize his expanded capital, and perhaps even to appropriate a surplus profit. In this sense competition is the manifestation of the tendency to overproduction inherent in the social form of capitalist production.

Marx argues that production usually expands rapidly. This mainly stems from the increasing capital stock, improvements in technology and workers being more productive over time. However the market does not, and cannot, expand to meet this. This does not mean that surplus value is not realized (consumed), but the failure of the expansion of consumption to keep up with the expansion of production is one contradiction which forces the economic system to dramatic readjustments. If this confrontation between production and consumption is not mitigated, serious breakdowns probably occur.

Hence, in short, Marx sees the main problem of capitalism as overproduction not underconsumption. This is elaborated by Marx as follows:

> It is a pure tautology to say that crises are provoked by a lack of effective demand or effective consumption. The capitalist system does not recognize any forms of consumer other than those who can pay, if we exclude the consumption of paupers and swindlers. The fact that commodities are unsaleable means no more than that no effective buyers have been found for them, i.e. no consumers (no matter whether the commodities are ultimately sold to meet the needs of productive or individual consumption). If the attempt is made to give this tautology the semblance of greater profundity, by the statement that the working class receives too small a portion of its own product, and that the evil would be remedied if it received a bigger share, i.e. if its wages rose, we need only note that crises are always prepared by a period in which wages generally rise, and the working class actually does receive a greater share in the part of the annual product destined for consumption. From the standpoint of these advocates of sound and "simple" (!) common sense, such periods should rather avert the crisis. It thus appears that capitalist production involves certain conditions independent of people's good or bad intentions, which permit the relative prosperity of the working class only temporarily, and moreover always as a harbinger of crisis.
>
> (Marx, 1885, *Capital* Volume 2, chapter 20)

Pre-capitalist societies used to produce for the use values of commodities, rather than exchange values. People in these societies simply produce to meet their own needs. Hence overproduction was not a problem in them. But they suffered an underconsumption problem, originating from the scarcity of products determined by natural disasters and wars. This is in fact underproduction that leads to underconsumption. But the problem of overproduction is seen only in capitalist societies. The decision-making process of market societies is mainly decentralized and no planning pushes the intensification of competition that improves productivities in the production process, resulting in more products that are needed. But if capitalistic production were well designed, it would meet the basic needs of society. Hence Marx argues that the theory of underconsumption is not sensible.

The main problem is in the process of persistent capitalist accumulation, which implies both the concentration (increasing growth of the largest individual accumulations of capital) and centralization of capital (the increase of capital in the hands of a limited number of capitalists). The capital must search out new countries or markets to continue accumulating. If they cannot find them, they cannot place the surplus value to the production process, and a realization problem will emerge. This in short causes problems such as overproduction (goods that are not sold) and overaccumulation (the existence of excess capital).

After the Second World War, economic growth was the result of an effective combination of factors that accelerated the accumulation process, along with the development of the welfare states in advanced countries. During the period post-war, new global mechanisms were designed, which led to a new era of international relations. This is a phase of global accumulation in which capital was looking elsewhere for the realization of surplus value produced in the center.

Starting in the 1970s, the world economy (mainly advanced countries) experienced stagnation in growth and higher inflation. This induced liberals to dominate the economic and political debate. Their main argument was that the crisis was not associated with contradictions in the capital accumulation process. The crises, in their view, were mainly associated with mistakes made by governments that distorted the functioning of the markets. These views spread and got power in the US and UK at the beginning of the 1980s. They urged initiating the dismantling of the institutional structure that had promoted the globalization, and internationalization, of productive capital. The capital could no longer be constrained to a narrow geography. The capital demanded more mobility on a greater scale via mergers, acquisitions, and relocation of production plants. They thought that this was a new stage of accumulation to absorb surplus value.

The chain of crises in the USA, Asia, and Europe in the late 1990s and early 2000s, in the view of many analysts, was a result of overaccumulation. The foundations of these crises were laid by the booms in these regions in the early 1990s. On this issue, Rajan (2005, pp. 3–4) expresses this as follows:

> The current situation has its roots in a series of crises over the last decade that were caused by excessive investment, such as the Japanese asset bubble, the crises in Emerging Asia and Latin America, and most recently, the information technology bubble. Investment has fallen off sharply since, with only very cautious recovery.

Overcapacity was apparent in the New Economy in the 1990s and 2000s in the US. This was especially critical in the various large industries. Computer production capacity in the US increased 40% per year. This was much higher than the increase in demand. Similarly, automobile firms around the world were selling 70% of their production each year. And there was a similar excess capacity in the steel industry, around 20%, which was the largest gap between supply and demand since the 1930s (Bello, 2006).

Many scholars think that globalization and financialization are mechanisms designed to escape the pressures of overaccumulation and overproduction. In fact they worsened it. Especially along with global finance, overcapacity increased much more in several sectors, which was evident especially in the telecommunications industry. The excessive supply of capital, rather than demand, determined investment decisions. As a result, the telecom firms, under oceans and across the US, laid excessively long fiber-optic cables. One of the most serious factors increasing global overcapacity and overaccumulation has been the integration of China into the international economy. China's high growth during the last decades (about 8–9% per year) has created an enormous demand for the world economy. Hence China contributed too much to global overcapacity. Due to the increasing excess capacity, several countries such as Japan and other East Asian countries responded to this by reducing their investments.

This process of overinvestment was also intensified by transnational capital, which mainly was located in China in the late 1980s and 1990s. Transnational corporations saw China as the last frontier, the unlimited market that could endlessly absorb investment. However, since China imposed restrictions on foreign direct investment and trade, these corporations had to move the majority of their production structure to China, instead of outsourcing a limited part of their production. However, this led transnational corporations to overinvest in the countries (especially China) and build up a great production potential that is even larger than these countries or even the rest of the world can consume. As a result of this, for example, in some sectors such as steel, automobile, cement, aluminum, and real estate, idle capacity increased tremendously since the mid-1990s. As Bello (2006) points out, this results in the fact that over 75% of China's industries are currently confronted by excess capacity. In short it seems that overproduction has been a very fundamental concern in the development of capitalist production all over the world, having the potential to create deep crises.

1.5 Disproportionality theory

Another cousin concept related to underconsumption and overproduction is disproportionality. There are two types of approach within disproportionality theory. One is called the anarchy of production theory that mainly asserts that the anarchical production structure of capitalism can lead to disruptions in the production process, which was mainly developed by Mikhail Tugan-Baranov (1865–1919). Another approach is that of Rudolf Hilferding (1877–1941) who focused on the disproportions between the two great departments of production, Department I producing the means of production, and Department II producing the means of (personal) consumption. The relationship between these production departments can be distorted, so that one of these departments produces more with respect to the other. This ends up with a crisis.

Tugan's disproportionality view was based on criticism of underconsumption theory on the basis of Marx's reproduction schemes, which asserted that disproportionalities were the only possible source of crises, and that such crises were not necessary but contingent, stemming from the ignorance of capitalists and intensified by the increased volume of credit which sustained the disproportional expansion of production.

Tugan argues that the tendency to overproduction arises from disproportionality in different production departments, rather than underconsumption, that is, some branches grow more rapidly than others. Therefore a crisis demonstrates itself in overproduction in one department (reaching its limits), then it creates a chain effect, spreading to another department. Hence it is not necessarily the case that the specific branches producing means of consumption tend to overproduce and there is no particular reason to mention underconsumption as a form of disproportionality. Tugan argued that disproportionality is not a state in which there is a secular tendency creating underconsumption; instead it is simply associated with business cycles. Crises, in his view, correct disproportionalities and restart the conditions for new accumulation. Hence there is no reason to think that each successive crisis will be more severe due to the fact that there is no secular tendency of capital accumulation. In Tugan's view, moreover, instead of this secular tendency, ignorance of capitalists is critical in disproportionalities. So he advised more planning and regulations that would limit the expansion of credit to mitigate the cyclical tendencies of accumulation.

As mentioned above, the second group disproportionality theory was developed by Hilferding. He, in his book titled *Finance Capital* (1910), aimed to advance the Marxian analysis of capitalism. Instead of focusing on underconsumption, he emphasized the role of disproportionality on crises. In this sense, he drew attention to cartels and monopolies and credit mechanisms of financial institutions, thus mainly banks. Hilferding argued that the domination of finance capital was the new stage of capitalism. Banks captured industrial capital. This mainly arose from the fact that industrial capital needed a large amount of capital to make investments. Firms' increasing scale of production financed by banks reduced their capital mobility. Thus along with their cartelization tendency, firms having large industrial capital could not move easily and lost their flexibility to changes in the economy, leading to disproportionalities. In this sense, in Hilferding's view, these kinds of barriers to the equalization of supply and demand were the source of crises.

The capitalist dynamism, in Hilferding's view, was removed with large and capital-intensive firms, which reinforced the tendency of cartelization. Hence he focused on divergences in the rate of profits between different production departments. He tried to define the barriers to the equalization of the rate of profit. In fact, any emerging disproportionalities between branches due to difference in the rate of profit would disappear if capital was mobile between branches of production. Hence, in Hilferding's view, the source of instability in capitalist production is the impediments to capital mobility, equalization of the rate of profit constituted by fixed capital, cartels, and the subordination of productive to banking capital. Along with these barriers, sound connections between different branches of production are lost, leading to systematic disproportionalities via the barriers creating distortions in price mechanism. Hence Hilferding argued that only well-designed planning could prevent the tendency to crisis. He expressed this in the following:

> Planned production and anarchic production are not quantitative opposites such that by tacking on more and more "planning" conscious organization will emerge out of anarchy. Such a transformation can only take place suddenly by subordinating the whole of production to conscious control.
>
> (Hilferding, 1910, p. 296)

According to Hilferding, the disproportionalities that led to crises would not arise from the nature of the capitalistic production, but would occur in its developed stage of finance capital. With the introduction of large fixed capital and cartels that distorted the structure of profits, the disproportionalities would emerge. They did not emerge as accidental results of anarchical functioning of markets as Tugan pointed out. In this sense, crises were a result of fierce competition for profit. This is better elaborated as follows:

> The possibility of crises is implicit in unregulated production, that is to say, in commodity production generally, but it only becomes a real possibility in a system of unregulated production which eliminates the direct relationship between production and consumption characterizing other social formations, and interposes between production and consumption the requirement that capital shall be varicolored at a particular rate.
>
> (Hilferding, 1910, p. 241)

Hilferding emphasized the investment cycles that manifested themselves in disproportionalities, in which the main properties of the capitalist production process such as cartelization and dominance of finance would prevent avoidance. In this context, Hilferding identified a crisis as general overproduction, thus a sort of overinvestment cycle. Hence it was not related to underconsumption; instead it arose from the fall in profits leading to the fall in investments. The fall in profits originated from increasing physical capital (investment) or an increase in the organic composition of capital as Marx argued. This would stop new investments. Thus a crisis simply would start with the fall in the rate of profit. However, the fluctuations in the rate of profit were cyclical rather than secular, as opposed to Marx. Thus, the cycle would start with expansion of fixed capital due to the emergence of new markets and developing new technologies, etc.

Notice that even though Hilferding generally benefited from the conceptual tools of Marxism, his thoughts on crises did not move from the capitalist mode of production. Instead he identified crises as the result of market imperfections.

1.6 Concluding remarks

Depending on the political and economic environment, underconsumption crisis theory has taken different forms over time. The scholars were mainly divided into underconsumption, overproduction, and disproportionality crisis theorists. Although their initial arguments to explain crises were not that distinct, they diverged from each other much more over time. But in later periods, the disproportionality theories were sidelined by the other two theories.

In the 1960s Marxian scholars mainly started to emphasize the role of declining profit rates in the cause of capitalist crises. However, during the same period, differently from this view, Sweezy and Baran focused on the overproduction/underconsumption argument. At the same time the profit squeeze theory (mainly the fall in profits due to increasing wages) became highly popular among some Marxists. The main reason behind the increasing interest in state of profits was that Keynesian demand management policies could not mitigate the negative effects of the crises in the 1970s. And these crises did not have any connection with underconsumption, but rather seem to have been related to declining profits arising from capital accumulation and increasing wages.

Underconsumption theories explain economic slumps as demand-driven. As a result of this reasoning, the demand problem can be solved by creating new demand to counteract the fall in demand. A loose monetary policy (reducing interest rate) or expansionary fiscal policy can do this. The Keynesians argue that the Second World War ended the Great Depression, because the war played the role of expansionary fiscal policy. The policies of the New Deal were too small to stimulate the economy sufficiently. Similarly, to some economists, the governmental stimulus package was also small in the case of the global crisis in 2007–2008.

As mentioned earlier, underconsumption theory mainly claims that fall in demand leads to crises. In fact this is a kind of tautology, because recessions or crises are defined in the fall in national output, which is already decomposed as components of demand. The real question is why a slowdown occurs in demand, especially consumer demand, although underconsumption refers to all components of aggregate demand.

It is a fact that income distribution seems crucial in determining degree and patterns of consumption. This is more likely to lead to insufficient demand because those with lower propensity to consume save more as income inequality rises. This also causes another complication that is related to income inequality, which is the catch-up effect in consumption of the relatively poor people. They try to catch up with the rich in consumption when they observe that some people out there consume excessively. Hence they resort to credit to finance their consumption, and so the feelings of unjust suffering arising from a comparatively low level of consumption accelerate consumption. This naturally creates some distortions in the economy that can end up with economic crises at the aggregate level.

There are also under/overconsumption implications of global imbalances. Before the Global Recession, in 2007, personal consumption of gross domestic product (GDP) was twice as high as that in China. Thus while one country (the US) overconsumed, another one (China) underconsumed. Overconsumption in the US was financed by large levels of excessive borrowing, some fraction of which was financed by capital flows from China. Thus, the unbalanced structure in consumption (low saving) of the US was partially related to another type of structural imbalance in consumption (high saving) in China. And this was not sustainable. Notice that both countries were—in fact still are—quite bad in their income distributions. This caused different consequences. In the case of the US, this led to overconsumption and in the case of China this led to underconsumption. This mainly arises from the different economic and social structures of these countries. However, it is certain that levels of consumption, thus savings, of these countries played a critical part in development of the Global Recession.

Consequently I think that underconsumption, overproduction, and disproportionality all have a part to play in the occurrence and prolongation of crises. But each approach is one-sided. They are not mainly causes of crises, but rather features of one phase or another during the crisis. That is, they arise in the course of business cycles. The following chapters of this book will help us to see better the links between aggregate consumption and other related economic variables during crises.

Notes

1 Say's Law mainly states that everyone who sells something uses that money to buy something in return. So if a worker sells his or her labor, or a capitalist sells his products, they will use the money to buy. Because of this, there will always be enough demand in general.

2 The prisoner's dilemma is a standard example of a game analyzed in game theory that shows why two completely rational individuals might not cooperate, even if it appears that it is in their best interests to do so.

2 Debt accumulation

2.1 Introduction

Economists generally regard debt as a beneficial instrument that allows money to move from where it is least needed to where it is most needed by borrowers. Hence the deepening of national and international credit markets is thought to increase growth, since it makes it possible for more individuals to borrow from a bigger loan market at appropriate rates of interest. However, whenever a financial crisis occurs, debt turns out to be a problem, thus turning from a ladder into a chute. Hence in recent years the dynamics of debt and its relation with crises has become a much more important issue of economics.

During the global crisis period that started in 2007, a large number of defaults on mortgages occurred in the US. Financial institutions, especially investment banks, could not bear these defaults. Along with the contagion of defaults, banks with liquidity problems could not continue to lend, hence it spreading to the rest of the economy. Governmental rescues increased public debt as well. This also caused fears to spread about the solvency of sovereign debts of some countries in Europe, ending with Greece's collapse. Therefore, debt seems to have been both a cause and an outcome of the crisis.

However, until the Global Recession, in the mainstream economic models, debt was not regarded as an issue that could trigger a sequence of problems, hence it was not incorporated into these models. The main rationale behind this was that borrowers and lenders canceled each other out at the level of the economy, thus every dollar owed by someone was also owed to someone. Hence the incorporation of debt into economic analysis seemed trivial. However, we learn each time from austere times (during crises) that debt is critical in terms of triggering the problems and their deepening. Therefore, debt is a more complex issue and not a simple zero-sum game. Economists have started to deal with new complications by including debt in their economic models such as heterogeneity between debtors and creditors and discontinuity arising from collapse in economic relations.

The historical evidence shows the dangers of debt. The extent of these dangers created by increased debt depend on who has the debt (firms, banks, households or governments) and what kind of debt they have—depending on maturities (short or long) and financing types (loans or bonds) and types of currencies (domestic currency or foreign currency). In many diverse countries and periods, combinations of these forms can come to the fore. In one country, government debt can be a big problem, but in another country it can be private debt and with a short-term maturity, and it can even maybe be borrowed in foreign currency. Hence several forms of borrowing can emerge in different countries, so it can reveal itself in different problems.

Until the Asian crisis in 1997, economists were widely concerned with government debt. Along with this crisis, private debt became critical in understanding the crisis. The global crisis in 2007–2008 also showed that private-sector liabilities, namely household debt (the bulk of which was mortgages) and financial institutions (especially banks), was too high. In recent years, it also seems that household and corporate debt in many countries, especially in rich countries, have increased as a percentage of GDP. Households owed to financial firms, non-financial firms owed to financial firms and further at an increasing rate financial firms owed to financial firms. In particular the financial firms' debt structure has become more complicated over time; that is, borrowing from depositors and bondholders, borrowing from and lending to financial firms (lending to lenders). Hence they enter a huge debt and asset relationship at the same time.

It seems that systemic crises have a common feature, which is that they involve debt, without which there would be no crises. If the debt level is not controlled, it has the potential to hamper economic growth especially in consumer-based economies, since people have a tendency to tighten their belts during hard times. Under these circumstances, people often use their disposable income to reduce their debt, thus deleveraging. This deepens the problems in the economy further. Thus, excessiveness of these debts may not only lead to crises but can also prolong the pain of crises, especially due to debt reduction (deleveraging) that can impose heavy costs. In short, while leveraging or borrowing produces seemingly positive effects such as increasing consumption, investment, employment and asset prices and so on, the reverse case, namely deleveraging, generates negative chain effects and more painful outcomes.

In this chapter, essentially we will search the importance of debt accumulation in the emergence of crises, especially the global crisis in 2007–2008, and its deepening factor on them. There are different forms of debt such as private, public domestic and sovereign debts. Analysis of their trends and dynamics will help us to observe the dangers of debt accumulation in each form of debt. We will debate their own dynamics and inherent properties that can drive and deepen the financial crises in the following sections.

2.2 Increasing debt

In this section, we firstly look at the general trends in debt, in particular during the run-up to the global crisis in 2007–2008. Then we trace domestic and sovereign (foreign) debt trends in general in the following subsections.

Over the last decades, it is a well-recognized fact that households, firms and governments have been borrowing much more than before. And the widespread perception in particular that both the global financial crisis in 2007–2008 and the European sovereign debt crisis were caused by excessive borrowing urged scholars further to focus on this subject.

During recent decades, in many countries and sectors debt has grown in an extreme manner. As of the 1980s, private debt, namely debts of household and firms, grew strongly. Figures show that the total gross debt of the non-financial sector in several advanced economies was $12.3 trillion or 168% of the GDP of these countries in 1980. But these figures increased to dramatic levels in 2011. It increased tenfold, reaching the value of $128.5 trillion, which was 315% of their total GDP (Buiter and Rahbari, 2012).

In funding markets, individuals and corporates trade billions of dollars each day through several debt instruments. These debt instruments are mainly treasuries, repos, asset-backed commercial papers, mortgage-backed securities and money-market funds. They are used for managing their cash balances and short-term liquidity needs. These financial instruments seem to have created no problems for a long time. However, along with collapse of these funding markets in the global crisis in 2007–2008, new concerns have come to the fore about how they function and what kinds of problems they can lead to.

One of the main widespread potential risks in funding markets is that debt contracts are used as collateral. That is, for example, where asset-backed commercial papers are debt instruments backed by commercial papers which are also debt. Mortgage-based securities are one of these debt instruments because they are backed by mortgages which are debt. Repo is also such a financial contract that is based on other debt instruments as collateral. This points out the sequence of debt structure behind debt obligations. Any breakdown in this chain can trigger a financial collapse. Since liquidity provision for economic actors is extremely crucial for the real economy, any default in the debt chain can deepen the problems in the economy.

Trades in debt markets are predominantly made by financial institutions. By a financial institution, we do not mean only a traditional commercial bank but also other financial institutions which trade in debt markets. They do not collect deposits from households or non-households like banks but they function in debt markets in the same way as banks do. They are insurance companies, pension funds, hedge funds, investment banks and mutual funds, etc. All these financial institutions take place in funding markets, carrying out operations of buying and selling debt instruments in very great volumes.

As mentioned before, there has been an overborrowing tendency all over the world in recent decades. There are several explanations for this development. In addition to macroeconomic factors, continued economic growth and rising asset prices in recent years generated positive expectations for further increases in asset prices due to adaptive expectations. Along with these developments, real interest rates declined significantly because nominal interest rates fell further than inflation in many countries. This induced borrowing due to declining financing costs. Before the global crisis in 2007–2008, the volatility in financial markets had declined; this period was even called "Great Moderation" by Bernanke (2005). Due to declining in risk perception together with underestimation of risk by regulators and agents in the economy, there was an increase in credit demand and supply, increasing the degree of indebtedness. In Europe, the introduction of the euro in 1999 and rapid financial integration gave an additional boost to borrowing (domestic and sovereign debt) due to rapid declines in interest rates in many countries. Along with the introduction of euro, spreads over ten-year bonds of peripheral countries (like Greece and Portugal and Ireland) declined and hence their sovereign debts increased sharply.

There is another cause of this overborrowing problem: market failure. Markets can send out wrong signals to borrowers about the risks undertaken by all the agents in the economy. These wrong signals create perceptions that increased indebtedness is not a significant problem. For example, Greece faced such a situation. In the 1990s, the interest rate paid by the Greek government was much higher than the German 10-year bonds, around 5-6% higher. But this changed after Greece joined the Eurozone. The capital flowed into Greece, and consequently interest rates began to decline sharply, close to the interest rates valid in Germany. In 2005, the interest rates of 10-year Greek sovereign bonds were only about 0.2% above German bonds. This created a false impression that the Greek government could roll over their debts perpetually.

One another explanation behind excessive borrowing is that wages in the US have failed to rise in the last 30–40 years. This further led to a divergence in income equality. Debt became one of the financial tools to mitigate the stagnation of real wages in the US. People in the US have maintained a rising standard of living through borrowing when their real wages did not rise. This was especially seen in the dramatic rise in mortgage debt.

The situation in the US since the 1980s provides a good example: Although workers' productivity (the output per labor) increased by 70% over the 1980–2005 period, the average hourly wage increased only by 4.4% (ILO, 2010). In other words, the income that was generated during the production of output did not translate to sufficient demand, because most of the increase in output went to those at the top. In order to compensate for this, people tried to create additional purchasing capacity, and this was achieved through borrowing from deregulated credit markets.

Many scholars argue that there is no doubt that the dramatic increase in inequality during the 2000s accelerated the debt-fueled housing bubble and financial crisis. This is expressed by Piketty (2014, p. 297) as follows:

> one consequence of increasing inequality was virtual stagnation of the purchasing power of the lower and middle classes in the United States, which inevitably made it more likely that modest households would take on debt, especially since unscrupulous banks and financial intermediaries, freed from regulation and eager to earn good yields on the enormous

savings injected into the system by the well-to-do, offered credit on increasingly generous terms.

It seems that income inequality fed economic instability during the run-up to the Great Recession in 2007–2008 in two ways. First, stagnation of wages caused increased demand for credit, leading to a housing bubble. Second, the increased financial funds of the rich went to new risky financial products. Particularly risk-taking behavior of hedge funds, whose main customers were the rich, accumulated the total risk in the financial system, turning the whole system into a casino. This subject of inequality and crises will be discussed in more detail in later chapters of the book.

Household debt increased drastically over the same period as the income inequality went up dramatically. This is seen in Figure 2.1. During the 2000s, the debt-to-income ratio increased drastically, accompanied by stagnation of wages. The increased lending to the lower- and middle-income groups led to a boom in demand and increased the economic growth of the early 2000s. But it was soon seen that this was not sustainable; the housing market collapsed. Many households could not bear these high levels of debt with their low wages.

Globalization over the last two decades provides an explanation of declining wages in advanced countries. Wages in high-wage countries have declined because of the competition of imports from low-wage countries; and capitalists discovered that they could employ low-wage workers to do the same work that was previously undertaken in high-wage locations. The main character of globalization of the recent period is precisely the geographical extension of the

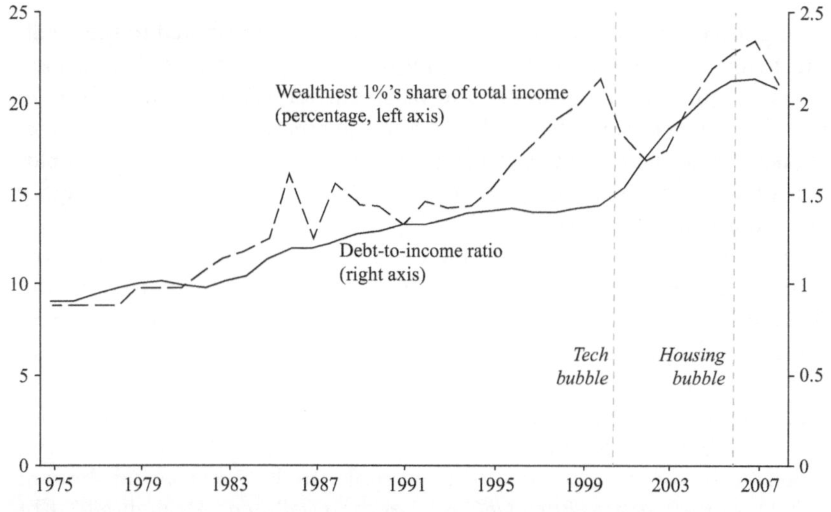

Figure 2.1 Household debt-to-income ratio and income inequality.
Source: The US Congress Joint Economic Committee (2010).

production circuit. As transnational corporations outsourced more and more stages of the production process to workers in low-wage countries, the division of the produced value between wages and profits became more unequal. This led to the emergence of a large segment of the labor force in the advanced economies who have been less formally employed and have been essentially competing with low-wage labor in the emerging economies. They have been forced to live with declining wages while firms have increased their profits.

In recent decades, a loosening of credit constraints by banks has also allowed these relatively low-wage households to increase their debt. Financial innovation driven by financial liberalization and deterioration of lending standards further urged this increase in credit availability. The deregulation of financial markets created long-standing effects on certain areas, from a lowering of prudential regulations in the financial institutions and markets to reductions on barriers on capital flows across countries. Compared to traditional banking firms regulated much more tightly, some other financial institutions and instruments have been regulated less. That is, lower capital and reserve requirements for some other financial institutions, products and activities caused the development of more loosely regulated institutions, which led to the emergence of the shadow banking sector.

Along with greater credit availability due to widespread deregulation around the world in the last decades, we observed many excessive-debt country cases. For example, the authorities in the Scandinavian countries reduced the regulations on financial products in the 1980s. In Iceland in the 2000s, households' access to debt was eased significantly due to liberalization of the banking system. Similarly, in Hungary, household debt grew about fivefold between 1999 and 2007 along with their prospect of EU membership (IMF, 2012).

Rising prices of financial assets and real estate also contributed to the credit boom, hence excessive borrowing. Many people expected these higher asset prices to continue in the future and to be sustainable. As the price of houses increased, more people participated in the housing market and more mortgages were taken. The increase in asset prices (mainly houses) induced households further to withdraw loans against equity in their homes (called home equity loans) to meet their consumption.

Compared to the developments in the 2000s, we also observe similar factors leading to excessive borrowing in the case of the roaring years of the 1920s in the US before the Global Depression. These years in both eras show that credit availability and optimistic expectations of economic agents induced further borrowing. In the 1920s, new innovative products such as automobiles and radios flooded the markets due to technological innovations. Households took loans to buy houses, consumer durables and automobiles due to the easiness provided by financial innovations. For example, in 1927 households bought two-thirds of their home appliances and cars on installment. Households' debt increased from 4.5% of personal income in 1920 to 9% in 1929. Furthermore, over the same period in the US the ratio of mortgage debt to national product increased from 11% to 28%. Even though these forms of debts (high-leveraged mortgage loans) were increasing at this time, they were not as complicated and risky as financial products in the 2000s (Snowden, 2010). Consequently, it is a very clear trend that debt burden of the agents (households, financial and non-financial corporations, governments) increased before important systemic crises such as the Great Depression in 1929 and the Global Recession in 2008.

2.2.1 Empirical trends in domestic debt

Domestic debt or internal debt includes private and domestic public debt. The total domestic debt in a country is owed to lenders within that country. Domestic debt's complement is sovereign or external debt in which the lenders are foreigners. Private domestic debt is debts owed by domestic households, financial and non-financial corporations while domestic public debt is the debt that the government borrows from domestic agents.

During the boom in the US during the period 2001–2007, the total debt of households (mortgage plus credit card debts) increased about twofold, from $7 trillion to $14 trillion. This change, namely the increase in the ratio of debt-to-income, has not been seen since the Great Depression (Shiller, 2012). Increasing this leverage was associated with the boom in home prices before the global financial crisis. Mortgage lenders presented a diverse range of financial products to households to ease their payments; for example, the lower down-payments mechanism very much induced home buyers to borrow more for buying more expensive homes.

In order to describe the extent of borrowing in the US, we can use another proxy for this: the number of credit cards per person. Just before the global crisis in 2007–2008, in the US each person had on average five credit cards compared to thirty-three persons per credit card in China. Until the crisis, advertisement of credit cards in the US became widespread and they were sent to everybody regardless of the fact of whether they could finance their purchases or not. Widespread use of credit cards signaled a serious problem. Increased use of credit cards before the crisis contracted likewise in a sharp sense after the crisis. In recent years, people increasingly recognized the fact that aggressive credit card promotions led to excessive debt.

Since the US was the center of the global crisis, we need to look at the detailed analysis of the US debt markets. It is evident that the role of the financial institutions in the US was crucial in increasing home prices. Starting in 1995 and until 2003, financial institutions used rather traditional methods in financing mortgages. But in 2003 the mortgage market reached its boundary, drying up. For this reason, mortgage lenders searched for a new market for their mortgage loans. They started to use non-traditional tools to expand this market. They looked for new customers for their loans.

This new situation created a new lending environment. Along with this, three developments were observed. First, individuals with risky credit history and less money were given mortgage loans to buy houses. Second, these newcomers entered the housing market once house prices had already increased too much. Hence they also took on mortgages, increasing further mortgage loans in the economy. Third, these newcomers were riskier customers; they were charged higher interest rates. This means that they were more exposed to more risk when house prices started to fall. All these developments increased further the damage of the market crash in 2007–2008 for these indebted people. When the markets crashed, an average home lost about a quarter of its value. This caused millions of homeowners to get into negative equity, and thus their homes' values were lower than the balances on their mortgages, which is also called an underwater mortgage[1]. Therefore they could not finance their mortgages and ended up in foreclosure.

The mortgage market in the US expanded exponentially over time. Its volume rose from $458 billion in 1990 to $4 trillion in 2003 (its peak value). Most of them were securitized as mortgage-backed securities (MBS). Figure 2.2 displays the sources of total loans during the period 1990–2008. The sharp increase in the mortgage market occurred in 2001, standing at $1 trillion a year. In this year, the dot.com crisis occurred. Hence, in order to mitigate its detrimental effect, the Federal Reserve Bank (the Fed) reduced interest rates sharply and this in turn led to a new refinancing and house-purchasing boom. In the following years, during the period 2002–2004, residential loans in the US went up from about $1 trillion to about $4 trillion. The reason for this rise

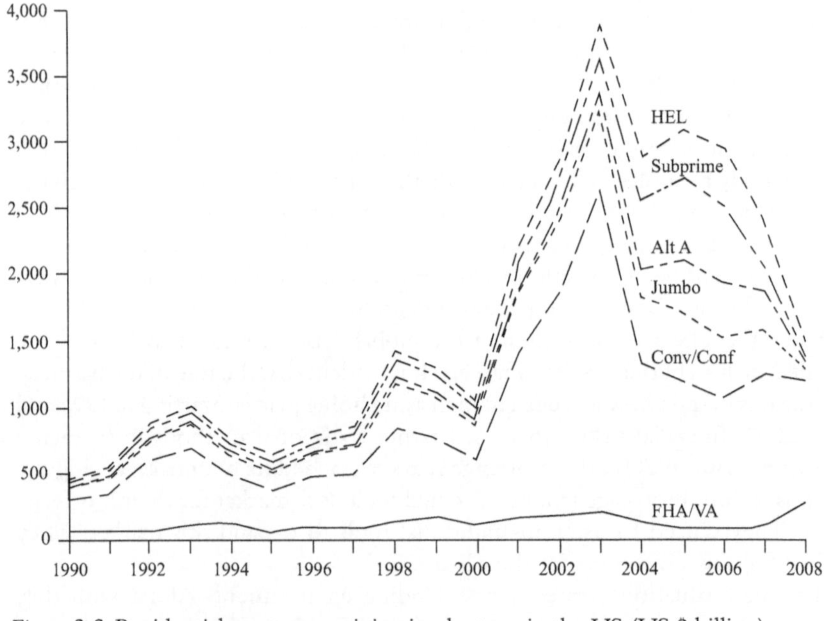

Figure 2.2 Residential mortgage origination by type in the US (US $ billion). Source: Inside Mortgage Finance (2009).

mostly originated from households' refinancing their mortgages to benefit from lower interest rates (Fligstein and Goldstein, 2010).

As seen in Figure 2.2, the banks increased their non-prime lending largely after 2003. They hunted for subprime groups. The transformation of the mortgage market can be seen in the figure. The Federal Housing Administration (FHA) and the Veteran's Administration (VA) were institutions that lent mortgage loans despite their limited share in the market. The largest market share of mortgage loans was conventional mortgages with fixed interest rate, most of which were securitized into MBS. It is evident that the important segment of the mortgage market during the period 1990–2003 was these two groups of loans. However, there was a drastic transformation starting in 2003, namely a compositional shift of mortgage loans. People were lent jumbo loans, whose sizes were larger and which did not conform to the guidelines of the government agencies. Home equity loans (HEL) were loans given in relation to the equity in houses purchased with mortgage loans. Alt-A and subprime mortgages (loans with lower credit quality) were given to households lacking an ability to make payments. In the history of the US, this was the first time that the sum of these four categories of loan became more than the conventional (prime) market.

It seems that there were two main reasons behind the fact that the banks preferred to make more non-prime loans. First, the traditional markets had dried up; there were fewer households with appropriate credit history. Second, subprime origination and securitization turned out to be largely profitable. Securitization was profitable because interest rates in the country were low, and naturally securities collateralized with mortgage loans (MBS) became attractive for their higher returns for investors. It also motivated the mortgage lenders to create more subprime loans as much as they could. In this way, they created more securities from mortgages where they earned fees for producing and selling these securities.

Subprime mortgages were attractive for both lenders and borrowers. Borrowers took these loans because they expected the house prices to go up. Adjustable-rate mortgages were also influential on their buying houses because they predicted the prices of houses they bought would increase and could pay their installments easily. Lenders also expected that house prices would continue going up in the short term, offsetting other credit risks and justifying lower initial interest rates. Borrowers, with expectation of increasing house prices, thought to refinance their loans using accumulated home equity before the mortgages reset to the higher interest rate. This incentive explains why about two-thirds of subprime loans during the period 2000–2006 were for refinance purposes rather than new purchases.

Domestic public debt is another important part of total domestic debt. Figure 2.3 displays the evolution of public debt and private credit by banks in the developed countries since 1870. It seems that there are two main trends in the development of debt. The first trend is about public debt ratio. It started to increase from the late 1970s until the mid-1990s. But later it tended to go down

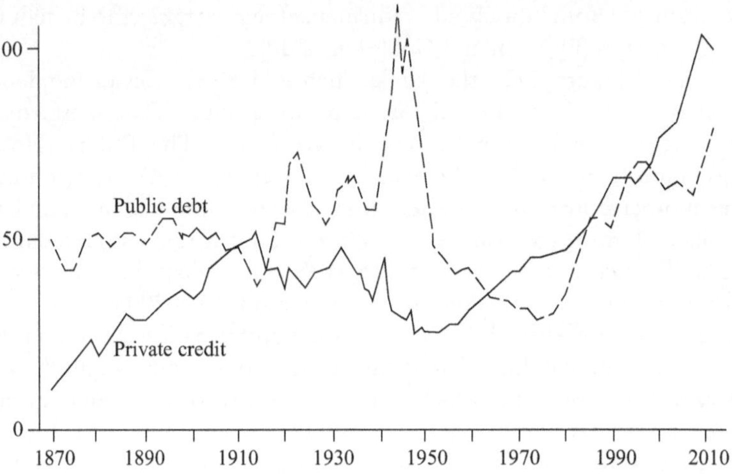

Figure 2.3 Public debt and private credit in advanced economies since 1870 (% of GDP). Source: Jorda et al. (2013).

toward its historical peacetime average before the crisis in 2008. The second trend is that private debt deviated from the historical pattern that maintained until the 1970s. It increased to unprecedented record levels prior to the crisis in 2008 (Jorda et al., 2013).

These trends represent the importance of private-sector borrowing in the development of the global crisis in 2008. Thus the risks loaded onto the financial system were generally concentrated in the private sector, not in the public sector. However, there were some exceptional cases of excessive levels of public debt such as Greece. Nevertheless in the most advanced countries, public debt levels before the crisis did not turn out to be a serious problem. But after the global financial crisis, the public finance of the countries in general deteriorated immensely through falling tax revenues and rising cyclical expenditures.

The historical record of defaults on domestic public debt shows that they are hardly rare even though they are less frequently seen than external defaults. Reinhart and Rogoff (2010) present a data set that includes 68 domestic defaults (compared to 250 post-1800 external debt defaults). For instance, as a more recent case, Argentina defaulted three times on its domestic debt during the period 1980–2001. Two of these defaults coincided with defaults in external debt in 1982 and 2001. The crisis in Turkey in 2000–2001 was also mainly a domestic public debt crisis, along with banking problems. In the period before the crisis, public-sector borrowing in Turkey was very high, and this was mainly financed by domestic debt. The level of external debt to GDP was relatively low. Along with a worsening banking sector, the sizable domestic debt facilitated the collapse in 2001 in Turkey.

2.2.2 Trends in sovereign debt

The economic literature mainly emphasizes sovereign or foreign debt owed to foreign creditors. In this type of debt, the debt to foreigners becomes more important as compared with domestic debt. Foreign debt is emphasized due to the "us vs them" distinction. Foreign or sovereign debt is in particular very critical for emerging markets.

Sovereign debt crises are a recurring phenomenon. Reinhart et al. (2003), for instance, point out that France defaulted on its sovereign debt eight times between 1500 and 1800. And there were thirteen sovereign debt defaults in Spain during the period 1500–1900. Similarly Tomz and Wright (2007) evidence that 106 countries experienced 250 sovereign defaults during the period 1820–2004.

Figure 2.4 displays the percentage of all countries that defaulted during the period 1800–2009. Throughout this period, many countries suffered foreign debt defaults. As seen there are five significant default cycles. The first cycle is during the Napoleonic Wars (1803–1815). The second cycle is the period 1820–1840, when about half the countries in the world defaulted (including all of Latin America). The third period starts with the early 1870s and lasts for two decades. The fourth period is the period 1930–1950. This period spans the Great Depression until the end of Second World War. About half of all countries went bankrupt in this period. The last period is the 1980–1990s period, where mainly emerging countries defaulted (Reinhart and Rogoff, 2011).

As the figure presents, default periods occurred in clusters, corresponding to successive expansion of lending and increasing large capital inflows. In the

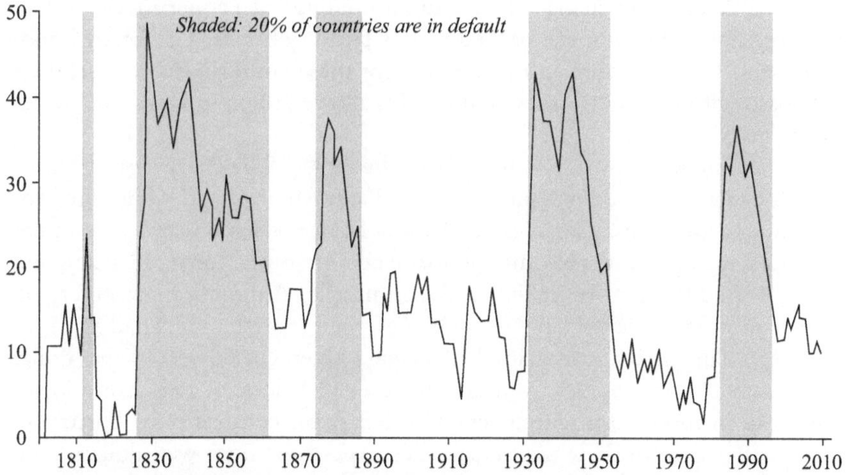

Figure 2.4 Sovereign external debt: 1800–2006 (% of countries in default or restructuring).
Source: Reinhart and Rogoff (2009).

20th century, the advanced countries faced defaults only during the Great Depression and the Second World War. However, throughout the 20th century, the frequency of defaults in particularly developing countries increased too much and after these crises they struggled to obtain funds from foreign capital markets for several years. Developing countries, especially Latin countries, experienced a wave of sovereign defaults in the early 1980s. The number of sovereign debts in default also peaked in the 1990s; for example, the Russian sovereign debt crisis in 1998. More recently the European sovereign debt crisis of 2009–2012 occurred.

Since the Second World War, the issue of sovereign default has been mainly associated with developing countries. The third-world debt of the 1980s was the biggest. The banks in the developed countries had expanded their credits in the 1970s, in part by recycling the surpluses generated by the oil-exporting nations. Increased oil prices increased the revenues of oil-producing countries in the 1970s. These countries gave more loans to governments and state companies in Latin-economic countries such as Mexico, Brazil, Argentina, and other developing countries. The foreign debt of these countries increased tremendously. With this foreign money, they financed their large trade deficits.

However, Mexico and other developing countries met with unpleasant developments, for example, the interest rates charged to them increased in the international capital markets and their export revenue declined drastically. Hence Mexico could not meet its debt repayments and the crisis quickly spread to the rest of Latin America, such as Brazil and Argentina at the beginning of the 1980s. The US banks were exposed to heavy losses. But the so-called Brady plan (named after the US Treasury Secretary Nicholas Brady) came to the rescue. It allowed banks to exchange their illiquid holdings of Latin American debt into more liquid instruments, backed by US Treasury bonds. The Brady bonds in 1989 and 1990 provided an opportunity for these countries to convert their bank loans with the US treasury bonds. This allowed them to access the global finance markets again.

Debt problems were spread to Asia in the 1990s. The Asian countries, in general, had a much better reputation than Latin America and were noted for their rising economies, characterized by low labor costs and heavy investment in manufacturing. The economic performance of South Korea, Thailand and Taiwan caused them to be called an Asian miracle. Although these emerging Asian economies achieved rapid growth rates, their growth model had a serious problem. Many Asian countries had pegged their currencies to the dollar to maintain export competitiveness. However, US interest rates were lower than those in most Asian countries. This led Asian companies to borrow in dollars rather than in their own currencies. And these borrowed dollars were channeled to the domestic markets. This caused another speculative bubble, in which Asian companies borrowed from domestic banks to invest in commercial property. When the property bubble burst, and the banks collapsed, Asian countries had to turn to the IMF.

Notice that in the 1980s and 1990s, sovereign debt crises forced governments to turn to the IMF. The end of the Bretton Woods system had caused the IMF to be an important emergency provider of finance to the developing world. The loans by IMF to these countries often carried strict conditions that reflected what was known as the "Washington Consensus", forcing them to follow liberal policies in every area of the economy and stipulating that they would reduce public spending.

With the liberalization of financial markets since the 1980s, with help of the IMF, there have been repeated foreign capital cycles that many developing countries have experienced. Along with financial liberalization, capital flowed into developing countries. The capital inflows caused domestic assets to go up and their currencies appreciated. Appreciation of foreign currencies suppressed inflation in these countries and this opened the way to the central banks to continue their expansionary monetary policies. However, this was not sustainable due to increased current account deficits. The process for these countries generally resulted in large depreciations of their currencies. This in turn ameliorated the banking crises because there were large numbers of domestic borrowers who borrowed in foreign currency. The immediate sales of domestic assets (financial and real estate) during this stressful process caused their prices to plummet. The balance sheets of the banks deteriorated further. This led to the failures of banks. Hence in such situations there was a coincidence of banking and currency crises.

Global boom-bust cycles, in fact, have been prevalent since the 1980s. This created a pattern in the direction of capital flows: During a global boom phase, capital flows from the core countries to the peripheral countries and then, suddenly, back to the core countries. During the phases in which money flows back to the core, a number of peripheral countries suffer from crises. In this way, these countries have regularly experienced several boom-bust cycles since the 1980s. During the first boom phase in the second half of the 1970s, capital mainly flowed to Latin America. The bust came in the early 1980s, together with the very restrictive monetary policy in the USA at the end of the 1970s, and left a destructive effect in Latin America for a decade. In the early 1990s, after opening their capital accounts, the Asian and transition countries were flooded with capital flows. The so-called Tequila crisis in Mexico in 1994 only interrupted this boom cycle for a short time. The boom phase continued until the Asian crisis broke out in 1997. In the 2000s, a new wave of increasing capital flows to emerging countries started, which was interrupted with the end of the global crisis in 2009. But with low interest rates in the core countries after the global crisis, capital flows again began to flow to peripheral countries.

Empirical evidence also indicates that a foreign debt default for a country can stem from various reasons. Tomz and Wright (2007) evidence that during the last 200 years, 62% of defaults occurred in the years when the country's growth rate was less than its long-term growth rate. In a similar manner, Broda (2004) documents that fluctuations in terms of trade (ratio of the price of exports to the price of imports) were especially a critical element behind the crises in some emerging economies. Moreover, great events such as wars or civil conflicts can also lead to sovereign defaults because they lowered their revenues and tax sources. Sovereign defaults may also be triggered by a devaluation of the local currency when a relatively large fraction of the sovereign's debt is denominated in foreign currency and its revenues rely heavily on the taxation of non-tradable goods. The magnitude of crises triggered by a devaluation of the local currency can be intensified by currency mismatches of households, the non-financial corporate sector, or the banking sector.

The recent global recession in 2007–2008 clearly generated a great amount of sovereign debt through the collapse of sources of tax revenues that the sovereigns had depended on. The measures to provide fiscal stimulus and the bail-outs of banks, other financial institutions and sometimes non-financial companies also increased sovereign debt-financed governmental expenditures. This was seen first with the collapse of Iceland's banking sector in late 2008, with the recent cases of Greece, Ireland, Spain and Portugal.

In recent decades, sovereign debt crises seem to have been significantly associated with developments in the banking sector. Sovereign debt crises, as argued by Reinhart and Rogoff (2011), coincide with or follow banking crises. But in fact the occurrence of twin sovereign debt and banking crises is not as common as that of cases that include a currency crisis. The recent European sovereign crisis was an example of this, the coincidence of twin crises, namely both a banking crisis and a sovereign debt crisis. Due to the single currency it was not a currency crisis.

Bank assets are mainly composed of loans and securities. These securities are either issued by the private sector or sovereigns. During normal times banks will hold sovereign securities as a means to maintain liquidity, but, during times of sovereign debt stress, banks prefer to hold risky sovereign securities to get more return. This happened during the recent European sovereign crisis. There were several reasons for this from banks' perspectives. First, sovereign securities became the safest asset for domestic banks of the countries in Europe when the private sector seems riskier. Second, central banks regarded sovereign securities as collateral in their operations with banks. Third, banks held sovereign debt securities to avoid holding more capital requirements because their risk weight in capital requirements was minor in most cases[2].

During the course of the European crisis in 2010, these developments induced the banks in the core countries in Europe, especially German and French banks, to finance the southern countries' (periphery countries) trade deficits. This resembles the process of the case where the increasing petrodollars of the oil-exporting countries in the 1970s were invested in the US and European banks. In the 1970s, the banks in the US had made sizable loans to emerging economies, especially Latin American countries. The banks became vulnerable when these countries could not pay their debts back in the early 1980s. In the same manner, the banks in Germany and France experienced the same problem during the sovereign crisis in Europe. The southern European countries had difficulties with paying their debts back.

Here I would like to finalize this section with theories aiming to explain currency crises, which are mentioned above in several places. Currency crises are critical for emerging countries which generally borrow in foreign currency rather their own currency. They do not have the privilege of countries like the USA and some other developed countries which can accumulate foreign debt in their domestic currency. Hence boom-bust cycles damage developing countries more than developed ones during currency crises. A theoretical analysis of this kind of crisis can help us to trace the mechanisms leading to them.

Theories on currency crises have evolved over time as the nature of such crises has changed. In particular, the literature has evolved from a focus on the fundamental causes of currency crises to emphasizing the scope for multiple equilibria, and to stressing the role of financial variables, especially changes in balance sheets, in triggering currency crises. Three generations of models in the literature are mainly employed to explain currency crises that took place during the past four decades.

First-generation currency crisis models explain the cases of fiscal policies that are not compatible with exchange rate policy. When countries follow up expansionary monetary policy (printing money) to finance their budget deficit, they get into trouble due to the phenomenon called the trilemma: Open economies can simultaneously choose only two out of the three policy targets of control over the exchange rate, monetary policy autonomy and free capital mobility. In an environment with flexible capital flows across borders, trying to expand money supply to support a fiscal deficit causes the fixed exchange rate regime to become unsustainable and ends eventually in a currency crisis. The first-generation models were mostly developed to explain the crises which occurred in Latin America in the 1960s and 1970s. The deterioration of the fundamentals resulting from inconsistent economic policies in these countries led to financial crises. These models' main focus was on the dynamics of speculative attacks against a currency at the root of which fundamental imbalances take place.

However, the onset of the European exchange rate mechanism (ERM) crisis in Europe in the early 1990s showed that the first-generation models were incapable of explaining crises such as the ERM crisis. The crises of EMS in 1992–1993 cannot be related to expansionary monetary policies since most of the European countries implemented strict and converging policies in accordance with the Bundesbank in order to promote the single European currency. In this sense, the second-generation models were developed by economists to explain them. According to these models, these crises were better described as the outcome of self-fulfilling speculative attacks and herding behavior by investors rather than the unique equilibrium described by the first-generation models. Instead of an inconsistency between the fiscal and monetary policies followed, the critical reason for this kind of crises was elaborated as the outcome of a game between investors on one side and governments on the other with each having well-defined goals and objectives.

Although first- and second-generation currency crisis models have been successful in explaining former currency crises, they could not explain the East Asia crisis in 1997–1998. Some properties of the East Asian crisis were not observed in previous crises. For example, the crisis countries had sound macroeconomic fundamentals such as low budget deficits or surpluses, low unemployment and low current account imbalances, which make first-generation models inapplicable. Furthermore, these economies were not facing any exchange rate stability problems, which also makes second-generation models inapplicable. Hence, the Asian crisis of the late 1990s led to a third class of models being proposed. These models focus on increasing evidence of a close link between banking sector problems and currency crisis episodes.

In the case of Asian countries, macroeconomic imbalances were not at dangerous levels before the crisis—fiscal positions were often in surplus and current account deficits appeared to be manageable—but vulnerabilities associated with financial and corporate sectors were large. Models show how balance sheets mismatches in these sectors can give rise to currency crises. For example, if local banks have large debts outstanding denominated in foreign currency, this may lead to a banking cum currency crisis. Some authors use the notion of moral hazard as a possible explanation for the Asian crisis. They analyzed financial and currency crises as interrelated phenomena and defined moral hazard leading to the undertaking of excessive risk by borrowers and creditors prior to the outbreak of the Asian crisis 1997–1998 to be the common factor underlying the twin crisis (currency and banking crises).

2.3 Why and how can debt cause and deepen crises

2.3.1 Why is debt critical

Since the global financial crisis of 2007–2008, scholars have increased their interest in the relationship between debt and economic activities. For this, countless academic researches have been made. They mainly argue that debt, "domestic or sovereign" or "private or public", can be critical not only at the occurrence of crises, but also to their duration and severity. That is, it started to be recognized that large debt accumulations in any form can create important problems, even by mainstream economists. In fact, views on problems of debt are not particularly new. For example Fisher (1933) considered the perils of debt by mentioning the problem of debt deflation. However, it has never been the focus of mainstream economics. Now that it has been changing, the role of debt in the economy is more emphasized.

Historically, we can observe the importance of the impacts of lending by banks or other actors. For example, during the Tulip Mania in 1630s, people bought tulips on credit from sellers. Otherwise they could not maintain their demand for tulips. The price of tulip bulbs kept increasing continuously; this in turn led the Dutch economy to expand. However, when prices fell, the boom stopped. A similar process occurred in the cases of both the South Sea Bubble in London and the Mississippi Bubble in Paris in 1720. The share prices of these two companies increased for a while when they were financed by credits from newly established banks. As a relatively new example, there is the asset bubble inflated by excessive lending in Japan in the mid-1980s; increasing supply of credits in Japan caused asset price bubbles in the mid-1980s. And the last global crisis showed us the immense debt accumulation actualized in new and risky financial instruments and markets during the last decades.

The usual or normal definition of debt involves a transfer of money between a unit who lends and a unit who borrows. In this sense, financial intermediaries just intermediate these units. Hence debt flows are expected to have no impacts on the macroeconomic dynamics because every dollar paid by a debtor will be received by a creditor. This will not lead to a fall in demand either (leave aside the case of foreign debt). As argued by Eggertsson and Krugman (2012, p. 1471) that "debt is money we owe to ourselves".

However, this view seems naive. In order to better understand the impacts of debt at the aggregate level, we need another conception of debt. The conception of debt in standard economic models is not enough because their basic structure is simple and does not take into account complications of debt. At the macroeconomic interaction level, such a view is not refined enough. Recently economists have drawn more attention to banks' money-creating power rather than just their intermediary role. They have started to consider that banks are not just an intermediation unit, transferring funds from surplus units (depositors) to deficit units (borrowers), but rather lending money in the form of deposits to borrowers. After accepting the deposit, the bank lends this to someone else. This is recorded into the borrower's deposit account. If this money is drawn and spent on products in the economy, it will push up demand, leading to increase in production. In short, bank lending will increase both debt and national growth.

In fact, loans obtained from the banks can be spent on diverse areas of the economy, rather than being spent according to how production increases. People, with loans, can buy existing assets, such as financial assets, homes or other firms. Their purchases do not contribute to national income because they already exist. That is, while debt accumulates, production does not go up, because the money borrowed does not go to the production process but goes to existing assets. During the run-up to the global crisis, due to the increasing value of houses and other assets, the net worth of the households in the US went up despite their increasing debt. Borrowing has a self-reinforcing effect; more borrowing increases the prices of assets and this in turn induces other investors to borrow to purchase assets whose prices are increasing. That is, borrowing induces more borrowing by incorporating new people to benefit from increasing prices of assets.

In the end, the excessive accumulation of debt leads to critical problems. Borrowers became aware of the fact that their income is not sufficient to repay their debts. In this situation, a cycle runs in reverse; that is, asset prices go down, collateral constraints become tighter and borrowing opportunities are contained. This results in further falls in asset prices. However, in contrast to falls in asset prices, the debts of households and firms do not fall. The value of their debts stays constant even though the prices of their assets decline drastically.

The causal relationship between private debt and financial crises has been discussed in the literature, even if not that often, in the past such as in Fisher (1933) or Minsky (1977). Even if some economists emphasize the role of sovereign debt in crises (see Reinhart et. al 2012), recent academic researches emphasize the unstable dynamics resulting from private debt accumulation, that is rapid expansion of credit, as the first trigger of the financial crisis. They focus on the situation in which systemic financial crises tend to be preceded by rapid expansions of credit.

The accumulation of household debt can amplify downturns and weaken recoveries. In order to better understand the impacts of debt accumulation on depth of slumps, some economic models look at the case in which they differentiate between borrowers and lenders and incorporate liquidity constraints. These models, for example those developed by Eggertsson and Krugman (2012) and Hall (2011), show that distribution structure of debt among the actors in an economy is significant. This is pointed out by Tobin (1980, p.10) as follows:

> the population is not distributed between debtors and creditors randomly. Debtors have borrowed for good reasons, most of which indicate a high marginal propensity to spend from wealth or from current income or from any other liquid resources they can command.

In parallel to this, Kumhof and Ranciere (2010) show that household debt of lower income and wealth groups increased much more in the US during the 2000s. A negative shock to debtors having a high marginal propensity to consume leads them to cut down their debt, thus deleveraging. This results in a decline in consumption, hence production at the aggregate level. The decline in consumption can accelerate along with increasing perceptions of uncertainty due to the need for precautionary saving. Households will cut their consumption abruptly.

Sovereign debt crises have significant effects on economic activity due to the fall in credit extended by banks. Along with sovereign debt crises, countries cannot access international debt markets easily. The financial (mainly banks) and non-financial firms cannot reach foreign sources of credit. As a result, the lack of credits required for the economy will affect the macroeconomy negatively. This is a direct effect of sovereign debt crisis. However, sometimes sovereign financial stress can have indirect effects on other countries which had not suffered a sovereign debt problem directly. Thus, sovereign financial stress can also be transmitted to other countries through global banks. As banks with large international operations face capital shortfalls due to losses on sovereign exposures, they may reduce their cross-border lending arrangements in the form of syndicated loans. For example, European banks with significant exposures to sovereign securities during the European sovereign crisis reduced their global syndicated lending significantly.

When a country is dependent on international financial markets, it mainly needs money to finance private or public investments or to finance existing debts. If the financial actors in the markets do not trust that a country might be able to repay its debt, it is likely to face sovereign default because it will not be able to obtain new loans to pay its debt. For example, even though Spain had lower public debt to national income in comparison to that in Japan (that is, 60% in Spain versus 210% in Japan), Spain had more difficulties with borrowing in the capital markets. It implies that the debt rate is not sufficient to enable a country to default but expectations about a country in a more general sense are much more important.

For governments to mitigate problems in the economy, their debt margin should not be high before the crisis. This situation will provide an opportunity to intervene in the economy without increasing their debt level too much. Otherwise governments caught with high debt margin in a crisis cannot play that role positively. And if they cannot intervene in the crisis as required, the crisis will be prolonged. What is similar to this case happened during the crisis in Europe in 2010. The economic crisis in 2010 has urged some European countries to increase their public debt to contain the negative effects of the crisis. These expansionary fiscal policies would not be a problem in themselves. But the problem is that they already had a high level of debt before the financial crisis.

Some scholars like Reinhart and Rogoff (2010) argue that a country's rate of economic growth starts to deteriorate once the debt-to-GDP ratio passes 90% of GDP. However, this argument has attracted a lot of criticism. For example, it should be mentioned that correlation does not imply causality. It could be that debt-to-GDP ratios rise rapidly when countries get into economic trouble (i.e. GDP falls faster than debt rises). The most likely adverse economic impact of high government debts would come from the "crowding out" of private-sector investment; the government would absorb all of the nation's savings, leaving nothing for business. Hence, the budget deficit, not the stock of debt, might be the key criterion.

In recent decades debt intolerance of countries has increased[3]. Debt intolerance shows itself in many emerging markets at debt levels that would seem quite manageable by advanced-country standards. For these countries safe debt thresholds fall to very low levels, namely debt-to-GDP ratio ranging from 15% to 20%. These ratios are mainly determined by macroeconomic environment of the countries such inflation, growth and political environment. That is, debt intolerance originates from weak institutional structures and tensions in the political system. For this reason, global investors are suspicious about the government's motives. Hence, the upper limit to market access is lower when governments suffer from an intolerance to repayment but not to borrowing.

When investors become cautious about the potential of any country to repay its debt, the first thing they do is to charge higher interest rates to the country in question. They want to compensate increased risk with higher interest rates. The second event is not to lend at all. International investors are always cautious about the money they grant to other countries. They may not get their money back. This is why they force the countries directly or indirectly through international institutions such as the IMF to make efforts to gain trust with investors by reducing their public deficits. However, the timing of implementing these policies is mostly not appropriate because during bad times of economies it is hard to increase taxes and to reduce government expenditures. In fact these policies should have been followed before any problems existed.

As mentioned in the above sections, banking crises are frequently related to debt crises in the sense of timing, either following each other or coinciding. Serious problems in the banking sector have spillover effects on the economy in general. Hence governments try to prevent these effects. The recent European crisis represents this case, in which when the government tried to bail out their banks, the problems in the financial sector easily turned into fiscal sector problems, increasing public debt. More concretely, the banking crises in Ireland in 2008 and in Spain in 2012 indicated that the troubles in the liquidity and solvency of their banking sectors became a fiscal problem and then in turn caused a sovereign debt crisis.

Banking crises can also turn into sovereign debt crises due to two important channels. The first channel is related to the role of the government in undertaking bad liabilities of the financial institutions. The second channel is related to the existing domestic structural macroeconomic conditions during the crisis.

The first channel is about the critical role played by the government providing a safety net to the banking system. When the government supports the banking sector via explicit or implicit bank liability guarantees, it can end up with higher sovereign debt levels. For example, about 30% of EU GDP in 2011 was given as government guarantees on bank liabilities to the member countries of the European Union (EU) for the period 2008–2012. There was an important dispersion in the value of guarantees across these countries, with Ireland providing the most guarantees at about 250 percent of 2011 GDP. The sharp increase in the sovereign Credit Default Swap (CDS) premium in Ireland strongly suggests that the provision of guarantees by the government to the banking sector resulted in an important risk transfer from the banking sector to the government.

Moreover, during the same period 2008–2012 state aid to the banking sector in EU members (in the forms of recapitalization, asset relief interventions, and liquidity measures) reached the value of about 5 trillion euros, or about 40% of EU GDP in 2011. The extent to which the liabilities of the banking sector were socialized and the costs were transferred to taxpayers depended significantly on the resolution regime adopted for the stressed banks in the respective country.

The second transmission channel is related to the macroeconomic conditions of the country in the crisis. There are two components of this channel. First, banking crises commonly precede currency crises. For this reason, when a banking sector is vulnerable to foreign currency liabilities, it may be hard for the government to intervene due to extreme costs and therefore banking problems can lead to a sovereign debt crisis. Second, banking crises reduce economic growth due the contraction of loans and thereby taxes collected decline and budget deficit increases. Hence the collapse in tax revenues and the increase in public expenses from automatic stabilizers are generally accompanied by a surge in public debt, sovereign credit rating falls and, on occasions, sovereign debt defaults.

2.3.2 Leverage and deleverage cycles

It is now recognized that the process of leveraging (increasing excessive debt with respect to equity) before the crisis and deleveraging (reducing debt burden drastically) after the crisis is critical to analyze the impacts of debts on the agents in the economy. This process needs a detailed analysis.

As often mentioned in the literature, there are certain tendencies of financial institutions. They strongly increase their leverage prior to the crisis. But they act in reverse during the crisis, thus reducing their deleverage during the crisis. Therefore their leverage behavior is pro-cyclical. However, such conclusions are often based on using book-value data, which does not necessarily reflect current market prices, since book values are infrequently updated. The path of market leverage around the global recession in 2007–2008 is shown in Figure 2.5. Even

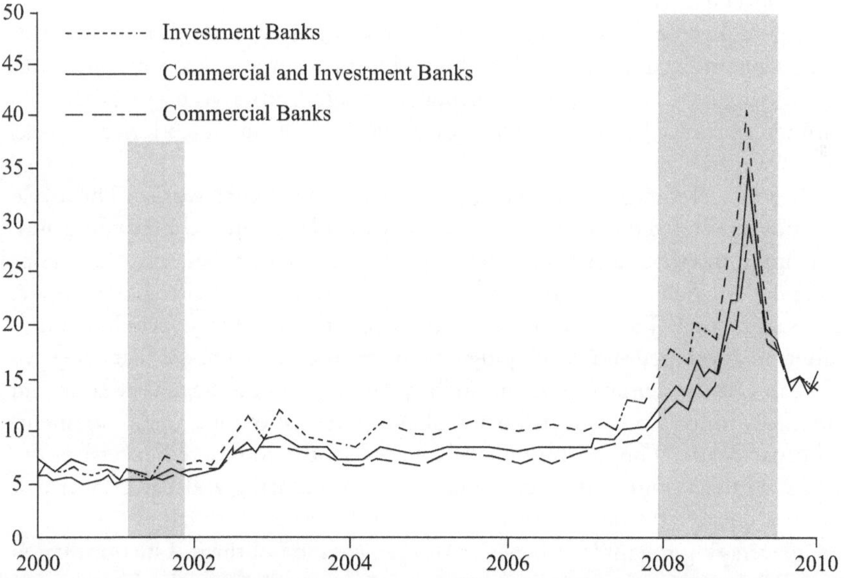

Figure 2.5 Market leverage in the US.
Source: Derived from Federal Reserve Bank of St. Louis statistics.

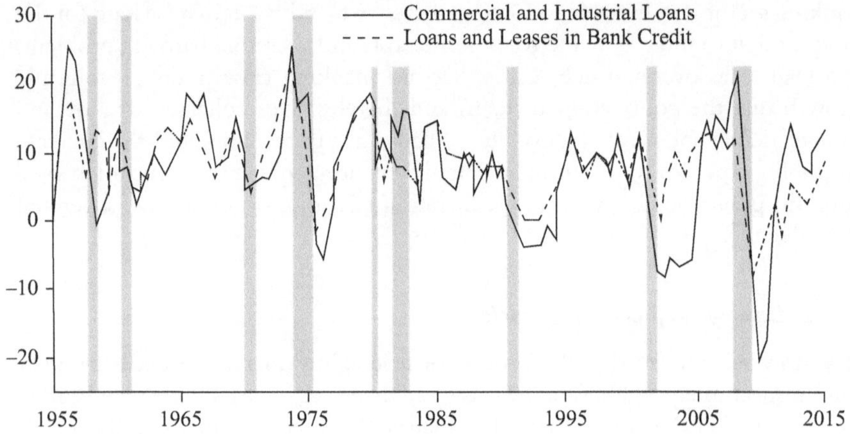

Figure 2.6 Pro-cyclical lending in the US (% change).
Source: Derived from Federal Reserve Bank of St. Louis statistics.

though financial institutions strongly increased their balance sheets during the run-up to the global recession in 2007–2008, that is, increasing their debt and assets, market leverage remained relatively stable and rose only mildly. This is mainly due to the fact that asset prices also increased, lowering leverage. However, during the crisis, the market prices of assets declined dramatically, faster than the fall in debt, leading to a sharp jump of leverage; and hence the market leverage seems acyclical.

Empirical evidence also shows that lending is pro-cyclical—both volume as well as lending standards which tighten during recessions and ease in boom periods. Figure 2.6 shows the percentage change from a year ago of the US commercial banks' lending, which strongly declines during recessions and picks up afterwards.

There is a leverage cycle that extends over the whole world. The cycle does not have a fixed period, and there may be a long interval between crises. Leveraging or overindebtedness develops during boom times, and then stops suddenly. In such cycles the overindebtedness can be individual, corporate, or governmental. There are at least two specific reasons why overindebtedness matters in developed and developing economies today. The first is that excessive debt can cause systemic crises, and such systemic crises can have very large and potentially long-lasting effects on actual and potential output, unemployment, and capacity use. The second reason is that if debt is considered excessive, the process of deleveraging (reducing debt) can be enduring and hard, even if it does not create a financial crisis or even after the crisis phase has passed.

Deleveraging resembles Keynes's so-called paradox of thrift. Uncoordinated gross deleveraging among the sectors in the economy can lead to serious problems at the aggregate level even if not at the individual level. Hence the detrimental effects of large debt reductions can create immense problems. Policy makers are supposed to take into account the probable costs of decentralized deleveraging.

Irving Fisher argued that the leverage cycle ended in debt deflation in 1930s, which deepened the Great Depression. When prices fell after 1929, real debt of borrowers increased, thereby while debtors were damaged by this, creditors benefited from this. The net effect was negative. The debt overhang then created negative spillover effects in the economy[4]. This overhang debt problem was also seen in the 2008 crisis in an environment of excessive debt relationships that deepened it[5].

Another serious cost of high household debt in the presence of a shock comes from the forced sale of durable goods. This is the forced sale of durable goods like houses. During crises, unemployment increases; this in turn lowers people's ability to service their debt, meaning a rise in household defaults, foreclosures, and drastic falls in prices at fire sales. Campbell et al. (2011) estimate the effect of foreclosures on the prices of nearby houses. For example, the price of a neighboring house falls by 1% when a single foreclosure occurs, but this reaches 30% if there occurs a wave of foreclosures. These negative effects of the fall in prices trigger chain effects such as fall in the value of collaterals, worsening balance sheets of banks and declines in credits. These kinds of fire sales, namely reduction in people's net worth, lower the potential of banks and firms to lend and borrow, thereby distorting the economic environment. In the case of the US during the global crisis, due to a housing bust on the back of fire sales, house prices undershot their equilibrium values.

There are some quantitative studies that analyze the effects of leveraging on economic growth using individual countries and cross-section data. These studies evidence the negative effects of overleveraging. They mainly show that excessive debt not only creates financial vulnerabilities but also pushes up their cost. Buiter and Rahbari (2012) estimate the effects of high leveraging in their study for the period 1980–2011. They divide the country sample at hand into two groups according to the changes in debt-to-GDP ratio during the four years before the crisis. Figure 2.7 shows that the growth rate in the countries that experienced larger-debt increase fell about twice that in the countries that experienced smaller-debt increase after the crisis. Moreover, the countries that had smaller debt increase turned to their growth trend much sooner than the other group of countries.

2.4 Concluding remarks

The frequency of debt crises has increased across the world since the deregulation of lending and global financial flows in the late 1970s. More people and countries have become more dependent on debt over time. The financial crisis that began in 2007–2008 was in particular a crisis in debt markets. Despite the fast recovery in stock markets, the problems in debt markets still continue more or less. Therefore in order to understand the global crisis and other relatively minor crises, we should focus on debt markets more.

Although the identity of the borrowers in each leverage cycle differs historically, the debt was a significant problem that led to crises in the associated countries. For example, the borrowers were governments and state companies in Mexico and other developing countries in the early 1980s. The borrowers were homeowners and real estate companies in Japan in the late 1980s and banks and homeowners in Finland, Norway, and Sweden in the early 1990s. The borrowers were banks that used external sources in emerging Asian market countries in the late 1990s. The borrowers were primarily house buyers in the US in the mid-2000s.

During recent decades, we see that there have been many factors behind the increase in debt, including financial innovation, a fall in lending standards, a rapid increase in house prices, a global fall in real interest rates (due to saving glut), and the perception of a fall in macroeconomic volatility and of enduring faster growth. During this period, these factors have led both the shifts in supply and the demand for expanded credit and thereby helped the occurrence of the financial crisis.

Some scholars support the view that the cause of crises, especially the global crisis in 2007–2008, is not overborrowing but it is just the effect of income inequality. To these scholars, an underlying cause of the global financial crisis was the rise in income inequality. This induced poor people to borrow excessively and rich people to engage in speculation on risky financial assets. While lower income groups became more dependent on borrowing, the higher

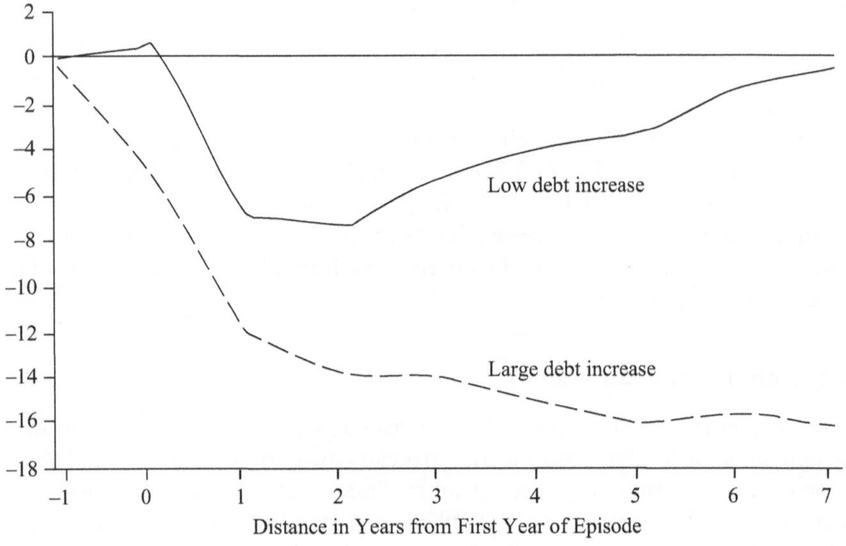

Figure 2.7 Real GDP versus pre-crisis trend after banking crises (% growth), 1980–2011.
Source: Buiter and Rahbari (2012).

income groups spent less of their increased income. With financial deregulation, inequality fueled lending activities and prepared the ground for the crisis. The relevance of income inequality will be analyzed in more detail in the following section of the book.

Concerning the sovereign debt crisis in Europe, some scholars see this crisis through the lens of public finance. They draw attention to the point that governments did not stay within reasonable limits of their budgets. For them, in order to prevent another crisis, stricter fiscal rules—a better Maastricht—should be imposed. However some other scholars argue that the main problem is private borrowing rather than public borrowing. In this view, the crisis in Europe (except for Greece) is the result of credit booms and housing bubbles that originated from the private sector. However, when this bubble burst, the governments had to undertake these bad liabilities of banks, hence placing the public sector under stress.

There are some policy lessons that we can learn from debt crises and propose some policies to tackle them. In particular governments should strengthen market regulation to reduce the risk of market failures. In this sense, they should follow policies that sustain financial stability and take prudential regulatory and supervisory measures that prevent excessive borrowing. In fact, most of these reforms are still at various stages of implementation but their impacts should be checked out continuously and they should be refined when new problems are observed.

Notes

1 An underwater mortgage is a home purchase loan with a higher principal than the free-market value of the home. This situation can occur when property values are falling. In an underwater mortgage the homeowner may not have any equity available for credit. An underwater mortgage can potentially prevent a borrower from refinancing or selling the home unless they have cash to pay the loss.

2 In Europe the problem of excessive government debt in some countries was compounded by European bank regulators, who imposed zero capital requirements on banks' holdings of euro-denominated government debt. This regulatory decision meant that government defaults could also bring down banks.

3 This state is built on the empirical fact that debt crises in emerging economies tend to occur at levels of debt that may not be considered excessive. Thus, they become intolerant to even low levels of debt.

4 Debt overhang is a debt burden that is so large that an entity cannot take on additional debt to finance future projects. Debt overhang serves to discourage current investment, since all earnings from new projects would only go to existing debt holders, leaving little incentive and ability for the entity to attempt to dig itself out of the hole.

5 When people's debts exceed their assets, many problems are created for the economy. When firms or households hold a lot of debt, even a small fall in the value of their assets can bring them to the brink of bankruptcy. If a family owns a $100,000 home and owes $90,000 to the bank, their net worth is $10,000. But if the value of their home drops by 5%, their net worth halves, falling to $5,000.

3 Financialization and neoliberalism

3.1 Introduction

In last three decades, changes in capitalism have been commonly described in terms of neoliberalism, globalization, and financialization. Even though there has been much academic research on the first two of these, much less attention has been given to the third. However, it is widely recognized that financialization has been becoming the overwhelming force behind economic activities. Thus, the dominant character of capitalism has been becoming financialization. This means that economies, particularly those of advanced countries, pass from one stage to another, where the gravity of economic activity shifts from production to finance. That is, the nature of capitalist accumulation has been passing through a profound transformation.

Financialization has increased the dominance of money. By the late twentieth century the principles of privatization and financialization had entered into our personal lives. People have been encouraged to see their security in money terms backed by personal financial assets. This weakened the collective perspectives to social issues. Collective entities such as trade unions were undermined and social policies such as pensions and various social insurances were integrated to the financial sphere. Everything has been regarded as a financial asset. A house is no longer a house, but a financial asset. Hence financial expansion started to dominate economic and social relations more deeply.

This chapter mainly reviews the economic consequences of financialization and its relevance to crises. We also analyze the connections between financialization, neoliberal policies and crises. In this sense, we look at neoliberalism and its consequences on financial crises in the context of financial deregulation in the following sections of this chapter.

3.2 What is financialization

In addition to neoliberalism or globalization, financialization has become one of the most comprehensive notions to specify the current phase of capitalism. Although in the mid-1960s some heterodox economists had already drawn attention to the growing weight of finance, the widespread use of the financialization concept occurred in the 1990s. Widespread use of the term generated various perspectives from authors of diverse theoretical background, and hence a commonly accepted definition of such term does not exist.

The concept of financialization is often employed to stress the growing importance of finance in contemporary economies. But it is still a controversial concept. According to Callinicos (2010), it has three meanings. The first meaning implies a fusion of banking and industrial capital, which was elaborated by Rudolf Hilferding in the 1910s. But the evidence is not compatible with this meaning. That is because ways of financing have been changing across time and country. For example, although industry relied strongly on bank finance in Germany and Japan (although this also declined over time), it has not been so in the UK and the US because they relied rather on capital markets. Moreover, the contemporary direction of fusion is not from finance to non-financial but rather from non-financial to finance. That is, non-financial corporations have started to gain a significant part of their profits from financial activities.

The second meaning of financialization is the fact that the finance sector has become increasingly autonomous. This mainly implies that finance has announced its independence from reality and only acts in its own interest without taking into account the general health of the economy. And the third meaning is the increasing domain of finance. Finance started to dominate almost all financial actors and integrated them with each other with the help of new financial products or its expansion to the whole economy.

In line with the third meaning, Epstein (2005) defines financialization as *"the increasing role of financial motives, financial markets, financial actors and financial institutions in the operation of the domestic and international economies"*. This definition captures what has been going on around the world, especially in the advanced countries. Financial markets and actors have spread everywhere because of a combination of neoliberalism and information technology. This growing impact is also reflected in a *"pattern of accumulation in which profit making occurs increasingly through financial channels rather than through trade and commodity production"* (Krippner, 2005, p. 174).

In fact, financialization has been the result of a historical trend since the late 20th century. Finance became the pronounced factor in the functioning of economies, especially those of the advanced countries. This process accelerated particularly post-World War II. It describes current economies in which finance has dominated the other parts of the economy. This process is described as a profound shift from production to finance since the 1970s. It affected each part of the economy: (1) rising share of financial profits in total income; (2) the growth of FIRE (finance, insurance, and real estate) as a share of national income; (3) rising debt relative to GDP; (4) proliferation of risky financial products; and (5) increasing financial asset bubbles.

More evidently financialization of the economy shows itself at three levels: industry, firm, and household. Finance, at the industry level, has become the

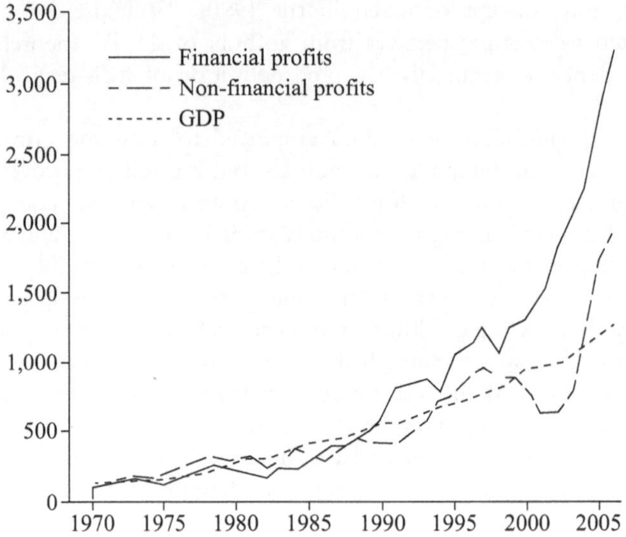

Figure 3.1 Financial and non-financial profits index in the US (1970=100).
Source: Foster and Magdoff (2009).

most profitable industry in the US. Its share in national output went up from 15% in 1960 to approximately 23% in 2001, which was more than the share of manufacturing in the 1990s. Its profits reached high levels, peaking in the years just before the crisis in 2008 (Krippner, 2005).

At the firm level, we see financialization in the behavior of corporations. All corporations started to emphasize maximizing shareholder value more. In corporate governance, primacy of shareholders became prominent. This is seen in the primacy of financial executives. Another behavior change that came along with financialization at the firm level is that non-financial corporations engaged more in financial activities, which constituted a significant part of their profits. The share of their financial profits has increased since the 1970s. This has been a new mode of capital accumulation, which is different from accumulations originating from production and trade.

Figure 3.1 displays the trends of financial, non-financial profits, and GDP in the US. It indicates that their growth trends were almost the same the until 1990s. However, in the late 1990s, as mentioned by Foster and Magdoff (2009, p. 123),

> finance seemed to take on a life of its own with the profits of US financial corporations (and to a lesser extent non-financial corporate profits too) heading off into the stratosphere, seemingly unrelated to growth of national income, which was relatively stagnant.

At the household level, we also see that financialization has been expanding. Households have started to hold many more financial assets in their total assets over time. This mainly arises because of households' increasing involvement in stock markets and liquid funds and the shift from defined benefit to defined contribution pension[1]. Households' increasing debt was also critical in this development. They accessed credit markets much more mainly due to stagnation of their wages.

3.3 The development of financialization

3.3.1 A historical overview of financialization

The Great Depression had shown the dangers of a market without regulation. Hence the authorities introduced several regulations in the 1930s to truncate the financial incentives that could put society into jeopardy. To achieve this, the authorities in the US enacted regulations such as the Banking Acts of 1933 and 1935, the Glass–Steagall Act of 1933, and the Security and Exchange Act of 1934. The main objective of these regulations was to limit systemic risk and increase transparency of the financial actors.

In the 1950s and 1960s, there was a well-established balance between finance and real parts of the economy in the US and the other developed countries in general. But there were some developments starting in the late 1960s that threatened the profitability of banks. The high inflation levels in the late 1960s led to decline in real interest rates, which in turn lowered the banks' profitability. Moreover, the tight monetary policies narrowed banks' lending opportunities. Following these changes, banks began several innovations to increase their profitabilities. Through new financial products, they mostly aimed to evade the regulations in the 1960s and 1970s. Additionally, non-bank institutions started to emerge due to the fact that they were not subject to regulations that bound the banks. Many non-financial corporations began to establish financial subsidiaries; for example General Motors and Ford [2].

From the late 1960s to early 1970s, the profit rate in manufacturing fell about 40%. Brenner (2006) mentions that this decline originated from the downward pressure on prices mainly as a result of acceleration of international competition along with the entry of Japan and Germany into the global markets. Brenner argues, *"... due to such precipitous growth in world trade, new producers, without warning, began to supply radically increased fractions of the world market, supplanting long-ensconced incumbents" (p. 110)*. That is, there was a fall in profits in manufacturing in the US, leading to the problem of overcapacity. Naturally, the manufacturing firms shifted to investment in financial assets, rather than further real investment.

In the early 1970s, the oil crisis created one unexpected side effect, which accelerated the financialization process. The excessive gains of oil-producing countries due to increased oil prices flowed to the banks in the US and Europe. These so-called petrodollars increased the funds that they could lend. Most of these funds went to foreign countries rather than domestic agents. The funding at that large scale affected the financial environment of the world. Increasing capital flows, along with increased volume of trade, kindled liberal thoughts. With these liberal thoughts, the Washington Consensus developed and shaped financial activities in the US as well as other countries. Hence it generated new incentives not only for the US firms that started to engage more in financial activities but also for the US government.

Keynesian measures in the 1970s failed to obtain desirable results, and hence the policymakers shifted more to monetary policies and austerity policies. The Federal Reserve (Fed) followed anti-inflation policy persistently. This in turn caused interest rates to rise and naturally the profits of banks went up. Price stability became prominent with the policy of higher interest rates in the 1970s and 1980s (Epstein, 2005). Such a monetary policy accelerated further financialization in the early 1980s. Ronald Reagan, starting in 1981, began to deregulate all the markets by relaxing labor markets, lowering high taxes, and reducing government regulations. In particular the obstacles in front of firms were reduced; for example capital gain taxes were reduced and more flexible federal policies concerning large mergers were introduced.

In the 1980s the firms' profits were continuing to fall. Brenner (2006) pointed out overproduction and overcapacity, mentioning

> ... With low returns on capital stock discouraging long-term placement of funds in new plant and equipment, money went increasingly to finance and speculation, as well as to luxury consumption, the way being paved by an undisguised lurch in state policy in favor of the rich in general and financiers in particular.
>
> (p. 189)

Starting in the 1980s, neoliberal policies reduced the size and scope of the state. Almost all markets, particularly financial markets, were deregulated. This policy was mainly based on the presumption of self-regulating markets and their efficient allocation. Based on the prominence of individualism, public interest was not valued because in this view there were only individuals rather than a society as a whole.

Hence, in the 1980s, financialization had already become an indispensable part of the economy in the US. There were signs of this development. One of these was the place of institutional investors in the economic system. They were main beneficiaries of the financial markets that were deregulated and new financial products that were introduced to the system. Along with these developments, this class of investor seized control of the system. They emphasized what was financial much more. The interests of shareholders, rather than corporate stakeholders, dominated the perspective of corporations. In line with this, the structure of corporate governance also changed in parallel with these developments. The firm owners aimed to handle the principal–agent problem by making the incentives of their firm managers compatible with those of the shareholders. This resulted in increasing concern of the managers with financial outcomes.

All these developments helped financialization to diffuse and deepen in the US and other developed countries. This kept going in this way, without any interruption, until the global crisis in 2008. The deregulatory acts in the 1990s, such as the repeal of the Glass–Steagall Act in 1999, accelerated this process further. During the peak years of financialization in the mid-2000s, financial profits accounted for a little over 40% of total US business profits, nearly twice the average value of post-World War II. However, even though the global financial crisis in 2007–2008 changed the landscape of the financial industry, it would be too early to assert that the economic crisis marked the end of financialization.

3.3.2 The developments in financial markets before the global recession

In this section, firstly I will try to show the magnitude of the great wave of financialization starting with the beginning of the 1980s and then I will elaborate reasons for this process.

The extent of financialization in the US can be better seen in Figure 3.2, displaying the trends in the debts of the financial and non-financial sectors as a percentage of GDP. Starting in the 1980s, the debt of non-financial corporations

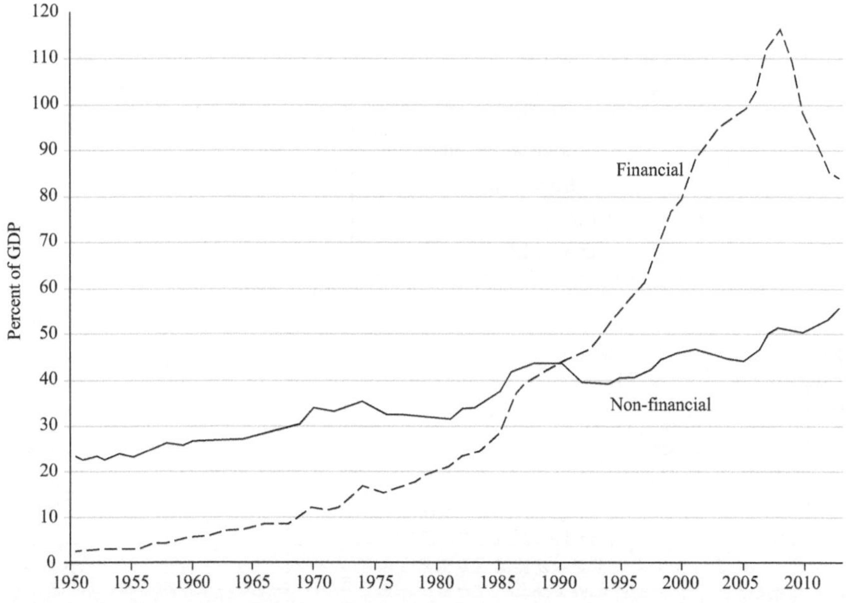

Figure 3.2 Non-financial and financial corporate debt (% of the US GDP).
Source: Magdoff and Foster (2014).

as a percent of GDP went up on a large scale. But surprisingly the debt of financial corporations also increased substantially. In the last three decades, financial corporate debt rose from about 20% of GDP to 116% of GDP (Magdoff and Foster, 2014). During the post-crisis, there was a significant fall in financial debt as a share of GDP but its level still stayed high.

Figure 3.3 illustrates the expanding size of financialization from another perspective (all numbers there are normalized to 1970). In recent decades, the gravity of the economic system has shifted from a bank-based toward a market-based financial system. As seen, there is a huge increase in securities markets relative to banking. The increase in assets of the banks was in parallel with the increase in national income. But the assets of non-bank financial institutions went up immensely in comparison with the increase in GDP. However, in this more diverse and complicated financial structure the connection between banks and non-bank institutions continued because of securitization.

During the last few decades, prominent changes have occurred. First of all, there were changes in financial actors and institutions. Several non-banking institutions have emerged and grown greatly. They range from pension funds to insurance firms, investment funds, money market funds, hedge funds, private equity funds, and special purpose vehicles. These financial institutions, compared to banks, have been subject to less regulation through financial innovations developed to circumvent traditional banking regulation. But they almost perform similar functions to banks. This new structure is called shadow banking. And this new structure has been the bearer of financialization.

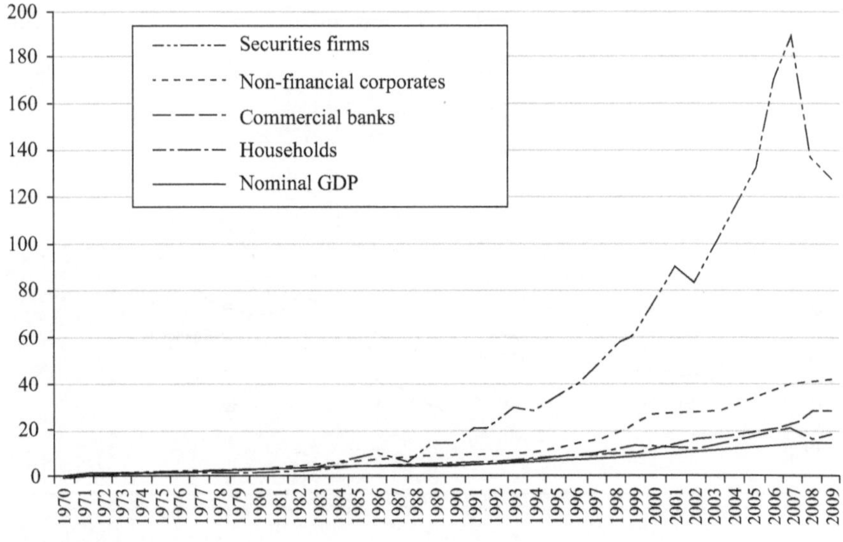

Figure 3.3 The financial assets of economic units in the US.
Source: Bibow (2010).

During this period the activities of the banks from which they obtained their profits have also changed. They shifted from interest income to fee-generating business. They sold their mortgage loans in the form of asset-backed securities (namely originating loans and then selling them to investors in the form of securities, which is called the originate-and-distribute model). Furthermore the subject of lending, that is, who is financed, changed. They started to lend to households more than to firms. Mortgages were the most important segment of these loans. And the way that the financial institutions dealt with risk has changed. The extent and prevalence of risk undertaken has changed tremendously along with the emergence of new financial products. For example, with increasing securitization (simply the transformation of loans into securities), they sliced risk into different parts (by means of different securities) and allocated it to different actors who wanted to hold. This means that new conflicts of interest and new areas of risk emerged. For example, securitization increased the financing potential of banks; it transferred the risk of the originator (loan maker, mainly banks) to the buyers of securities.

Along with these developments, we observe that banks were no longer the only significant source of credits. Instead the securities traded by diverse investors such as hedge funds, mutual funds, and pension funds gained the leading role in providing credits. With the simultaneous introduction of complex and obscure financial innovations, finance turned out to be a highly risky business. Furthermore, speculation activities also intensified. In this speculative process, banks played an active role, because the large expansion of financial wealth had been sustained by banks directing a lot of credit towards asset buyers to finance their speculative trading with a high degree of leverage.

In fact, this high acceleration of financialization received help from technology. The information technology developed by powerful computers and smart software reduced the transaction costs of calculation and trading of complex financial products and contracts. They both accelerated financial transactions and allowed complicated risk calculations. However, the critical point here is that these technological innovations could not solve the problems of intrinsic uncertainty involved in future events; moreover they created a kind of illusion that the financial operations were prudent, almost risk-free.

The complicated and risky assets increased immensely until the Global Recession. In 2007 the sum of securitized debt was three times bigger than in 1990, and the total of derivatives was six times bigger. Financial innovations, particularly derivatives, securitization and structured investment vehicles became critical for the whole economic structure. In the technical analysis of financial crisis, we need to understand these important developments in financial markets prior to the crisis. They are categorized as (1) commercial paper conduits, structured investment vehicles and asset-backed securities; (ii) leverage buyouts; and (iii) derivatives contracts.

(i) Commercial paper conduits, structured investment vehicles and securitization

There have been two important financial institutions developed in the financial structure in the US, which are commercial paper conduits and structured investment vehicles (SIVs). Their common aspect is the financing of long-term assets by shorter-term securities. They earn profits from the difference in yields between the typically short-term securities they issue, such as commercial paper and medium-term notes, and the longer-term assets they purchase, typically the product of securitization, which is the transformation of loans (in the assets of financial corporations) into securities, a procedure allowing for the sale of these loans to investors by the originators of the loans. This is a potentially very profitable activity, but also highly leveraged and risky, and this explains why banks developed it off-balance sheet. It was at the origin of large borrowings on the part of the financial sector.

Commercial paper conduit is a non-bank financial institution that issues short-term liabilities, commercial papers, to finance medium- to long-term assets. In particular banks generate them to finance their assets in an off-balance sheet way to avoid capital requirement regulations. They are regarded as a part of shadow banking. Similarly, a structured investment vehicle (SIV) is also a non-bank financial institution to make profits by benefiting from interest differentials between wholesale and retail financing. But their financing is instead based on medium-term notes (an unconventional bond note with a maturity period usually between 5 and 10 years), supplemented by commercial paper. They invest in longer-maturity corporate bonds and lower-rated structured credit products, such as traditional long-term assets, ABSs, and collateralized debt obligations (CDOs), which are a structured financial product that pools together cash flow-generating assets and repackages this asset pool into discrete tranches that can be sold to investors. Before the crisis in 2007, the total assets of the conduits reached the value of $1.4 trillion in the US, and that of SIVs worldwide about $400 billion (Duménil and Lévy, 2011).

(ii) Leverage buyouts

A leveraged buyout (LBO) is a financial transaction in which a company is purchased with a combination of equity and debt. Private equity firms generally follow such strategies and show the assets of the firms bought as collateral. They aim to repay their considerable borrowings by selling the firms to other firms.

The growth of LBOs in the US and Europe is seen in Figure 3.4. Until the early 2000s, the amount of LBO operations was not high, about $12 billion per year during the period 1993–2003. But after that it increased tremendously; for example it reached at its maximum in 2007 the amount of almost $380 billion, about thirty times higher. Figure 3.4 also shows a similar wave of LBOs in Europe, peaking at $290 billion in 2007 (Duménil and Lévy, 2011).

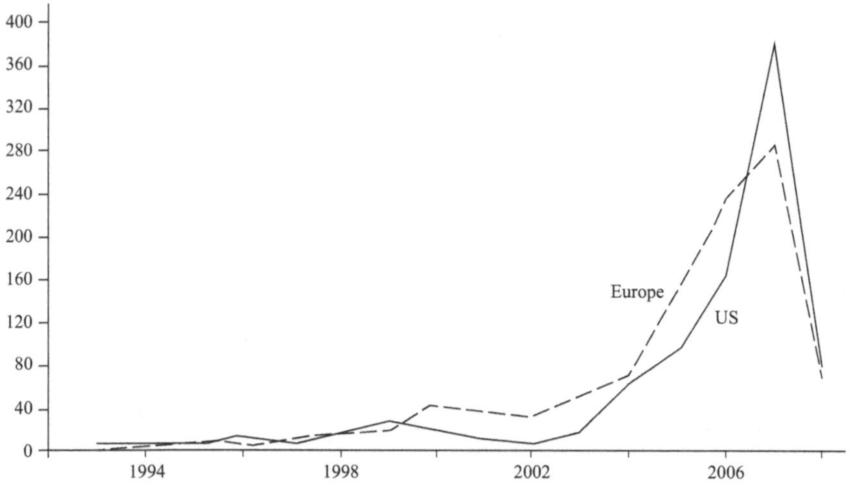

Figure 3.4 The flows of LBOs in the US and Europe.
Source: Duménil and Lévy (2011).

In fact, LBOs show another dimension of financialization. Increasing borrowing opportunities induced newly emerging firms such as private equity firms to buy firms with a highly leveraged financing. Private equity firms, like hedge funds, benefit from cheap funds to engage in speculative trading. However, it is important to note that their trading is not financial assets but companies. They specialize in buying and selling firms. In fact they are mostly asset strippers. They buy companies in trouble or separate them into different units and then sell them to other firms. A report published in 2009 by Ernst and Young shows that private equity firms gain their profits mostly from using debt (about half of their profits) and the rise in the prices of shares of firms bought (about a third of the profits) rather than increasing efficiencies of the firms they buy (only a fifth of their profits).

(iii) Derivative contracts

Another major financial development before the crisis in 2007–2008 was the rise of derivative markets. They became an important source of profits, but turned out to be an important source of extreme risk. It was realized that derivative markets could have potentially detrimental effects on the financial markets, as seen during the global crisis in 2007–2008.

A derivative is a financial contract that obtains its value from an underlying asset. The counterparts of these financial contracts try to benefit from possible fluctuations in the prices of underlying assets in the future. The underlying assets range from commodities to various financial assets such as bonds, currencies, commodities, stocks, interest rates, and market indexes. The derivative contracts can be bought or sold to hedge risks but they are generally

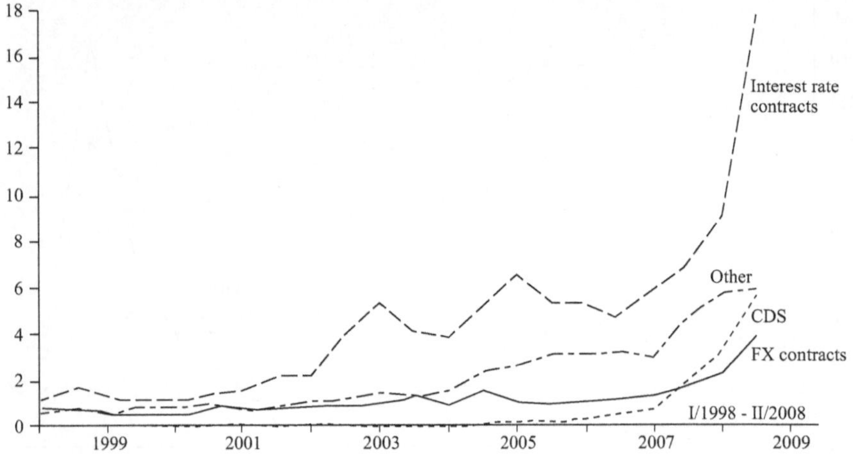

Figure 3.5 Gross market value of OTC derivatives worldwide (trillions of dollars, semiannual).
Source: Duménil and Lévy (2011).

used for speculation to make larger profits. They are highly leveraged and contain too much risk.

The total notional value of derivatives grew dramatically during the neoliberal decades. They have reached huge levels over time, starting in the 1980s. Their notional volume worldwide went up from $72 trillion in 1998 to $684 trillion in 2008. Total global output was around $60 trillion then.

Hedge funds are one of the main players in derivative contracts. Their risk-loving appetite pushes them to deal with highly speculative transactions. Their very high levels of leverage also create great potential for financial volatility.

Interest rate derivatives accounted for the largest component of derivatives, amounting to $458 trillion in 2008. Another derivative contract that developed immensely in recent decades is credit default swaps (CDSs), which is a financial derivative that enables an investor to "swap" or offset his or her credit risk with that of another investor. CDSs were created in the mid-1990s and grew to $58 trillion. Figure 3.5 displays the drastic rise of derivative transactions after 2002 (Duménil and Lévy, 2011).

During the last decade, financial investors have also begun to increase commodity futures in their portfolios. Due to the growing interest of financial investors who are not commercial participants, the volume of commodity investment has increased substantially since 2000. This process is referred to as the financialization of commodity markets. The Commodity Futures Trading Commission in the US reports that the number of speculators in commodity derivative markets in 2010 was three times as many as the conventional traders who protect themselves from price volatilities.

Financial investors increased their investment in commodities to reduce the total risk in their portfolio due to the low correlation between the commodity markets and financial markets. However, the increased role of financial investors in the commodity markets has increased the association of commodity with stock markets since the mid-2000s. But this was not considered thoroughly until the crisis in 2007. It was seen that the bubbles in commodity prices could be associated with speculation in commodity futures markets. Thus, the synchronized boom and bust cycle in 2007–2008 in a large number of commodities across the energy, metal, and agricultural sectors has led to a heated debate regarding whether speculation in commodity futures markets caused a bubble in commodity prices.

Financialization also transformed the actions of real firms, non-financial firms. In particular the increased role of shareholders was effective on this. This was seen in the change in the behavior of executives of the firms. They became more concerned with the short-term motivations of shareholders. Hence they shifted from the policy of "retain and reinvest" to the policy of "downsize and distribute", and thereby financial motives have become more important for firms. Another change is that firms have become more exposed to takeovers by institutional investors. Firms could be the victims of institutional investors. As mentioned before, leveraged buyouts by private equity firms remain an external threat for real firms.

In addition to these changes, the economic environment that firms faced also changed. Increased volatility, thus risk, in financial markets had devastating effects on the business environment for non-financial firms, discouraging them from undertaking physical investment projects. The weak performance of investment compared to profits can be seen in Figure 3.6. The decline in the investment-to-profits ratio since the mid-1980s can be observed in all major economies.

3.3.3 Financial innovation

Here I must create a new section to show the importance of financial innovation in all these developments even though it has been debated several times in this chapter. It deserves separate analysis of the main personal and structural motives behind financial innovation.

Financial innovation played an important role in the development of the global economic crisis in 2007–2008. It was soon realized that the destructive effects of some of these innovative products and structure were important in the collapse of the financial system in the US. For example, it was realized that collateralized debt obligations (CDOs) and mortgage-backed securities (MBSs) were riskier than thought. Those holding them could not dispose of these risky assets easily.

As mentioned before, starting in the 1970s, the financial system in the global economy has begun to change. New financial products have emerged over time. It has been a combination of factors determining the developments of

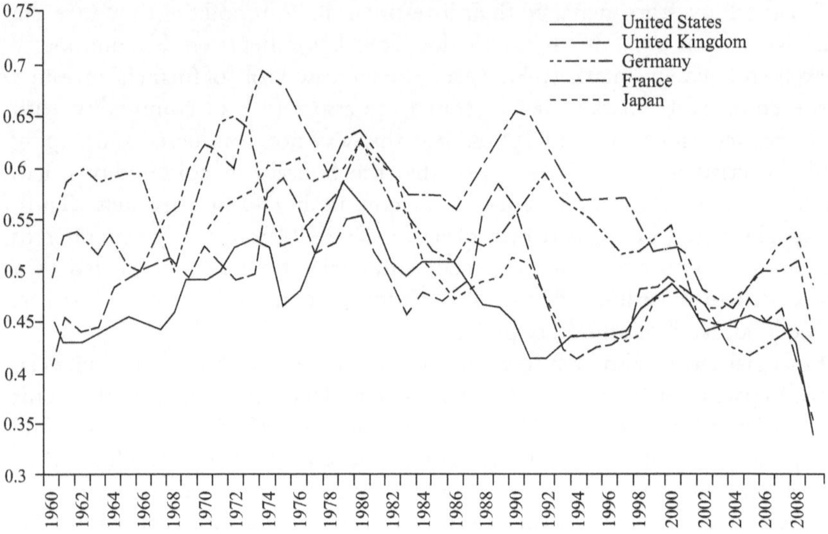

Figure 3.6 Investment to operating surplus.
Source: Stockhammer (2012).

financial instruments, such as financial deregulations worldwide, technological advancements in information and communication, globalization, and theoretical developments in finance. Consequently what we experienced was a gradual shift from the traditional financial products and more static structure to the highly complex and risky financial products and a dynamic structure. We have had new actors, new financial products and new institutions. The new system fundamentally altered the landscape and gave rise to a new set of actors, many frequently misunderstood.

Developments in the sciences of economics and finance also facilitated the introduction of various financial products. In particular, financial theorists developed theoretical foundations of new financial products and with the help of information technology they were applied to financial markets. In particular the financial models based on the Black–Scholes option pricing and the copula probability formulas caused a rapid growth in derivatives and structured products respectively. Hence these two formulas facilitated financial institutions in developing new risky products that meet the demands of risk-loving investors.

Macro-economy driven demands also played a key role in deepening and expanding the demand for new financial instruments. This is, for example, more concretely seen in the use of commodity derivatives after the increased volatility in prices of production inputs during the 1970s. Another example is the widespread use of interest rate swaps after interest rate volatility increased in the early 1980s. The use of CDSs expanded after the dot.com crash due to increased corporate defaults. Investment banks played a key role in developing these products to earn fees in an ever more competitive landscape. Those innovations coordinated economic actors, creating increasingly interconnected, homogeneous and sizable markets. Regulations also created incentives for developing derivatives and structures investment vehicles to circumvent them. For example, Regulation Q enacted in 1933 in the US (various restrictions on the payment of interest on deposit accounts) enabled the growth of money market funds, which would quickly become a systemic player in the financial system. Overall, these financial innovations have generated an extensive web that connected many actors. Hence economies have been loaded with riskier instruments and have been more susceptible to external shocks.

Meanwhile it should be mentioned that the growth of derivatives and structured investment vehicles can also be associated with governmental actions. For example, the Financial Modernization Bill in 1999 in the US exempted derivatives from being regulated. And Basel regulations reduced capital reserves against securitized assets, when compared with the identical loans on a bank's balance sheet, and thus banks found it beneficial to seek greater securitization.

The development of the shadow banking system is critical in understanding financial proliferation and innovation. Along with the collapse of the Bretton Woods system and increasing globalization in later periods it induced the development of the universal banking model. This banking model firstly started in Europe, then spread to Japan and finally to the US. The banks in the US were highly regulated and had some disadvantages in the sense of competition in comparison with the banks in Europe and Japan. Along with the enactment of the Gramm–Leach–Bliley Act in 1999 after the repeal of the Glass–Steagall Act of 1933, the banking system in the US passed to the universal banking model. This induced the US banks to expand their financial activities that were not regulated by the authorities. They created new institutions that enabled them to integrate various financial operations into their domain, for example they brought together the operations of retail banking, wholesale banking and insurance under a common legal entity. This change in banks' activities is called shadow banking. Shadow banking was first regarded as the activities outside the realm of traditional banking but it was realized immediately that it was a new version of banking that had transformed over time. In this way, the banks have exited the traditional financial areas and participated in and introduced many new, risky and complex interconnections in a financial sense.

It is generally proposed that when an innovation is introduced, both issuers and buyers benefit from this. However, it happens that all the effects of innovation on individual institutions and their stability are not thoroughly scrutinized. Laeven (2013, p. 234) elaborates this: *"the literature on financial innovation primarily focuses on the good or the dark sides of innovation but not on the incentives that the owners of financial institutions have to exploit such innovation"*. This mainly arises from the fact that there are some definite disciplinary biases and preferences in economics and finance. Policy makers, regulators and the majority of financial economists in the field believe that financial innovations lead to better-functioning markets. Llewellyn et al. (2009, pp. 26–27) mentions as follows:

> By increasing the range of financial instruments, the financial system [moves] closer to the Arrow–Debreu (1954) ideal where all transactors can ensure for themselves delivery of goods and services in all future contingencies, and the system comes closer to approximating the number of "states of nature" . . . , therefore financial innovation has the capacity to significantly enhance the efficiency of the financial system for the core of its functions.

But the problem here is that these economists did not take into account institutions and their mechanics, hence the fundamental motivations of the financial business actors are not considered well.

3.4 Financialization process and its linkages with other economic developments

Financialization is not by itself an isolated development in the economy. It has affected and been affected by some important trends in the economies. Now we look at the critical ones.

Financialization and growing indebtedness

The growth in total debt relative to GDP remained moderate after World War II until 1980, rising moderately from 126% in 1952 to 155% in 1980. However, it increased tremendously during the liberal decades, increasing up to 353% in 2008. With regard to the debt of the financial sector, it is seen that it was 3% of GDP and 20% in 1952 and 1980 respectively. But it went up substantially during the liberal decades, rising to 119% of GDP in 2008, just before the global crisis. Table 3.1 also indicates that the financial sector's debt exceeded that of households in 2008 (Duménil and Lévy, 2011). This development represents an important transformation of debt burden. Financial firms are highly indebted in relative to the past.

The financial sector's increasing debt is related to the developments defined above, which are a combination of supply, demand, and governmental actions in financial markets. Through financialization, financial actors focused on more funding activities among themselves to obtain higher returns, rather than lending to the real sector. More new financial products were supplied and more demanders for these products were out there and moreover the government facilitated this via deregulation. At an increasing rate, a variety of assets, loans or securities were transferred among financial institutions themselves. Hence the financial sector emerged as a major borrower during the neoliberal period starting in the 1980s.

Table 3.1 The debts of all US sectors (% of GDP)

	1952	*1980*	*2008*
Non-financial sectors	124	136	234
Households	25	48	96
Business	30	51	78
Government	68	37	60
Financial sector	3	20	119
Total	126	155	353

Source: Duménil and Lévy (2011).

Financialization and income distribution

Although income inequality was already on the rise as financialization took shape, the economic developments shaped by the increasing size and importance of the financial sector further contributed to inequality. First of all, the increasing power of financial firms impacted the distribution of the growing profit share among different sectors of the economy. They benefited most from this. This is evident in the historical trends in their profits. While the share of profits was about 1% in the 1960s, it went up sharply from the early 1980s to the present day, reaching 15% in 2007 before the crisis (Reed and Himmelweit, 2012).

Along with the expansion of financialization, non-financial corporations have become ever more dependent on this growing financial sector. This interdependence changed the real firms' governance manner. They became more concerned with short-term financial gains. In this sense they valued shareholders' interests more and emphasized more short-term profits (Stockhammer, 2010). This perspective induced firms to cut labor costs and to reward top executives for having a short-term horizon. This implies unemployment, stagnation of wages, and swollen payments of the top employees of the companies, leading to increasing inequality.

In fact there are many other factors that caused the share of wages to fall, such as advancements in technologies, globalization, and the weakening power of labor institutions. Hence it is difficult to decompose these effects. However, there is increasing evidence that determinants such as technological change combined with globalization are not sufficient to explain the fall in wage share. For this reason, recently more attention has been given to the weakening labor institutions such as union and collective bargaining, and increasing financialization as important determinants in the wage share. The distribution of the growing profit share among different parts of the economy revealed the financial sector as the prime beneficiary.

Another critical aspect of finance is its relationship with wealth inequality, which is more extreme than income inequality. Deregulation in financial sectors mainly worked out in favor of financial actors, which increased income and wealth inequality further. Deregulation also triggered a combination of other factors that increased wealth inequality such as profit-making from an explosion in now deregulated credit, especially for property and financial speculation, and pushing up household consumption, mortgage acceleration of shadow banking activities and the growing hedge funds sector pursuing highly leveraged investment strategies. Furthermore, increased wealth inequality due to deregulation of financial activities also opened up more room for regulatory capture. In this process, regulators were increasingly controlled by those who are supposed to be regulated. Hence regulatory capture benefited some minor rich groups and loaded a great risk on the whole system.

Mobility of capital has encouraged governments to further lower their taxes in a race to the bottom to draw capital or keep it in the country. Dramatic reductions in tax rates have played an important part in wealth accumulation. Many countries attempted to draw capital by applying sharp reductions in tax rates (tax race among countries) and creation of tax havens. This also favored financial capital and opened up the wealth gap between financiers and non-financiers.

3.5 Theoretical approaches to the links between financialization and crises

3.5.1 Marxist tradition

Some economists argue that the recent economic crisis in 2007–2008 calls for a return to a debate at the center of Marxism. This debate is related to the notion of financial capital, which can help us to comprehend the dynamics of capitalism. In the early 20th century, Rudolf Hilferding pioneered such a debate. In his view, finance capital was dominating power at the monopolist or imperialist stage of capitalism. However, later Sweezy (1994) suggested a new concept, which was monopoly-finance capital. In his view, this term defines the nature of capitalism.

Sweezy was familiar with the studies of Hilferding. He knew how finance played a role in capitalist accumulation in continental Europe. Sweezy's argument, which became the main foundation of the Monthly Review school, on financialization was extremely influential. Political economists in line with this thought have drawn attention to the contrast between stagnation and the increasing role of finance in explaining the crisis of 2007–2008. The main argument here is that capital has looked for financial profits to compensate for the decline in profitability in real production. But increasing financial transactions eventually ended up with the crisis.

The authors of the journal *Monthly Review* focus on three crucial trends in contemporary capitalism: the stagnation of growth, monopolization, and financialization. Sweezy explains this as follows. He begins with analysis of financialization from the production process. He argues that the growing production of large firms is not absorbed, thus, there is not enough demand to buy their products. The large capacity of these firms cannot be sustained. Therefore they switch their capital to other areas. The financial sector is one of these. The increasing capital flows to financial markets lead to swollen prices, thus bubbles arise periodically.

This means that financialization mainly stems from the obstacles to the process of real accumulation, serving as a force counteracting the tendency towards stagnation. This is stressed by Foster and Magdoff (2009, 18–19) in this way: *"the largest of the countervailing forces during the last three decades is financialization—so much so that we can speak today of 'monopoly-finance capital'"*. They imply that financialization itself is not a cause of crises. But they keep saying:

> rather than being a modest helper to the capital accumulation process, it gradually turned into a driving force . . . the economy could not live without financialization (along with other props to the system such as military spending) and it could not in the end live with it.

In short, they argue that financialization occurs due to real firms' declining profit (thus a symptom of stagnation) but then itself turns into a driving force of bubbles.

However, increasing financialization, in the view of the Monthly Review school, creates other complications; financial firms reduce corporate profits, which discourages productive investment. One of these complications is that high financial profit opportunities lead to higher financial investment and result in a decline in real investment. Another is that increased financial payments can decrease the funds available for real capital accumulation. And modification of managers' incentives is another important effect of increasing financialization on business corporates. This shows itself in a shortening horizon of the planning production process. The executives of real firms focus more on short-term profits rather than the benefits of long-term real production, leading to further decline in real investments.

The financial and credit policies of neoliberalism that are developed in the financial markets do not take into account the problem of overcapacity or lack of sufficient demand. They cannot find policies to provide a stable foundation for renewed accumulation. Some policies such as increasing availability of credits or reducing interest rates can mitigate these problems to some extent. But they just lead to new problems such as overborrowing and asset bubbles, as long as the underlying overaccumulation problem remains in place.

As said above, those in line with Marxian thoughts mainly regard financialization as a reaction to declining profit opportunities in the real sector. This is to treat the financial sphere as a "superstructure" wholly dependent upon a "material base" in the real economy. However, this view may not be enough to understand the dynamics of capitalism. Financialization has also been influential on the restructuring of capitalist relations. That is, it is not only a passive response but also a constructive power. Innovations in the financial system have the potential to restructure production processes and spread them into the global level via the internationalization of capital. It is clear that the extensive development of finance and financial motives have been critical in the evolution of neoliberalism.

The authors of the Monthly Review school argue that money capital, bank capital, credit and speculative capital are all necessary stages of capitalism. Capitalism is inconceivable without them. Fictitious capital and indeed all the credit generated by the financial system is inherent in money-form and a necessary part of capitalist accumulation, even if ultimately dependent on the "real" economy for its revenues (that is, capitalism rests on the production of commodities not just their circulation). Capitalism needs them in order to function well and creates financial innovations to generate new financing opportunities. Moreover, they do not contemplate an inherent tendency of the capitalist system to trend toward crisis during financial accumulation. Therefore the crisis is not an inevitable result of the process of accumulation. It should rather be looked at in terms of new patterns in class relations and forms of state power. It is the particular context in which the crisis emerges. Moreover the proponents of the school mention that crises can be avoided if the disproportionality between capital goods and consumption goods departments of the economy is mitigated and ineffective demand can be restored by well-defined redistributive policies.

3.5.2 Post-Keynesian analysis

Even though Post-Keynesian analysis of financialization emphasizes to some extent the connection between stagnating production and increasing finance as argued by the Marxists like those in the circle of the Monthly Review, Post-Keynesian economists primarily focus on the detrimental effect of rising finance on productive activities. In this sense, the problems in the real sector are associated mostly with the expansion of the financial sector. That is, they move from finance to real, rather than from real to finance as in the case of Marxians.

In this sense, according to Lapavitsas (2011), Post-Keynesian analysis of financialization is mainly related to the notion of rentier. He thinks that the Minskian analysis is not directly associated with Post-Keynesian analysis. It focuses on financial theory of investment rather than the balance between finance and the rest of the economy.

The rentier, whose emergence is partly the result of neoliberal economic policy, has increased financial profits at the expense of industrial profits. As a result, financial motives have discouraged investments and led to stagnation in developed countries. The concept of the rentier is important for Keynes's analysis. He argues that the rentier derives his profits from the scarcity of capital and his financial motivation suppresses real investment. For Keynes, a healthy performance of capitalism needs the situation known as the "euthanasia of the rentier" to be effected through low interest rates. In this way, the rentier should be removed from the economic system; at least his role in the economy should be mitigated. However, in Marxian studies, the rentier class does not have a critical role, making only fleeting appearances.

The rentier is a monied capitalist. They do not make investments in the real sector but lend those who make real investments. That is, it is other capitalists who make productive investments, rather than monied capitalists. However, the former capitalists pay a fraction of their earning to the latter capitalists who lend to them. Some fraction of their surplus goes to the monied capitalists. Therefore there is a conflict of interest between them. The existence of monied capitalists has a negative effect on profits of the real sector, by constraining available investment funds and/or lowering the returns of industrial capitalists.

A categorization of stages of development of capitalism is also inherent in the Post-Keynesian approach. In line with this, the most recent stage of capitalism is specified as finance-dominated capitalism. In this structure, the demand side and distributional implications of financialization are analyzed in a macroeconomic framework. From this perspective, financialization is defined as a combination of three developments: firms' rising shareholder value orientation; increasing debt-financed consumption and redistribution of income from employees to firm owners and managers.

With regard to the first development, namely an increase in shareholder value orientation, it can be said that it leads to two effects on the management of a firm. First, more dividends are distributed and thereby internal funds decline for financing new investments. This naturally leads to the fact that investment is increasingly financed by debt with higher cost. Second, the payment structure of managers changes. They are paid in the form of bonuses and stock options. This changes the motivation of the managers, leading them to focus on more short-term profitability rather than long-term sustainability of the firm.

With regard to debt-financed consumption as a second development, as mentioned in different parts of this book, increasing financial capacity of the economic system has encouraged further consumption due to debt and wealth effects of increasing asset prices (Dünhaupt, 2016). Finally, the third development, according to Post-Keynesian economists, is that financialization also impacts on the distribution of income. Regarding functional income distribution, it is argued that shareholders' rising demand for dividend payouts comes at the expense of the share of wages in national income. Thus, along with increasing financial concerns, more dividend payments to shareholders are targeted and this generates reducing wages of employees.

Post-Keynesian economists discuss financialization in the models of growth and distribution. They define two different growth models with regard to financialization. They are the "finance-led model" and the "profits without investment model". The finance-led growth model incorporates the situation of increasing shareholder value. This creates a positive effect on growth. It is because even though it creates a redistribution from labor to rentier income, consumption is strong due to a high propensity to consume out of rentiers' income and debt-financed consumption related to a strong wealth effect. Moreover, through accelerator effect, investment also increases.

The second growth model, namely "profits without investment" is in fact similar to the first growth model. But there is an important distinction, which is that there is no stimulation of investment in the second model, as in the first model. In this model, demand comes from other sources such as consumption, fiscal expenditures by the government or increasing net export. In this sense, Dünhaupt (2016) argued that growth in the US was generated by increasing household consumption rather than investment expenditures made by firms since the 1980s, except for the period of new economy in the mid-1990s. Similarly, until the global crisis in 2007–2008, the US economy grew mainly from consumption financed by debt and increasing government expenditures rather than increased investments. This was not sustainable and eventually collapsed in 2007–2008.

3.6 Neoliberalism, deregulation, and financialization

3.6.1 The rise of neoliberalism

Neoliberalism developed as an intellectual current among conservative circles in the US and Europe in the 1950s and 1960s. Departing from neoclassical notions of self-regulating markets and emphasis on individual decision making, they elaborated the views that the improvement in the welfare of human beings is compatible with an institutional structure supported by strong property rights, free markets, and free trade. Since then, these views have formed the intellectual and ideological background of the developments that refer to neoliberalism.

In the post-Second World War period, socialist parties in European countries were very strong and the political influence of the Soviet Union was effective all over the world. Socialist parties had large popular public support in many large capitalist countries. The governments in these countries developed new forms of solidarities with labor to avert the threat of revolution. But the threat of the socialist movement reduced in the West in the 1970s and leftist parties became reformist.

In fact, the rise of neoliberalism is associated with various interconnected processes. It is mainly a response to factors such as declining profitability, excess capacity, and accumulation of huge amounts of capital. Capital attempted to respond to this to avoid declining profitability. This showed itself in geographic relocation of production, increased labor productivity, the fall in unionization, and the reduction of social benefits. Within this liberal period, these changes created several diverse effects: the stagnation of real wages, a weakened welfare state, deregulation of financial markets, increased uncertainties in financial markets along with the collapse of the Bretton Woods system, increasing privatization, rising mobility of capital flows, intensification of global competition, outsourcing, monopolization, and fast diffusion of technological innovations.

Along with the collapse of the Bretton Woods system, exchanges became more volatile and mobility of capital intensified. This facilitated foreign

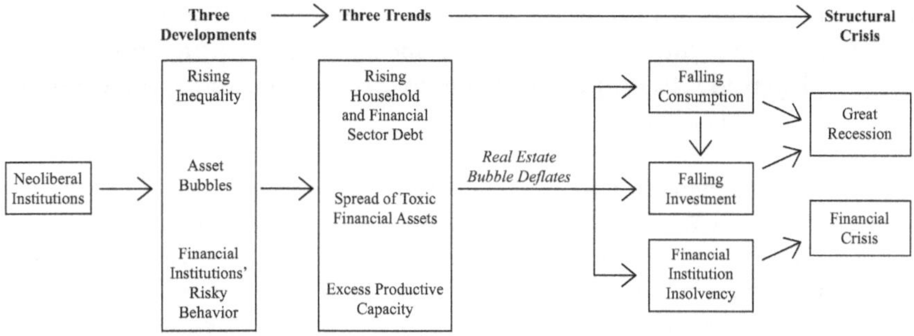

Figure 3.7 Possible causes of economic crisis.
Source: Kotz (2016).

exchange trading, risk hedging and speculation. Financial investors all over the world started to pursue new financial products. The constraints on the financial system were relaxed. For example, the controls on interest rates and the quantity of credit and barriers to international flows of capital were removed, capital markets were established and promoted and so on. Furthermore, the shift of weight to monetary policy led the authorities to focus particularly on the stability of prices, disregarding the concerns of inclusive growth and income equality.

In addition to these developments, there was also a new form of global competition starting in the 1960s and 1970s. This was mainly participation of countries such as Japan and Germany in the world economy. The growth of new multinational companies in the world led to a fall in profit rates. This also triggered the hostile takeover movement of the 1980s. All these resulted in a greater internationalization of the division of labor and transformation of the composition and location of workforce. Along with these, the advances in new technologies, especially in information technologies caused labor-saving and the suppression of wages.

All these developments during the spread of neoliberalism can be summarized under three main headings: inequality, financialization, and asset bubbles. All these developments that emerged through the institutions of neoliberal capitalism shaped the extent and degree of capital accumulation in the neoliberal decades. This mechanism is described in Figure 3.7.

The neoliberal institutions deepened income inequality further. We see this in developments such as: declining unionization, increasing casual jobs, cuts in social benefits, restraint of the welfare state, tax cuts for companies and rich groups, and excessive payments to company CEOs.

In finance, there occurred a critical shift from conventional financial practices to riskier and speculative activities. Many scholars think of financial deregulation as the main reason behind this. In fact, it was indeed deregulation of finance that allowed the shift in financial institutions' practices. Financial deregulation was not just a consequence of governmental initiative but also of mutual attempts of institutions at capitalism. Some of these are as follows: an intense competition in both the financial sector and the real sector; hiring highly-paid CEOs; the narrowing vision of corporates; and the rise to dominance of liberal finance theories.

It is a controversial question whether capitalism is inherently biased towards asset bubbles. It seems that there was no big asset bubble in the US from the end of the Second World War until the 1980s. However, along with neoliberal policies starting in the 1980s, the frequency of asset bubbles increased. Rising inequalities driven by neoliberal policies and developments that accompanied them induced the wealthy to engage in riskier and speculative financial transactions, causing asset bubbles to grow over time.

3.6.2 The relation between neoliberalism and financialization

It is generally recognized that there is a close relation between the financialization process and neoliberal restructuring but the critical question is which one has determined the other, namely the direction of causality or just coincidence.

It is widely recognized that a significant transformation occurred around the 1980s, from state-regulated capitalism to neoliberal capitalism. Financial liberalization was a crucial part of the neoliberal period. However, the relation between financialization and neoliberalism is not a simple matter. To some authors, the growing power of financial capital led to neoliberalism benefiting financial capital. However, as Kotz (2011) argues that this view has serious problems. He questions this argument.

For this, Kotz (2011) firstly reasons as follows: If interest in financial capital diverged from non-financial capital, there had to be a struggle between two. But there was no evidence of such struggle. Neoliberalism first took root in the US and UK at the end of the 1970s. In the US the shift toward neoliberalism appeared to have unified support from the capitalist class. A major part of big capital had earlier supported the regulated capitalist structure, in alliance with organized labor. At the beginning of the 1970s, most capitalists had common views on labor unions. They showed a kind of solidarity with labor unions. Later this changed. The big firms changed their alliance with labor, which accelerated the neoliberal process. As Harvey (2005) argues, when Prime Minister Thatcher began neoliberal restructuring in 1979 in the UK, even though there was no agreement among the capitalists, there was no strict stance of financial against non-financial capital. The opposition arose from old-school, aristocratic sections of finance and industry reacting to Thatcher's neoliberal policies.

Those supporting the view that the dominance of financial capital explains neoliberal change define finance capital very broadly. They do not make any distinction between financial and non-financial segments of capital. In this sense, finance includes all capitalists, rather than just financial institutions. Therefore the view that financial capital dominated non-financial capital has no explanatory power at all. But if, in the narrow sense, financial capital is different from non-financial capital, the question of how financial capital obtained a dominant position is more worth answering.

It is known that non-financial capital was dominant in the post-war economic structure. But at the same time, in the US, financial institutions, mostly banks, had some important concerns about the constraints placed on their transactions. However, these concerns were not taken into account until the liberal period. Liberal ideas pressed to remove these limitations by spreading the notion of efficiency of free markets. This led to the beginning of neoliberal restructuring in both the financial sector and other sectors of the economy. This supports the view that financialization was driven by neoliberal restructuring, rather than another perspective that finance determined the path of neoliberal restructuring.

3.7 Financial deregulation

The crises of the 2000s in the developed and developing countries raised profound questions regarding financial regulations and their effects on the performance of economies. Along with the wide spread of financialization, it has become a more prominent issue. In this section, we now consider the broad parameters of financial regulation since the end of the Second World War focusing on the scope of and prospects for regulation in the context of financialization and neoliberalism.

Regulation after the Second World War: market-negating regulation

From the end of the Second World War to the mid-1970s, there were various regulations and controls on domestic and international finance levels in the world, trying to constrain and negate all the markets in general, the financial markets in particular. Theoretical and ideological justification for tight controls over finance was provided by Keynes's view on financial excess, calling for the "the euthanasia of the rentier" by following economic policies that would strengthen the role of productive capitalists. The regulation of finance was an integral part of this so-called Keynesian period.

The regulation of financial markets and institutions mainly started after the Great Depression in the 1930s. The major institutional and legal change of this era took place in the US with the introduction of some important regulations such as the Glass–Steagall Act in 1933, which separated commercial from investment banking and imposed limitations on bank interest rates (Regulation Q). The Glass–Steagall Act represents the general approach to financial regulation until the gradual emergence of the liberal period.

The system of regulation applied to both money and finance, domestically as well as internationally. It relied on the role of the dollar as world money under the Bretton Woods Agreement and on administrative controls on prices, quantities, and functions within the domestic financial system. Three elements characterized financial regulation generally across mature capitalist countries during the Keynesian period, although there always have been some differences between various financial systems such as market-based (Anglo-Saxon) and bank-based (German–Japanese) financial systems.

First, there were limitations on interest rates applied by banks. Credit interest rates were frequently determined administratively, and were kept deliberately low with the aim of supporting productive capitalists. Interest rates on deposits were even more tightly controlled, often being zero for a range of deposits. Further, there were also controls on the quantities of credit and the direction of credit flows. Second, the business areas of financial institutions were restricted. This aspect of financial repression again varied according to the historical and institutional trajectory of particular countries, but several features were in common across both developed and developing countries. Commercial banking was generally kept separate from investment banking through legislation. Banks that provided long-term investment funds were also generally kept separate from other commercial banks, through special privileges in obtaining liabilities (for instance, issuing long-term bonds). Third, the mobility of international capital flows were restricted, operating as a necessary extension of the Bretton Woods agreement that guaranteed convertibility of the US dollar into gold. In effect, gold still functioned as the global means of ultimate money among states, even though the dollar was used generally for payments as well as for store value internationally. International monetary transactions occurred at largely fixed exchange rates. For this reason, the restrictions on capital mobility were required to sustain stability in foreign exchange rates.

The period that followed the end of the Bretton Woods system was characterized by great volatility of exchange rates; moreover, inflation rose sharply in the 1970s contributing to volatility of interest rates. For financial institutions active in the world market it became important to remove controls on international capital inflows precisely to confront the risks generated by the new volatilities.

Removing international capital controls and relaxing domestic regulations laid the groundwork for financial liberalization. An important step was the partial abolition of Regulation Q in the US in the 1960s, thus freeing some interest rates on bank liabilities. Equally important was the introduction of Competition and Credit Control legislation in the UK in 1970s which began to dismantle international regulations constraining British banks. Financial deregulation accelerated in the 1970s and became the norm in the 1980s in many countries. The end result was substantial disappearance of controls on financial prices, quantities, and functions, thus of the very substance of systemic market-negating regulation.

Financial liberalization also spread to developing countries in the 1970s mostly on the grounds that low interest rates had failed to encourage investment by productive capitalists. Funds for development could presumably be internally generated as domestic saving would respond positively to rising interest rates.

These ideas and policies began a trend that eventually led to the Washington Consensus in the late 1980s, which was mainly based on the view that financial repression was counterproductive because it led to weak and inefficient investment. From this perspective, the appropriate approach to finance in developing countries was to allow interest rates and all attendant financial magnitudes to be determined freely by financial markets. Here we have to note that financial liberalization in developing countries has always had a different character. Unlike developed countries, liberalized finance was partly imposed on developing countries through pressure by multilateral organizations such as the IMF and World Bank. The force behind the imposition of financial liberalization has mainly been conditionality attached to international loans given by multilateral organizations and the fact that developing countries were caught up in the repeated crises of the last decades.

Regulation under conditions of financialization: market-conforming regulation

The dominance of financial liberalization does not mean the absence of regulation. Finance has always been regulated, both domestically and internationally, but regulation has been of a very different type from that of the period immediately after the Second World War. The prevalent approach can be characterized as market-conforming regulation in contrast to the market-negating regulation that had set financial prices, quantities and functions.

The characteristic form of regulation in the years of financialization has been market-conforming especially after the 1980s. This type of regulation has tended to apply primarily to individual financial institutions, rather than to the financial system as a whole. It has often aimed to affect the balance sheets of financial institutions by imposing some limitations. Note that market-negating regulation after the Second World War also affected the balance sheet of banks, including the asset side. Thus, both loans and reserves were subjected to controls to ensure the direction of credit as well as the availability of adequate liquidity for banks. In contrast, market-conforming regulation in the years of financialization has shifted regulatory attention to the liability side of the balance sheet, above all, to the adequacy of own capital with a view to ensuring bank solvency. This approach to regulation has been designed in the Basel Accords (known as Basel I, II, and now Basel III)[3]. All these Basel Accords are highly compatible with market-conforming regulation[4].

Capital adequacy regulation became apparent as the movement of banks toward mediation in open markets continued to develop apace in the 1990s, including derivatives trading. Heavy involvement of banks in financial transactions meant new dangers of losses due to changes in asset prices; these gave rise to market risk. For this reason, a critical step in the development of the Basel Accords was the introduction of amendments which made provision for market risk. For the largest banks this meant the introduction of advanced models of calculating risk based on value at risk (VaR)[5]. Bank balance sheets thus began continually to reflect the movement of securities prices in the open markets, a factor that proved important in the development of the crisis of 2007–2008.

The crisis of 2007–2008 shows evidence of the failure of Basel II. One consequence, therefore, has been the further development of the regulatory framework through the Basel III Accord that began to take shape in 2010–2011. The underlying logic of Basel III is similar to that of the previous two accords: market conducive regulation designed by the financial system and aiming to strengthen the solvency of individual financial institutions by improving capital adequacy. But one important difference is the stronger emphasis on risk deriving from open-market trading particularly in connection with derivatives.

In the course of the crisis of 2007–2008 it became apparent that heavy use of credit default swaps (CDSs) by banks and other financial institutions created new sources of credit risk arising out of market trading. The integration of derivative instruments into the accounting practices of banks has been instrumental in creating these new risks, a development that has become gradually evident in the 2000s. In the bubble of 2007–2008, we observed that banks bypassed Basel II regulations. Securitization has involved setting up new institutions, such as structured investment vehicles, that issued asset-backed liabilities. Banks assets were moved off-balance sheet to avert capital requirements. In short, market-conforming regulations induced banks to securitize assets in order not to be subject to higher capital requirements.

This process has been referred to as regulatory arbitrage. It implies that those regulated have always try to bypass the regulations. The bypassing of Basel II, for example, is merely an instance of the spontaneous tendency of the financial system to avoid costly regulations. It is because Basel II had created opportunities for large banks to engage in regulatory arbitrage due to new capital adequacy regulations. But it is misleading to assume that market-conforming regulation could ever be designed permanently to avoid the danger of regulatory arbitrage. The best that could be hoped for would be continually to revise the regulatory framework to contest the efforts of financial institutions to bypass existing regulations.

The failures associated with market-conforming regulation in the context of financialization have led to a search for new approaches to regulation. Ideas have been put forth in the way we should treat the financial system as a network or as a biological system, but these have not led to concrete suggestions regarding regulation. There have also been attempts to explore macro prudential regulations, but they have hardly amounted to anything more than establishing a range of early warning signals, or of discretionary levers of intervention, to help regulators deal with crises.

3.8 Concluding remarks

Financialization is a transformation of capitalism based on the changed conduct of financial and non-financial agents. The transformation has taken place during the last four decades along with neoliberal ideology and was shaped through deregulation of financial markets and other markets.

There have been dramatic changes in financial institutions and products in recent decades. Increasing securitization, proliferation of new financial products, particularly derivatives, the growth of hedge funds and the shadow banking sector, the changes in regulation and a long period of deregulation transformed the landscape of financial markets and institutions completely. Finance has shifted from an integrated functional form to a market-mediated chain involving actors, products, structures, and arrangements.

Financialization changed the conduct of economic agents in several ways. One of these is that financial institutions emphasized the dividends of shareholders as a criterion of performance, especially in Anglo-Saxon countries. Firms have started to downsize the workforce where possible and distribute corporate earnings to shareholders, instead of retaining corporate earnings and reinvesting them in the business and returns to workers. The horizon of firms has shortened, focusing on more short-term profits. Another important change coming along with financialization has been an increase in debt. Economic actors, especially households, have been systematically induced to borrow further.

I think that financialization is not simply the outcome of policy changes that dismantled the regulations. Its development has been associated more with neoliberal ideas. The crisis of 2007–2008 and its aftermath, furthermore, indicate that financialization is persistent. Dealing with its problematic outcomes will induce us to think more about the regulatory framework of finance. We need a visionary perspective that recognizes interactions, market failures, and externalities in financial markets. It should not be constrained to periodic monitoring, stress tests or other routines. In this sense, with an integrated perspective, all supervisory agencies should oversee the financial system in its entirety rather than just the individual institutions or agents within certain markets.

Notes

1 A defined benefit plan is "defined" in the sense that the benefit formula is defined and known in advance. Conversely, for a "defined contribution retirement plan", the formula for computing the employer's and employee's contributions is defined and known in advance, but the benefit to be paid out is not known in advance since the returns from the contributions that are invested, at the participant's direction, in mutual funds, money market funds, annuities or stock offered by the plan are unknown in advance.

2 Take the case of General Electric:

> You probably think of it as a maker of lightbulbs and appliances, right? And in 1980, manufacturing did indeed account for 92 percent of its profits. But by early 2008, GE's financial business accounted for 56 percent of its profits. (Its GE Capital subsidiary happens to be the largest nonbank lender in the United

> States.) Now consider General Motors: It makes cars, doesn't it? But before its financial arm, GMAC, got caught up in the subprime mortgage crisis of the late aughts, GMAC routinely accounted for 60 to 90 percent of the parent company's profits. (GM sold off GMAC but has since replaced it with a new financial division, GM Financial.) When the wildly leveraged US economy crashed and burned at the end of 2008, many predicted that Wall Street's era of economic dominance had ended. But by March 2011, the Wall Street Journal could report that the financial sector once again was creating about 30 percent of corporate profits in the United States. While still short of the 2002 peak, when finance generated fully 44 percent of corporate profits, 30 percent was the financial sector's average during the subprime bubble
>
> (Noah, 2012, p. 156)

3 The Basel Accords are three series of banking regulations (Basel I, II, and III) set by the Basel Committee on Bank Supervision (BCBS). The committee provides recommendations on banking regulations, specifically concerning capital risk, market risk, and operational risk. The accords ensure that financial institutions have enough capital on account to absorb unexpected losses.

4 The Basel Accords are the product of the Bank for International Settlements (BIS) a body established to promote cooperation among central banks through a variety of institutional methods, including regular meetings.

5 The VaR approach simulates changes in the market value of a bank's portfolio and calculates a capital requirement based upon possible mark-to-market losses

4 Income inequality

4.1 Introduction

The distribution of income and wealth has been a significant matter in economics and the social sphere since the 18th century. There has been a long tradition in economics that emphasizes the effects of distribution on economic processes, seen in the books of Smith, Ricardo, Marx, and Keynes. Economists, especially those belonging to Marxist and Post-Keynesian schools, continue to explore the implications of income inequality.

However, interest in issues of income distribution declined post-Second World War; this was mainly due to the fall in inequality during this period. Hence, mainstream economists have not given an important role to income distributional considerations in explaining financial crises. As Atkinson and Morelli (2015) succinctly pointed out, prominent scholars such as Kindleberger and Aliber (2011), Krugman (2009), and Reinhart and Rogoff (2009), do not even mention income distribution in their studies. Moreover, in a relatively recent study, Robert Shiller's The Subprime Solution (2008), again inequality does not appear. The US Financial Crisis Inquiry Commission, set up in 2009 to investigate the global crisis did not refer to inequality at all. Thus, several economists either disregarded the macroeconomic effects of inequality or regarded it positively due to its creating the opportunity to expand credit to those who demand it.

Recently many researchers have started to point out that income inequality is one of the most important problems of our era. Inequality has significantly increased in many countries over the last few decades. Some researchers blame income inequality for several social ills. Richard Wilkinson and Kate Pickett claim that if the UK halved inequality, *"murder rates would halve, mental illness would reduce by two thirds, obesity would halve, imprisonment would reduce by 80%, teen births would reduce by 80%, and levels of trust would increase by 85%"*. Moreover, economists like Paul Krugman claim that high levels of income inequality polarize society and put our democratic institutions into jeopardy. As a mainstream economist, Raghuram Rajan also draws attention to the role of income inequality in the global crisis in 2018.

In fact, economists have always been interested in income inequality for political, sociological and egalitarian policy reasons. However, in recent years, especially after crises, the character of that interest has evolved into analysis of its effects on macroeconomic variables such as unemployment and growth. There has been such a perspective in Keynesian tradition. But now these ideas have started to infiltrate into mainstream economics. Starting in the 2000s, especially along with the global crisis in 2008, some mainstream economists have been concerned with the reasons and effects of increasing income inequality. They have begun to debate more and more the role of income inequality in the development of the crisis. The debate entered the public sphere particularly with the book by Rajan (2010), *Fault Lines*, where the author points out the links between indebtedness and income inequality, causing the global recession in 2007–2008.

As is known, the US was the center of two great crises in the world—the Great Depression in 1929 and the Great Recession in 2007–2008. Interestingly, there is an important similarity between these two great crises. It is that before both crises income inequality increased drastically. These similar trends before the two great crises further induced economists to draw attention to the probable role of inequality in the crises. In this sense, in this chapter, with the help of theoretical approaches, we also aim to discuss the empirical dimension of the relationship between increasing inequality and the occurrence of crises.

4.2 Evidence of increasing income inequality

Income inequality patterns in recent decades can be traced via trends in functional income distribution (income shares of labor and capital) and personal income distribution (income shares of different income groups). The trends in these two categories of income inequality allow us to observe structural and agent-based changes in the sphere of income inequality over time.

Functional income distribution is a conception of distribution that cares about the distinction between labor and capital. The income share between labor and capital is estimated; in this way we can evaluate whether the developments in an economy happen in favor of labor or capital. If the share of labor income increases in disfavor of capitalists' entrepreneur income (that is, profit), it is said that there is an improvement in income distribution.

Personal income distribution is different from functional income distribution. It focuses on income distribution among individuals, households or different economic or social groups, rather than the distribution between two income categories such as labor and capital. We use various quantitative methods to estimate the level of personal income distribution, some of which we employ below.

4.2.1 Trends in labor share

Labor income share was stable until the 1980s. It was seen as a stylized fact of the economy all over the world. However, in recent decades, this development has changed. Empirical evidence shows that there has been a steady decline in the labor share in many developed and developing countries. From 1990 to 2009, the labor income share went down from about 66% to about 62% in 26 countries (OECD, 2012). In another recent study by OECD, it seems that the average adjusted labor share (including self-employed income) in G20 countries declined by about 0.3 percentage points per year between 1980 and the late 2000s. However, for the emerging and developing countries, the results are not that clear. Although there have been sharper declines in Asia and North Africa, the fall in wage shares in Latin America has been minor and stable; further there has even been a little improvement in some countries in Latin America. Similarly, using its annual macroeconomic database (AMECO), the European Commission estimated labor-share trends in the G20 countries plus Spain. It is seen that there has been a decline in the labor share in the vast majority of countries (Figure 4.1).

Notice that there is a widespread perception that the decline in labor's share of national income is limited to the US. However, both as seen in Figure 4.1 and in other studies this is clearly not true. For example, in their study Karabarbounis and Neiman (2013) analyzed data from 56 different countries and found that 38 of these countries demonstrated a significant decline in labor share. This indicates that the decline over a period of ten years had been larger than that in the US. In particular the decline in China was dramatic, falling three times the US.

Here we have to draw attention to another point, which is that the share of labor income declined unevenly in favor of top income earners in the advanced countries. In the years between 1990 and the mid–2000s, the share

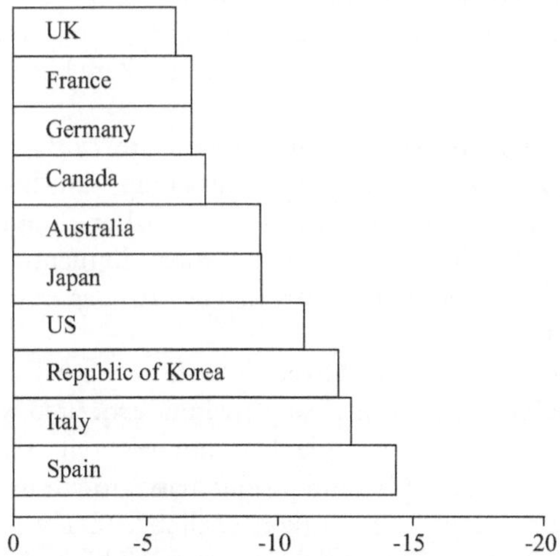

Figure 4.1 Decline in labor shares in G20 countries in advanced economies 1970–2014 (%).
Source: AMECO.

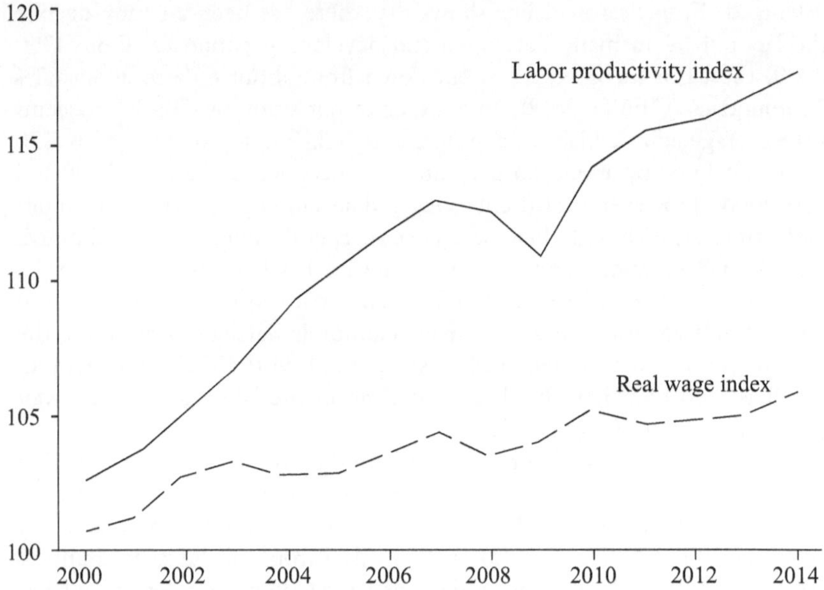

Figure 4.2 Evolution of average wages and labor productivity in selected advanced G20 economies (indices, 2000=100).
Source: ILO (2015).

of labor income of the top 1% in the OECD countries went up about 20%. This was due to the fact that while labor income of workers was stagnant, the income of executive employees increased dramatically in forms of high salaries and excessive bonuses. That is, if the income of high executive employees is excluded from total labor income, the size of the drop in labor share becomes much higher.

There are some fundamental reasons for declining labor share worldwide. They are mainly technological advancements, the increasing skill-biased technology and its diffusion, capital deepening, and entry of labor-abundant countries to the global economy. These factors seem more influential in developed countries, compared to developing countries. They have aggravated income inequality further over time.

The advances in technology that have occurred over time have led to significant increases in productivities. However, what is striking associated with this development is that the increases in productivities have not been reflected in wages for a long time. Wage growth lagged behind productivity growth in the G20 countries and hence the income share of workers declined. In advanced countries, this can be seen since 2000, as displayed in Figure 4.2. This is clearly apparent in the economies of the US, Germany and Japan. This trend can be also seen in other advanced and emerging countries, like Italy, the UK, South Korea, and Mexico.

Improvements in technology may not affect all the inputs used in production evenly, that is, affect their marginal productivities differently. This is considered as it may be more biased toward some inputs than others. For example, technological changes such as more complicated software, factory automation, advanced technologies in inventory management, and computer controlled machines replace routine and clerical work done by workers. However, newly emerging technologies like big data and high-speed communications have caused improvements in data-driven reasoning and hence contributed more to engineering, creative jobs, and design skills. These technological changes, in short, have changed the structure of the demand for labor. While the demand for low-skill labor declined, the demand for high-skill labor increased. This process is called skill-biased technical change, thus technological change has been in favor of people with high human capital.

Many studies show that American workers all enjoyed high wage growth before 1973. Until then, regardless of their educational levels, the rising trend of productivity increased workers of each group. However, along with the massive oil shock and recession of the 1970s and introduction of liberal economic policies in the late 1970s, the gains of workers began to diverge in opposite directions, increasing the gap between incomes of different groups with different human capital. Thus, for example, in the early 1980s, employees with college degrees started to see their wages growing. However, workers with no college degree (mainly those having only high school diplomas) were confronted with worse conditions, and their income declined in relative terms; thus their wages stagnated or fell. In fact the personal computer revolution that started in the early 1980s was the signal for this development.

In addition to technological changes, globalization seems to have affected tendency in labor share. Especially with the introduction of intense competition and the entry of countries which are primarily labor-abundant into the global economy, as some studies show that it reduced labor share in the developed countries. In particular China and India have had an important role in this development. This reduced the bargaining power of workers in the advanced countries, especially in the sectors with low-skill workers. Low-cost products of these countries flooded into the advanced countries. The demand for workers with low skills declined and thereby the power of the unions, whose members were these kinds of workers.

Changes in labor-market policies and institutions are another pronounced factor behind the decline in labor share. The declining power of labor-market institutions affected workers negatively, but especially lower- and middle-income workers. Here we can summarize some important changes in labor-market policies and institutions: (i) Decline in unionization rate, as empirical studies show that increasing inequality is related to declining unionization rate. For example, IMF Staff Discussion Note (SDN) evidenced that half of the fall in Gini coefficient in developed countries stemmed from the decline in unionization. Some other studies also verify this finding, even though the impacts that they found were not that strong. The decline in unions' power also caused unions to lose their power in influencing policy makers in directing economic policies improving the welfare of workers. They almost lost their power to affect redistribution polices, like progressive taxation rates. (ii) Declining power of other labor-market institutions: In addition to declining unionization and collective bargaining rates, other labor-market institutions lost their importance. For example, employment protection, unemployment benefits and minimum wages deteriorated. They became less effective in reducing inequality through wage and employment channels. Some studies also show that along with this, development of less secure employment practices such as casual and part-time worsened inequality further.

Financialization, namely increasing the role of financial markets, has also been regarded as an important factor in increasing inequality and declining labor share. Financial actors undertook an important role in the development of the economy in recent decades. They pursued higher profits and emphasized short-term interests of shareholders like the prices of shares and dividends, rather than welfare of their workers.

4.2.2 Trends in personal income distribution

Widening inequality in personal income distribution all over the world during recent decades brings similar implications regarding the decline in labor share. Personal income inequality (in both market and disposable income) as measured by the Gini index has increased greatly in most developed countries[1]. This development is more dramatic in the top income group. The share of the top income group has been rising, developing in disfavor of the bottom groups. In particular the share of the bottom 40% declined drastically in many countries. In the US, the top 1% received half of the increase in national income during the period 1979–2007. Similar things happened in Europe as well. This indicates that while the top 10% of the wage-earners gain 25% of total wage payments, the top 10% of capital returns captures 60% of total capital gains (OECD, 2011; Atkinson et al., 2011).

However, changes in income distribution in emerging markets seem to have mixed results. For example income inequality in Turkey, Brazil, Argentina, and Mexico has fallen since the mid–2000s. While this fall was more visible in Turkey, Argentina and Brazil, it was not that high in Mexico. In contrast, in other emerging countries such as China, India, Indonesia, and the Russia, income inequality went up over the same period. However, this rise was not as high as in advanced countries.

The tendency of increase in income inequality in many countries except for some has been persistent for about three decades. During downturns, this changes a bit but during the following recoveries, it starts to go up again; in other words, the short-term improvement in inequality during the recession reverts to its long-term trend. For example, the income share of the top 10% fell from 47.6% in 2000 to 43.8% in 2002 during the crisis in the US. But it

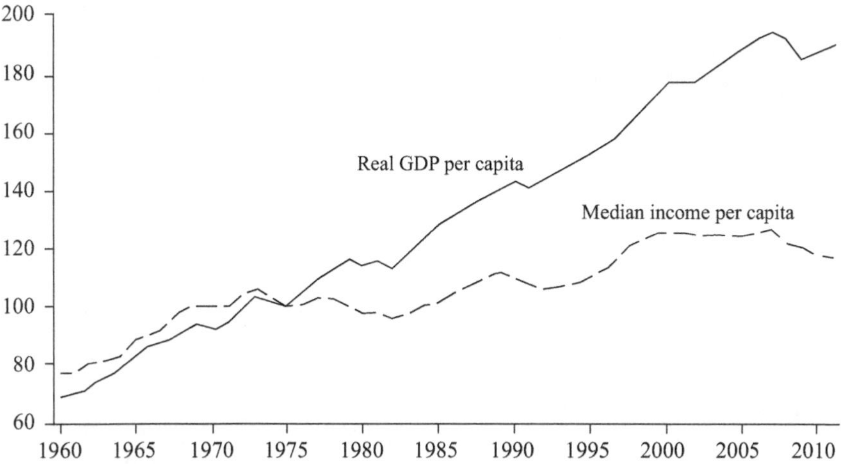

Figure 4.3 Mean and median income divergence in the US (indices 1975=100).
Source: Author's own calculations.

soon went up during the following recovery, even reaching the highest value before the Great Recession in 2008.

From the early 1970s, the US economy grew impressively, hence there was no stagnation in the country, and productivity was on the rise. But there was a shift occurring in the distribution of these gains. Thus there was a significant reallocation between different groups. In order to see this, average income can be compared with median income. In normal times, the changes in average and median income do not diverge from each other too much. But the reverse occurred in recent years, and thus the divergence between mean and median incomes increased significantly. This is shown in Figure 4.3. During the period 1973–2011, productivity grew at about 1.56% on average, and even rose to higher levels in the more recent years (1.88% during the period 2000–2011). However the median hourly wage did not change at all (merely 0.1% per year) because the increased productivity did not benefit the lower wage-earners, concentrating on the top income earners. Hence the median income did not increase as much as average income.

The relative changes in income shares of different income groups in the US are also striking. Figure 4.4 shows that middle-class incomes did not change too much, becoming stagnant. Thus, while the rich-income groups have become richer, the middle-income groups could not reach them, falling behind. During the period 1967–2008, the incomes of the top 20% in the US increased by $70,600—about a 70% increase. The middle quintile's income growth was much less, just $10,200, an increase of nearly 25%.

Long-run trends in income inequality in the UK, Germany, France, and the US are documented by Piketty and Saez (2006). In their study, it indicates

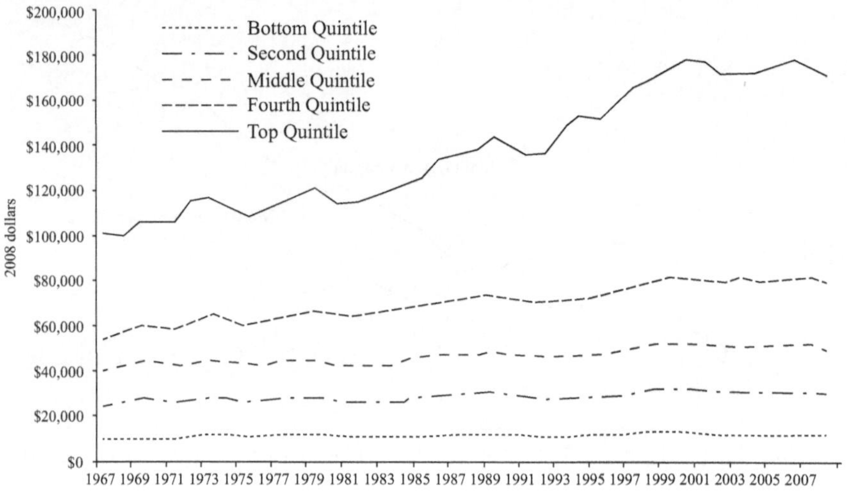

Figure 4.4 Average household incomes by quintile (in 2008 US $ thousand).
Source: The US Congress Joint Economic Committee (2010).

that income inequality was relatively stable for a long period. However, there was a great decline in inequality due to the first and the second World Wars. Starting in the 1980s, several studies, particularly those of Piketty and Saez (2006), Piketty (2014) and Atkinson et al. (2011), document that top incomes have dramatically risen especially in developed countries (particularly in the US and UK) but also in emerging ones like India or China. The rise in income share at the top has been associated with the rise of the top wages, those of employees in high executive positions. Figure 4.5 displays how the share of the top decile evolves in France, the UK, Germany and the US. The downward tendency changed its direction at the end of the 1970s and early 1980s. Thereafter, the top decile income shares in all these countries increased in a continuous trend.

According to Piketty, the increase in incomes of the top income groups has gone to high-skill employees. That is, increased inequality originates from the result of the increase in incomes of top bankers, corporate chief executives, and the shareholders of capital. This is seen in Figure 4.6. During the period 1990–2005, while the wages of workers rose by 4% and minimum wage fell by 9%, the average payments made to CEOs went up 298%, even exceeding the rise in corporate profits of 107%. At a speech at Georgetown University in May 2015, President Obama pointed out that the top 25 hedge fund managers earned more than all kindergarten teachers in the US combined.

All we argued above was related to income inequality but we know that wealth inequality is more dramatic. Wealth distribution is a more complicated problem because its conceptual boundaries are more elusive and data on wealth

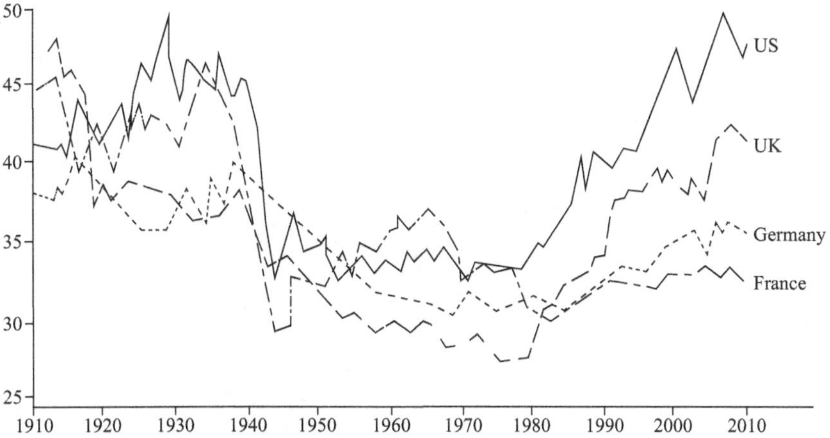

Figure 4.5 Top decile income shares, 1910–2010 (%).
Source: Piketty (2014).

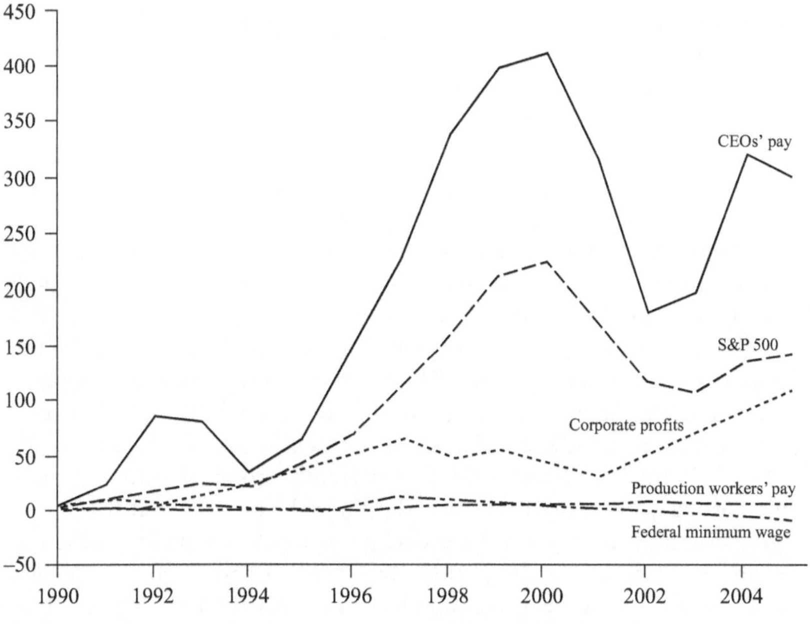

Figure 4.6 Gains of different actors from 1990 (% of 2005 US $).
Source: Domhoff (2006).

is more difficult to obtain. Data collection on wealth is less reliable when compared to income, which can be obtained by tax authorities and other institutions. People do not share information about their wealth. However Piketty collected data on wealth with a great effort. This is shown in Figure 4.7.

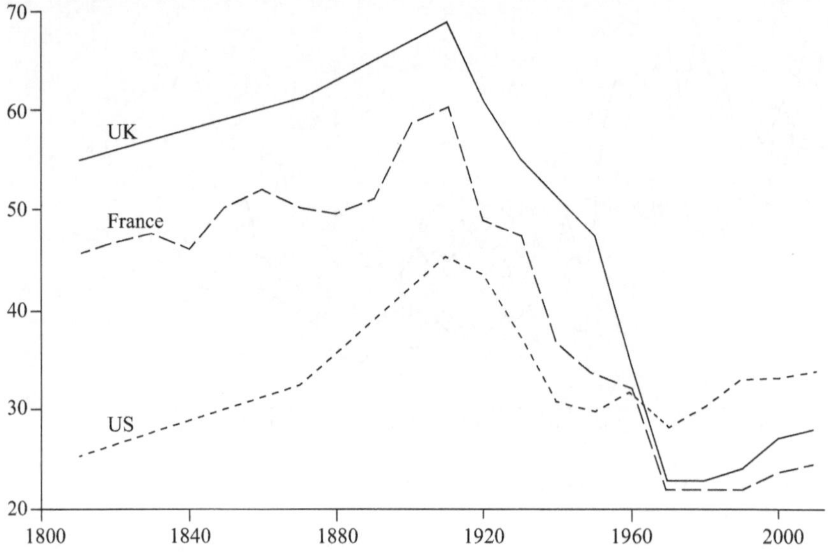

Figure 4.7 Wealth shares of the top 1% in three countries, 1800 to 2010 (%).
Source: Jones (2015).

Piketty reaches several findings from this data. First, inequality in wealth distribution is much deeper than that in income distribution. Figure 4.7 shows that the top 1% of families captures around 35% of wealth in the US in 2010, but a newer study by Saez and Zucman (2014) says it is 40% versus 17% of income. The top 1% of families corresponds to 1.5 million families in the US. The Walton family alone (the owners of the Walmart company) hold as much wealth as the bottom 40% of the American population put together. In 2015 the 62 richest billionaires in the world owned more than the poorer half of the world population (3.6 billion people). This number is down from 388 people in 2010 (Oxfam, 2016). Second, in comparison to the period 1810–1960, current wealth inequality in the UK and France was much lower. While the top 1% received 60% of total wealth in 1910, it is currently around 25–30% in these countries. Along with two world wars, the Great Depression and the rise of progressive taxation, there was a sharp decline in wealth inequality in France, the UK and the US during the period 1910–1965. Third, Figure 4.7 shows that wealth inequality has been continuously rising for the last 50 years. This is more visible in the wealth share of the top 1% in the US in comparison to other countries.

4.3 Income inequalities before global depression and global recession

The financial crisis of 2007–2008 has induced researchers to search for similarities between the Great Depression of 1929 and the Great Recession of

2007–2008. Most of them point out that the common tendencies in both cases were low level interest rates, deregulation and increasing financialization. But such reasoning requires more profound and deep scrutiny. Maybe they can be proximate reasons, at the deeper level, as some scholars claim; income inequality could trigger all these consequences because income and wealth distribution became more unequal in both periods.

In fact, there were also several important distinctions in the economies that experienced the great crises in 1929 and 2008. One of these is, for example, that the share of government expenditures was only 3% of national income in 1929 while it was much more than this, around 22%, in 2008 in the US. Another difference was the degree of financialization and financial speculation. It was much more widespread in the 2000s in comparison to the late 1920s. Speculation concentrated on real estate in the 2000s, whereas the stock market was the subject of the speculation in the late 1920s.

Historically the periods of inequality in the US were the period 1860–1900, the period 1914 to the late 1920s, and the period the 1970s–2000s. In two of these three inequality periods crises occurred. In these two periods, the economic state seemed very prosperous. The economic growth rate and unemployment were 4.7% and 3.7% per year on average respectively during the period 1922–1929, and the growth rate and unemployment rate between the period 1993–2007 averaged 3.25% and 5.2% respectively. However, in both periods the increase in productivity exceeded wages. This created important distributional problems.

As seen in Figure 4.8, income inequality reached its peak values before the crises of the Great Depression and the Great Recession. In 1928 the top 10% obtained 49% of total income. Then we know that the deepest recession in history broke out in the US. Nearly 80 years later, before the global crisis in 2007, the share of the top 10% reached its peak level, which was 49.7% (The US Congress Joint Economic Committee, 2010). Similar trends are also seen in other income shares of the richest 5%, 1%, and 0.1%.

Furthermore, Phillips (2002, p. 11) mentions that the number of millionaires increased from 7,000 in 1922 to 30,000 in 1929. The reduction in corporate taxes and marginal income tax (from 65% to 32%) intensified the inequalities. In the same manner, real income of lower income groups declined in the decades up to 2008. Another similarity between the two periods is that the top income groups gained higher shares, especially the ultra-top group, the top 0.01%. Its share went up from 1.7% to 5% in the 1920s and from 0.9% to 6% in the 2000s (Wisman and Baker, 2011, p. 66).

Wisman and Baker (2011) also show that the increases in productivities significantly exceeded the increases in wage on the way to both crises, leading to declining labor share and rising share of capital. During the 1920s, stagnation of wages partially originated from labor-saving technological innovations mainly in manufacturing, which caused a demand shift from unskilled labor to skilled labor. Labor-saving technologies displaced the less skilled labor, and hence their wages declined relatively. This is also seen in the fact that even though

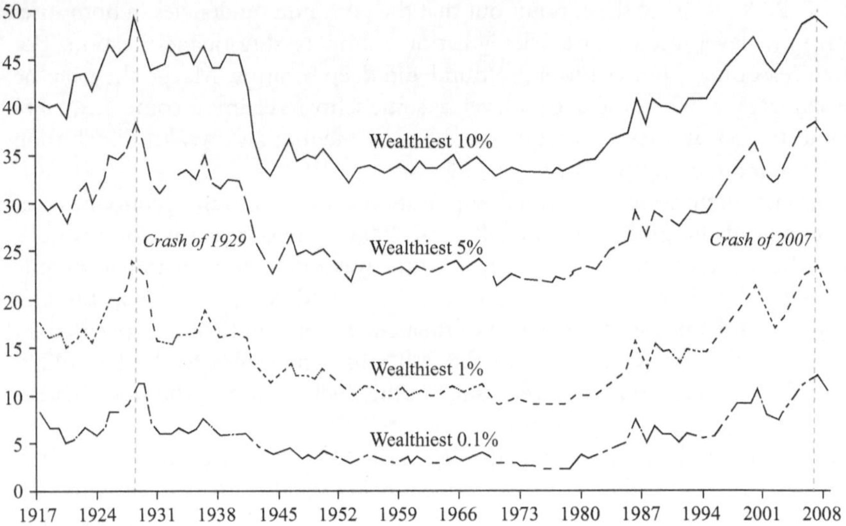

Figure 4.8 The income share of the wealthiest in the US (%).
Source: The US Congress Joint Economic Committee (2010).

the increase in manufacturing production was about 64% during the decade, the number of workers hardly changed at all. Similarly, as detailed above, during the last three decades before the crisis in 2007–2008, the increase in wages lagged behind the increase in productivity significantly because of labor-saving technologies as well as increasing international trade that destroyed domestic manufacturing jobs. Decreasing wage share, thus increasing capital share, naturally resulted in increasing saving by the wealthy and induced them to be involved in more financial transactions; we will discuss this issue later in more detail.

4.4 Theoretical perspectives on links between income inequalities and crises

In this section, we look at theoretical explanations for the links between income inequalities generally observed in the developed countries as shown above and crises that spread from these countries to all over the world. We can simply categorize these theoretical views under mainstream theories and non-mainstream theories under which Marxist and Post-Keynesian approaches will be argued.

4.4.1 Mainstream theories

In contrast to Post-Keynesians and Marxists—we will consider them in the section below—mainstream economists do not accept that crisis is inherent in capitalist production. According to them, economies have equilibrium tendencies; the forces of demand and supply will work out as an invisible hand that regulates them. Hence from this viewpoint crises do not occur in normal circumstances, since they are anomalies rather than an inherent tendency. This thought goes back to classical economists like Smith, Mill, and Ricardo. Based on this tradition, neoclassical theory argues that markets perform efficiently with fully informed agents maximizing their utilities. And financial markets function smoothly and efficiently. This is best expressed by the efficient market theory that elaborates that financial assets do not deviate from their fundamental values persistently; thus their prices are not persistently under- or overvalued and return immediately to their fundamental values.

In the neoclassical view, rationality and complete information play a critical role in preventing imbalances in economies. They ensure that financial intermediaries, basically banks, lend to credible borrowers, and that borrowers will borrow as much as they need to maintain their economic activities. Hence crises are not the results of systemic miscalculations realized in real and financial markets but they are rather the result of governmental distortionary interventions or unexpected external shock to the economic system (such as natural disasters and civil wars). In these cases, crises are in fact correcting mechanisms to balance the forces of demand and supply. They overcome exogenous disturbances and misguided government policies. This provides resilience to the economic system. Hence from this perspective crises are not endogenous, that is not originating from internally determined forces. In line with this view, since inequality is simply the result of variation in productivities, it will not have devastating and distorting effects on the economy.

Disregard of inequality by mainstream economics can be also observed in DSGE models (dynamic stochastic general equilibrium models), which are frequently employed by them. They are based on one representative agent. This implies that they are not concerned with distributive problems. Furthermore, in DSGE models, there is no excessive debt problem, therefore financial agents do not feature in these models. In short, according to most of the mainstream theories, inequality is not a serious problem. Its existence will not create a negative effect on aggregate demand. This mainly arises from the fact that fluctuations in income will be smoothed out by credits presented by financial markets (as asserted by the permanent income hypothesis).

However, even though general convention in the mainstream regarding financial crises has not changed too much, following the subprime crisis some mainstream economists have questioned the assumptions used and prominent economists have acknowledged that income inequality can trigger crises. Rajan (2010) was one of the first economists to put forward a theoretical link between inequality and the global crisis in 2007–2008. He argued that there has been a great transformation in skill-biased technology that changed the trends in inequality, deepening inequalities in the economy. The US government, in order to counteract this inequality, induced lending to households with lower income. This expanded credit volume in the economy. This was also supported by low interest rates and partially financed by increasing capital inflows especially from China. The eventual outcome of this process was overindebtedness, which no economy could sustain for a long time.

Rajan, as compared to other heterodox economists, does assume that the capitalist system is not prone to crisis. He emphasizes governmental failure in which the government distorts incentives for financial markets and poor households. He also focuses on the issue of educational failures, which is critical in increasing inequality. In this sense, Rajan develops some policy suggestions. For example, education is one of the policies to lower inequality. The government can correct the educational gap that occurs between different social groups, or otherwise this turns out to be income inequality in the long run. He also suggests that financial regulations should be designed in a way to reduce speculative activities, and international organizations should aim to mitigate global imbalances.

In parallel with Rajan, other mainstream economists like Roubini (2011), Reich (2010), Stiglitz (2009), and Milanovic (2010) also reject the mainstream view that assert no connection between inequality and aggregate demand. For example, in line with Rajan, Milanovic argues that politicians were eager to intervene in the disturbing problem of middle-income stagnation and wanted to ease the borrowing constraints of the lower income groups to increase their consumption. In a similar manner, Stiglitz (2009) also thinks that without the loose monetary policy of the post-2001 period, aggregate demand would not be enough due to stagnation of wages. Expansion of credits allowed people in the US to consume beyond their income. They caught up with their richer peers to maintain their consumption status. This reasoning resembles the view of Veblen's conspicuous consumption.

Additionally increasing power and rent seeking behavior of the rich, who successfully lobbied for less state intervention and less redistribution, and the decreasing power of the working class (due to deregulation, globalization, and weaker labor unions) coupled with existing skill-biased technological change, meant that polarization of incomes increased sharply prior to the crisis. However, this behavior was unsustainable in the long run as households became overleveraged and because the housing bubble could last no longer. Paul Krugman also recognizes that the influence of rich people on economic policies has been a major problem, but in contrast to Joseph Stiglitz, he asserted that not underconsumption due to increased inequality but overconsumption by poor and middle-income US households was a major problem before the crisis. He argued that there is a common causation between economic crisis and widening inequality, rather than the case in which one caused the other. In his view, both have the same roots, which are mainly triggered by excessive liberal policies.

Some mainstream authors also acknowledge that not only high inequality levels in the US, but also high levels of global inequality were important in the emergence of crises. For example, Vandemoortele (2009) especially focuses on this relation. In his view, within-country and between-country inequality are mutually reinforcing. While within-country inequality led to an aggregate demand problem, global inequality contributed to balance of payments imbalances (unequal capital flows and the accumulation of reserves). All of these have played an important part in the run-up to the crisis. This subject, in more detail, will be covered in the global imbalances section of this book.

4.4.2 Non-mainstream theories

Research on the impact of changes in distribution on economic processes and social matters has a longstanding history in economics and was discussed in the works of Smith, Ricardo, Marx, and Keynes. Although the topic became somewhat out of fashion in the last quarter of the 20th century, economists, Marxians and Post-Keynesians in particular, continued to debate the possible negative impacts of income inequality.

4.4.2.1 Marxian crisis theories and the role of income inequality

Marxian economists mainly explain crises through three different arguments, building on Marx's studies. The first group of Marxists argue that crises originate from problems during the accumulation process. During this process at a later stage increasing real wages due to unionized power of workers or increasing scarcity of workers reduce profits. This is called profit squeeze theory. The second group of Marxists explain crises as the result of the tendency for the rate of profit to fall, which is inherent in the capitalist system. This is called the tendency of rate of profit to fall. These two theories will be discussed in more detail in the following chapters of this book. The third group argues that crises originate from the realization of surplus value leading to overproduction or underconsumption.

In all these versions of Marxian crisis theory, the issue of distribution is a critical concept because all of them are associated with the class conflict between labor and capital. Marx says that the source of capitalists' profit is surplus value arising from the exploitation of labor. Thus, output can be divided into wages of workers and profits of capitalists. If the profits get bigger, it means that more surplus value generated by labor is captured by the capitalists. This can originate from increasing productivities of workers, lower wages or increasing working hours.

Marxians who support the view of falling profits point out that capitalist economies enter crises due to the fact that the degree of exploitation declines when these economies use more constant capital (more machinery or capital goods), that is, when the ratio of constant capital to surplus value goes up. The profits are falling because there is harsh competition among capitalists, which expands capital accumulation through increased investments. Hence the falling profits are not simply the result of growing worker resistance or rising real wages even though they accelerate this process. In this sense, inequality is the outcome rather than the cause of crises. However, proponents of the profit squeeze paradigm claim that an increase in inequality is not the cause of the crises but rather that a decline in inequality is the cause of crises. This argument is striking. It mainly means that an expanding scale of production leads to more employment, which strengthens the bargaining position of the workers. This lowers the capitalists' profits and leads to less capital accumulation. This in turn ends up in crisis.

The overproduction/underconsumption theory is the only relevant Marxist theory that directly proposes income inequality as a main cause for capitalist crises. From this viewpoint surplus value is not realized, and thus capitalists cannot sell their products because there is not enough demand. Competition among capitalists themselves pushes them to produce more. In order to increase their profits, they attempt to reduce wages. As a result, capitalists are constrained by effective demand due to an increase in supply of products and the fall in demand (declining wages). Marx (1993 [1857], p. 91) mentions this:

> Production mediates consumption; it creates the latter's material; without it, consumption would lack an object. But consumption also mediates production, in that it alone creates for the products the subject for whom they are products. The product only obtains its "last finish" in consumption. ... Without production, no consumption; but also, without consumption, no production.

Consequently, the spending capacity of economic units in any economy is the main determinant of how the economy evolves. The fall in employment level and wages can disrupt this spending capacity and lead to a crisis. Without adequate consumption demand, capitalists have no motive to increase their investment spending. They cannot sell their products for a profit. The fall in spending capacity or aggregate demand corresponds to an increase in inequality. Increasing inequality can cause an overall stagnation or a rupture in the economy due to a possible massive overproduction as pointed out by scholars such as Sweezy (1942), Baran and Sweezy (1966), and Foster and Magdoff (2009).

Furthermore, some Marxians whose thinking is close to the arguments above claim that unequal income distribution (declining wage shares) led to financialization and the increasing demand for debt. Thus this potential realization problem created different solutions; some of them (for example, the US) resorted to debts to overcome demand insufficiency, while some other countries (for example, Germany, Japan, and China) resorted to increasing exports to avoid insufficient domestic demand. And also some fraction of the surplus was diverted to finance. In this sense, along with the expansion of the financial sector, speculative investments replaced productive real investment. In this way, consumption was induced through inflated prices of financial assets, which created wealth effects. At the same time, more financial funds were transferred to households to maintain their consumption. This mechanism simply describes a growth model starting with inequality (stagnant wages and excessive salaries and bonuses) and then leading to overindebtedness showing itself in an increasing number of credits and subprime mortgages to households which they might not repay easily. As a result, from this viewpoint, the inequality that drove the debt-led growth model resulted in financial crisis.

4.4.2.2 Post-Keynesian crisis theories and the role of income inequality

Post-Keynesians mainly focus on how functional income is distributed between workers, capitalists and rentiers and how this affects effective demand. This forms the basis of their main argument. In this sense, Post-Keynesians associate performance of an economy with changes in income distribution. For their analysis, they start with making a distinction between functional and personal income distribution. As they have mentioned, functional income distribution is important for analysis of class. It shows how workers and capitalists share total production in an economy. But personal income distribution describes the effect of income inequality among individuals on aggregate demand in the economy.

From a functional distribution perspective, the direction of change in real wages can affect the functioning of the whole economy in different ways. For example, there can be positive and negative effects of an increase in real wages in an economic sense. Higher wages mean higher demand and higher production because the marginal propensity to consume is much higher for workers than capitalists. Hence firms make more investments and hire more workers (Palley, 2010a). However, at the same time the increase in wages may decrease the profits of capitalists because firms will have fewer incentives to invest, leading to less accumulation. Therefore the net effect depends on economic circumstances.

The change in personal income distribution has similar effects in terms of affecting the level of demand. But it is not concerned with the production cost effect of wages directly. Increasing inequality can have devastating effects on consumption because lower income groups have higher marginal propensities to consume than the rich groups. This perspective developed by some Post-Keynesian economists in fact resembles Marxian underconsumption theory. This is because severe inequality can lead to lower consumption, which in turn can distort the accumulation process.

Post-Keynesians also draw attention to the issue of inequality in a financialized system. In a highly financialized system, income inequality may not be apparent because consumption inequality is not that prevalent due to the fact that lower income groups have easy access to credits. Hence they become more overindebted due to a greater availability of loans. However, even though this situation initially may seem stable, eventually the large debt burden cannot be sustained and debtors are forced to save more (deleveraging) and consume less. And this is likely to lead to a debt-burdened recession and have a potential to cause a crisis.

In fact, there can be some economic developments that counteract the negative effects of increasing income inequality. For example, capitalists can decrease their saving and consume more luxury goods (increasing their propensities to consume) or they can increase their investment expenditure or external demand can increase (increasing trade surplus). However, as Palley says: *"A mass-production economy needs mass-consumption markets to support it [and] robust mass-consumption markets rest on a healthy distribution of income"* (Palley, 2002, p. 11). This reasoning is very much in line with Keynes's views. Keynes (1936, p. 372) argues that one of

> the outstanding faults of the economic society [is] its arbitrary and inequitable distribution of wealth and incomes and every weakening in the propensity to consume regarded as a permanent habit must weaken the demand for capital as well as the demand for consumption.

In the same manner, Kalecki draws attention to the issue of ineffective demand as the rich get richer, that is, their higher saving rates will reduce total demand in the long run. He mentions that unequal income and inadequate demand coincide.

Mainstream economists particularly emphasize the cost aspect of wages. Hence, in their view, a fall in wages has a positive effect on production and employment. But this is not verified with empirical data. For example, the average annual growth rates in GDP in the post-1980s were not high even though wages were stagnant for decades. However, the Post-Keynesians argue that wages have a dual role: demand effect and cost effect. A fall in the share of wages, reflecting an increase in inequality, reduces the total demand due to the fact that households' marginal propensity to consume is higher than the rich. This is demand effect. However, cost effect plays a role as well: Due to the fall in wages, the production cost will be lower, and profitability will go up. Additionally the decline in unit costs will also increase international competitiveness and therefore ultimately raise net exports.

Therefore there are various effects of a decline in wages: fall in domestic demand, increased profitability, and increased external demand. The net effect will be the combined effect of all these three factors. In the case where there is a big difference between marginal propensities to consume of workers and capitalists, a low sensitivity of investment to profitability and a low sensitivity of exports and imports to relative prices, then an increase in wages will have a positive effect on total demand. This regime is called wage-led, otherwise (thus if it has a negative effect) it is called profit-led.

These effects can change with respect to the circumstances through which countries pass. A wide range of empirical research has searched for these effects, and the results show three findings: (i) consumption responds more sensitively to a decrease in the wage share than does investment. This implies that in many countries domestic demand (sum of consumption and investment) is wage-led in countries in both the developed and developing world. In this sense, growth is determined by net export effects, which in turn depend on the price and labor cost elasticity of exports and imports to prices (ii) the international trade channel depends on not just the price and labor cost elasticity of exports and imports to prices but also the degree of trade openness (the share of exports and imports in GDP) and (iii) in a highly globalized trade environment, the effects of a change in wages are very constrained, and thus the competitive effect of decreased wages can be limited because countries follow the same strategy at the same time.

The outcome expected of this race to the bottom in wages since the 1980s generated a stagnation of demand in the global economy. So the question is now how the world economy grew before the crisis in 2007–2008 if there was a general stagnation in wage share. This case can be explained by two growth models: (i) the debt-led growth model in the advanced countries like the US and UK and in emerging economies and (ii) the export-led growth model in countries like Germany, Japan, and the Nordic countries and countries like China and some East Asian countries. Hence both the debt-led and the export-led growth strategies were followed at the same time in the world during the same period. It seems that both growth strategies aimed to avoid the persistent stagnation of demand due to declining wages.

Figure 4.9 summarizes all these arguments to describe what happened during the run-up toward the global crisis in 2007–2008. Since the world was in general in a wage-led regime, increased income inequality caused stagnant demand. In order to counteract this problem, countries adopted either debt-led or export-led growth models. As we know, the debt-led growth model led to a credit expansion and thereby increased demand. The countries that followed this growth model produced large current account deficits. However, some other countries followed another growth model, namely the export-led growth model. In this way, these countries benefited from other countries' demand because their domestic wage levels were stagnant. Both growth models are inherently unstable in that they each rely on high debt ratios. In the debt-led model, it is clearly seen that household debt has risen in these countries to allow for growth. In the export-led growth model, the high level of debt also occurred but in this case instead of increased domestic debt, foreign debt of other countries increased, mainly that of its trade partners.

As shown in Figure 4.9, increasing wealth concentration also helped to provide funds to maintain these fragile growth regimes. These funds provided by the rich generally flowed into riskier assets—such as asset-based securities (ABS) and collateralized debt obligations (CDOs). Particularly the super-rich played a crucial role in this development. Due to their increasing financial asset demand, the yield of traditional bonds declined. This in turn induced investors to seek alternative investments with higher yields. They became the main buyers of newly structured complicated and risky financial assets. Therefore they induced the financial institutions to produce new risky assets and caused the expansion of subprime loans provided by their funds, even if partially.

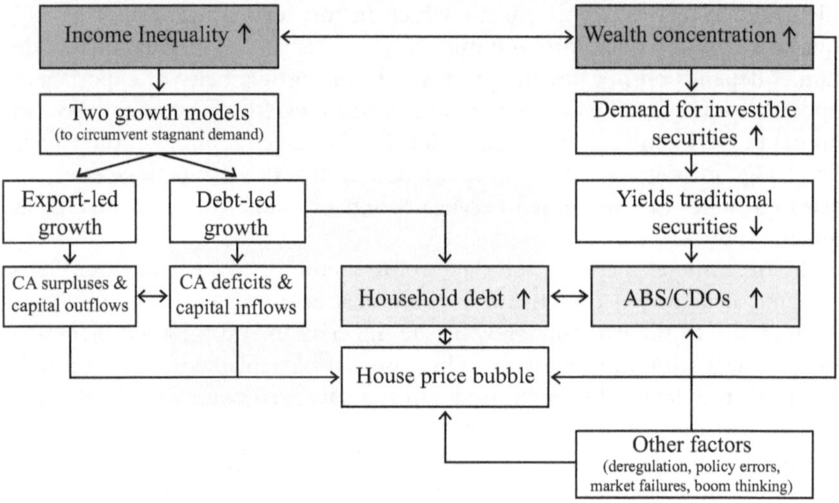

Figure 4.9 Rising inequality and growth mechanisms.
Source: Goda et al. (2014).

Moreover, they placed pressure on politics to design financial structure and deregulate it in parallel with their purposes.

4.5 Empirical analysis of linkages between income inequalities and crises

In this section we look at the main channels between income inequalities and other relevant important variables in a more concrete way, particularly focusing on the global crisis of 2007–2008.

Recent academic research is developing new explanations of the relationship between inequality and crises. This new emerging literature defines five channels, which are defined as: (1) Income inequality and weak demand (2) Increasing household debt and asset bubbles (3) Wealth inequality and financial speculation (4) Increasing inequalities and current account deficit and (5) Increasing inequalities and regulation. We will discuss all these channels from both theoretical and empirical perspectives below. In fact, they are more compact and concrete forms of theories discussed above and recognized by many more economists after the global crisis of 2007–2008.

Channel 1: income inequality and consumer demand pattern

Many countries have suffered a significant fall in the share of wages in national income. As mentioned above, several studies verify that growth rates depended on the trends in wages rather than those in profits. That is, if the wages went down, many countries experienced slowdown in their economies. Additionally the change in the distribution within wages has become critical over time. That is, the wages of top earners have increased much more than the wages of low and middle groups. This transformed the consumption pattern of wage-earners. It pressured the overall demand downward further because the higher wage groups saved more, thus not increasing their demand as much as those with lower saving rates. Hence the overall consumption rate of a country generally decreases in the case of high income inequality in comparison to the case of more evenly distributed income.

However, according to mainstream theories such as the permanent income of Milton Friedman and life-cycle hypotheses of Franco Modigliani and Richard Brumberg, saving and consumption at the aggregate level are not associated with the distribution of permanent income. In this sense, only if there is a high variance in transitory income, it will lead to higher precautionary saving. Moreover, according to this argument of permanent income, combined with the assumption of rational expectations, people smooth out their consumption with help of financial markets, even in the case in which the transitory component of income shows a higher variability. From this viewpoint, the rise in inequality until the crisis in 2007–2008 merely reflected a higher variability in transitory income and therefore households with lower income groups insured themselves through borrowing from credit markets.

Hence, according to permanent income hypothesis, an increase in household demand for credit originates only from transitory changes in the incomes of different income groups. However, this view is unable to construct a relation between rising inequality and declining aggregate saving rate and increasing household debt. It is expected that higher income instability should induce more saving if people think that uncertainty about their earnings in the future is increasing. However, it fell throughout the long period up to the crisis in 2007–2008. Although this subject has been explored contentiously since the period in which the saving rate began to fall in the mid-1980s, it remains a puzzle.

According to Piketty and Saez (2013), there has been a permanent income shift from the poor to the rich, rather than a transitory shift. They assert that an immense income shift occurred in the US since the early 1980s. While the top 1% and 10% became richer, the rest, the bottom 90%, became poorer. There was an income transfer from the latter to the former, about 15% during this period. Hence the explanation of the higher level of transitory income of the permanent income hypothesis of consumption is not good enough to explain the fact that was observed as a permanent shift of income from the bottom 95% to the top 5%. If the transfer was really permanent, the only way to explain such increase in debt, in the permanent consumption theory framework, is that households did not immediately perceive the income shock to be permanent.

In the last decades before the crisis in 2007–2008, households tended to reduce their saving but at same time borrowed more. Rajan (2010) links these developments to increased inequality during the same period. In his view, increased inequality mainly originated from "college premium". He claims that the general structure of education has been diverging from what has been required by advances in technology. Technological advancements exceeded the improvements in education. A large portion of society could not have opportunities to obtain qualified education. This further deepened inequalities between those who have been well educated and those who have been less educated. But those who have been less educated have kept consuming further, living beyond their income for a long time.

Researchers have started to think more about increased consumption not consistent with income levels as happened before the global crisis in 2007–2008. For this, they applied more to behavioral literature. They mostly benefited from the conspicuous consumption hypothesis of Veblen (1989) and the relative income hypothesis, developed by James Duesenberry, providing an intuitive explanation for this rise in consumption. The sociologist and economist Thorstein Veblen coined the term "conspicuous consumption" to explain consumption as a means of either attaining or maintaining a given social status. To some scholars, this incentive of lower- and middle-income groups speeded up the consumption that went beyond the means of these households during the run-up toward the global crisis in 2007–2008, hence triggering borrowing and eventually collapse of the economic system.

The relative income hypothesis points out that a household's consumption is independent of the absolute level of income; instead it is a function of two factors: (i) the household's position in the income distribution within its local reference group. This is an external criterion, expressed in terms of the past consumption of some outside reference group. This is also defined as "keeping up with the Joneses" and (ii) the relation between the household's current and past income. This is an internal criterion expressed in terms of the individual's own past consumption levels. It is generally defined as "habit formation". This perspective tries to explain the high level of consumption of households with relatively lower income even if their income sources had stagnated for a long time. In more technical terms, these two types of reference consumption imply that households have had "time non-separable" consumption functions.

The increase in the income of wealthy people has a potential to affect the consumption of the less wealthy. This happens through "expenditure cascade". This means that the change in consumption patterns of one group is associated with another group's consumption patterns. That is, one group's consumption can be regarded as a reference point by other groups. If people start to think that their consumption level is lower than that of people around them, they increase their consumption level, which triggers expenditure cascades. The main reason behind this is the increased income of the richest that reflects their consumption and its effects on consumption behaviors of low income. Stiglitz (2009) also emphasizes this case. He claims that the rise in borrowing is driven by the desire of poor households to maintain their living standards even in the case of income stagnation. They do not look at their income levels; what they focus on is others' consumption.

Rajan describes the consumption pattern of low-income households during the Global Recession as irrational. He mentions that

> ...the argument is that if somehow the consumption of middle-class householders keeps up, if they can afford a new car every few years and the occasional exotic holiday, perhaps they will pay less attention to their stagnant monthly paychecks.
>
> (Rajan, 2010, p. 8)

However, when Rajan's view on inequality (based on divergence in income between the well-educated and the not well-educated) is coupled with the relative income hypothesis, it becomes clear that from the point of view of low-income households, credit-financed consumption (the case of less saving and more borrowing) may have been a completely rational reaction in the face of rapidly increasing consumption by top-income households. This is why their reaction can be rational when they observe other people consuming more. Thus being influenced by other individuals' consumption standards may be a rational response on the part of consumers in pursuit of widely recognized goals.

Channel 2: income inequality and rising household debt and asset bubbles

As we showed, both the Great Recession and Great Depression were preceded by a large increase in household debt and increase in inequality. James Galbraith, in his book *Inequality and Instability* (2012), supports this fact and says: *"As Wall Street rose to dominate the US economy, income and pay inequalities in America came to dance to the tune of the credit cycle"*. He stresses that the expansion of credits was the main factor that related inequality to economic instability.

This pattern in the period before these two great crises is seen in the following figures. Figure 4.10 plots the evolution of inequality in the US before the Great Recession in 2007–2008 and household debt-to-GDP ratios. In the years between 1983 and 2007, there was a drastic increase in income inequality. The share of total income obtained by the top 5% of the income distribution increased from about 22% in 1983 to 34% in 2007. And Kumhof and Ranciere (2010) argued that in 1983 the top 5% had a higher level of debt (by 15%) than the bottom 95%. But in 2007, the debt-to-income ratio of the bottom 95% was twice as high as that of the top 5%.

In the 1970s deregulation spread in almost all advanced countries. This triggered credit expansion. The banks started to finance various activities, regardless of their default risks, especially personal loans for consumption, mortgages, and speculative areas. This expansion in credits caused asset bubbles. In the 2000s, this showed itself in a housing bubble. People increased their debt excessively to buy houses on the expectations of a rise in their prices.

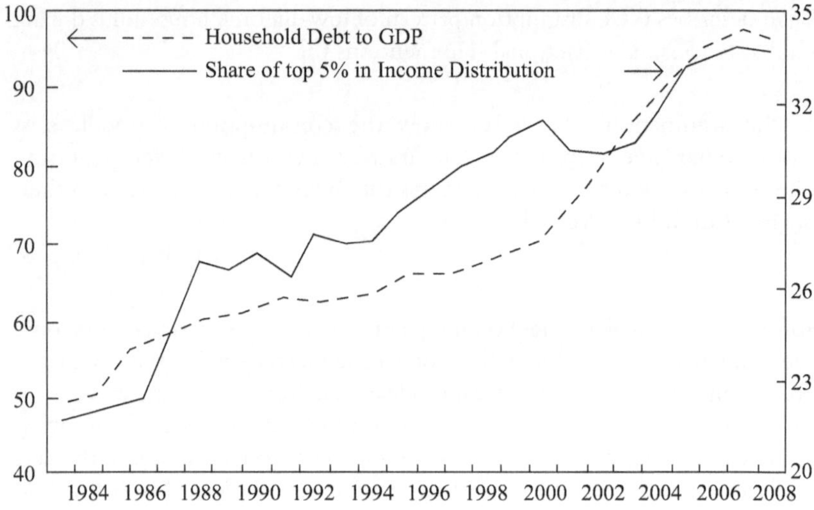

Figure 4.10 The US income inequality and household debt-to-GDP (%) before the Great Recession.
Source: Kumhof and Ranciere (2010).

Figure 4.11 The US income inequality and household debt-to-GDP ratios between 1920 and 1929 (%).
Source: Kumhof and Ranciere (2010).

Before the Great Depression, there were similar trends in income inequality and household debt-to-GDP ratios between 1920 and 1928. Figure 4.11 displays this. The income share of the top 5% went up from about 27% to about 35% between 1920 and 1928. The ratio of household debt to GDP also increased drastically, from about 17% to about 37% during the same period.

It seems that there were two complementary drivers of rising household debt in the context of income inequality. First, there was an increase in the demand for finance as households experienced wage stagnation and aimed to benefit from the increase in assets, in particular from increases in house prices. Second, the availability of credits for lower income groups increased because of lowered constraints on lending, global glut (funds flowing from Asian countries and oil producing countries) and the funds of the rich that transferred to the financial markets. The former view mainly implies that increasing inequality changed the behavior of the lower income groups. This led to the view that the crisis was caused by the poor by borrowing excessively. The latter view is associated with whether the excessive credit expansion was driven by inducement of financial institutions or by government policies that facilitated credits to middle-class voters. This is, in fact, a debate about whether the increase in the volume of credits originated from demand or supply factors. Hence it is about through what channels inequality affected the whole economy the most. This debate is in fact related to the subject of whom we blame. That is, whether we should blame predatory lending practices or whether we should blame immoral debtors who borrowed irresponsibly beyond their means.

The scholars differ over these two perspectives. For example, Barba and Pivetti (2009) interpret the rise in personal debt as a demand-side phenomenon. They argue that rising household indebtedness primarily derives from stagnant real wages and retrenchments in the welfare state. Similarly, Wolff (2010) also argues that the increase in household debt originates from the motivation of households to keep up their consumption level despite their stagnant wages.

By contrast, other scholars focus on developments on the supply side. For example, Kumhof and Ranciere (2010) argue that the higher credit supply resulted from increased saving of the rich who became richer over time. Lysandrou (2011) also stresses that the demand for risky financial products came from the huge accumulation of private wealth. In a similar context, some scholars raise their objection to the view that households in the US overconsumed and were caught in a kind of consumption fever. Warren and Warren (2004) denounced this, saying that driving forces in the financial sector induced households to borrow and consume, rather than the overconsumption myth.

Rajan also emphasizes the supply side but in a different context. He argues that the increased opportunities of finance were induced by the government. He argues that the governments in the US urged the government-supported financial institutions (such as Freddie Mac and Fannie Mae) to finance mortgages during the 1990s and early 2000s.

As part of this debate, there has been another important shift in the supply side. This is the change in monetary policy. The relationship between inequality and monetary policy has been widely ignored in the literature. Fitoussi and Saraceno (2010) say that *"an increase in inequalities . . . depressed aggregate demand and prompted monetary policy to react by maintaining a low level of interest rates which itself allowed private debt to increase beyond sustainable levels"*. This is in fact similar to the ideas of Rajan. According to this, monetary policy is associated with inequality, sparking borrowing that leads to a credit bubble.

Here there emerges a clear disagreement between the Austrian school and the Post-Keynesian school. Inflationary surprises, as Austrian economists elaborate, reduce real wages, hence raising profits, which in turn causes a transfer of income from workers to capitalists. Therefore expansionary monetary policies increase both the amount of credit and inequality at the same time. On the contrary, Post-Keynesians stress that the disinflationary policies of the Federal Reserve worsen inequality by reducing employment and wages.

Consequently, I think that it seems that it is hard to separate demand and supply factors that affect household borrowing. The answer is a complicated combination of both. Tridico (2012) gives an explanation from both supply and demand perspectives. He emphasizes both perspectives.

Channel 3: income/wealth inequality and speculative financial activity

Another important issue is whether there is any link between financial speculation / financial instability and income inequality. This issue came to the fore due to the fact that increasing wealth concentration at the top allowed those at the top to engage more in an increased propensity to speculate. They were involved in riskier assets than other groups. As several economists argue, the concentration of wealth at some groups' hands induced them to enter into a more reckless leverage and risk-taking stance.

Let us look at how this happens; namely how reckless behavior of the rich tends to put the whole system into jeopardy. It is straightforward that when the rich get richer, they have more opportunity to take on more risks with their money. According to statistical data given by the New Economics Foundation (2014), it appears that the wealth of a very small group of people doubled in the ten years preceding the crisis in 2007–2008 from $19 trillion to $41 trillion in the US. In fact, this has been one of the reasons for the development and build-up of risky products. It is also known that the rich owned more than half of the risky investment assets on the market—products such as collateralized debt obligations (CDOs) and derivatives. Thus wealthy people's desire for higher returns increased. This demand was met by new risky financial products created by the shadow banking system. The super-rich were the major buyers of toxic financial products. In fact, until 2002, the US market for CDOs was not that large, but after that it grew 12-fold in size over the subsequent 5 years. It is now widely recognized that these risky assets were generated by demands coming from those at the top end of the wealth distribution as a result of deepening inequality in the last decades.

It can be said that the increased supply of these kinds of financial products in the mid-2000s should have lowered their prices. But this did not happen. On the contrary, the demand for them increased. More investors and firms started to participate in the financial markets due to their lucrative yields. They

Table 4.1 Composition of financial assets across income groups in the US, 2007

	Percentile of the distribution of family net worth				
	0–50	*50–90*	*90–95*	*95–99*	*99–100*
Holdings of checking, savings, money market, and call accounts	6.5	33	11.4	26.2	22.9
Holdings of certificates of deposit	3.1	46.6	11.5	23.7	15.1
Direct holdings of publicly traded stocks	0.6	9	8	30.5	51.9
Mutual fundsother than money market mutual funds, and hedge funds	0.4	11.6	10.3	30.9	46.7

Source: Kennickell (2009).

shifted their resources from productive production areas to financial markets. From this increasing financialization process, economic income polarization increased further because the rich who were already rich benefited from the gains from the increases in asset prices. Survey data of the Federal Reserve shows that the rich household hold riskier assets. In 2007 the top 10% held about 60% of the holdings of checking, savings, and the money market, and about 50% of the holdings of certificates of deposits, but about 90% of direct holdings of stocks and 88% of bonds, 52% of mutual funds and hedge funds (Kennickell, 2009). This also verifies the fact that increasing wealth inequality pushes the richer to take on a riskier position in financial markets (Table 4.1).

Channel 4: increasing inequalities and current account deficit

In recent years, many scholars have started to focus on the causal relation between the inequality in the US and the global trade imbalances (e.g. Obstfeld and Rogoff, 2010; Fitoussi and Stiglitz, 2009). This perspective mainly addresses how increasing income inequality led to the emergence of export-led growth strategies developed by other countries. In particular, in Anglo-Saxon countries, along with developed financial markets, the poor- and middle-income groups easily borrowed from domestic and foreign lenders to finance their consumption. A significant part of these consumption goods contained imported products. In addition to the effect of inequality on international finance and trade balances, inequality in emerging economies, particularly China, also reinforced this process. Wages were already low in these countries and their financial systems were not developed enough to borrow. This resulted in insufficient demand and export-oriented growth. The creditors of these countries lent to foreign developed countries rather than to their domestic units.

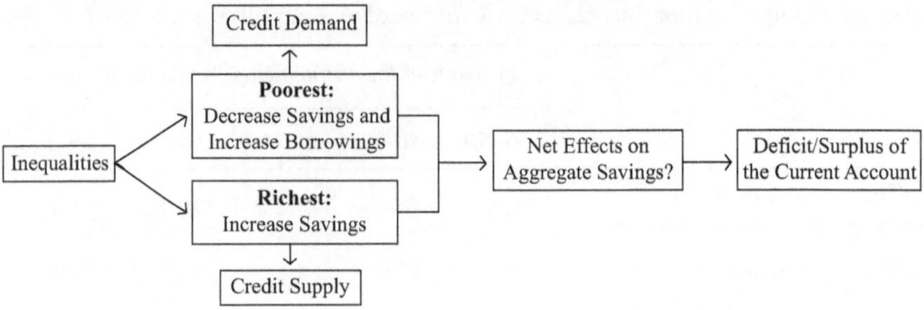

Figure 4.12 The linkages between inequalities and current account balance.

Form another perspective, the effect of inequality on current account is in fact related to saving behavior. This is derived from a simple relationship denoted by $X - M = S - I$, namely, net exports are equal to net savings. The saving countries have current surpluses and dissaving countries have current deficits. Inequality can affect saving behavior in two ways, one positive, the other negative: An increase of inequality is expected to affect people's position in income distribution. Those at the bottom in income distribution are expected to save less and hence borrow more; on the contrary, those at the top are expected to save more. Therefore the net effect of inequality on current accounts is ambiguous at aggregate level, depending on which segment of groups dominates. This mechanism is illustrated in Figure 4.12.

Channel 5: increasing inequalities and politics and regulation

Income polarization in the US also affected financial instability because it increased lobbying pressures on politicians to encourage policies of financial deregulation. The political pressure came from opposing ends of the distribution of income. Those at the bottom income put pressure on politicians to receive more credit as a substitute for rising household income. Those at the top income, who are more influential on the political process, also put pressure on politicians into liberalizing financial markets to increase their gains. As can be seen, these two different demands from different parts of society induce politicians to deregulate the system. That is, high levels of inequality induce a political or monetary response, which can lead to swollen credits, the accumulation of excessive debt, and increasing financial instability. In fact, this political process may be more complicated than we describe here but it captures the main motivations of different income groups whose demands are differentiated due to increased income polarization.

Rajan (2010) made an important contribution to this debate. He points out that increasing inequality in the US forced politicians to follow up policies to facilitate borrowing for the lower income groups. Redistribution of income via taxes and social spending policies is politically hard to enact. Instead of this, governments generally chose to support and enact policies that facilitate access to credits of the poor- and middle-income groups. This primarily occurs in the form of deregulations and funding opportunities for state-supported agencies. Rajan (2010, p. 39) mentions this in this way:

> Even if no politicians dreamed up a Machiavellian plan to assuage anxious voters with easy loans, their actions—and there is plenty of evidence that politicians pushed for easier housing credit—could have been guided by the voters they cared about.

Although this view is criticized because the US political system is mainly responsive to high-income voters. But I think there is a coincidence of wants between low-income groups and high-income groups. While one side wants to receive more credits, the other side wants to give more credits; hence wants coincide. This made the job of politicians easier.

Daron Acemoglu (2009) also participated in this debate. He asserts that it was politics that drove both inequality and the financial crisis. Hence there is coexistence, not causation between inequality and the financial crisis. Acemoglu argues that the politicians take into account the interests of the rich minority rather than the poor- and middle-income majority. The policies implemented generally were in favor of the rich rather than low- and middle-income groups. This is why, according to him, financial deregulation policies were implemented before the crisis in 2007–2008. In this sense, inequality leads to increased financial instability through a self-reinforcing process: (i) increasing inequality causes the expansion of political power of the wealthy; (ii) they use this power to design financial structure in their favor; (iii) this creates further financial fragility and increasing inequality; and back to (i).

4.6 Concluding remarks

Many scholars have started to emphasize the importance of the inequality that accompanied the global crisis of 2007–2008. To them, it was economic inequality that triggered a policy response which ultimately resulted in the economic crisis in 2007–2008. According to their view, the skill-biased technology change differentiated incomes significantly between low-skilled and low-educated and high-skilled and highly educated workers. Since the US did not have a refined redistribution mechanism, politicians resorted to other methods to appease the low-income groups. They attempted to facilitate home ownership by inducing the financial system to charge lower interest rates. This in turn led to build-up of debt, resulting in financial collapse.

All these arguments are mainly advanced by Rajan, and are called the Rajan hypothesis. This created a kind of controversy over inequality and its implications in the US. Some perceived his thoughts as suggesting that "the poor caused the crisis" together with misguided government policies responding to their demands. However, it is clear that Rajan does not take into account the explosion of incomes within the very top of the income distribution, instead focusing on changes in the 90/10 and 90/50 income differentials due to skill-biased technological change. The political process captured by the super-rich, which led to deregulations of financial markets, is ignored. In this sense, other scholars mention that inequality and financial instability merely coincided; this is not a causal relation. Perhaps financial deregulations can be codeterminant of inequality and financial instability.

It is clear that markets do not exist in a vacuum. They need political, social and cultural norms. In particular political processes are critical in determining the direction of markets. High-level economic inequalities create political inequalities. In such societies of high inequality, social welfare cannot favor everyone; some benefit more than others. This reduces social mobility as well.

Inequality is the natural outcome of capitalism. As Thomas Piketty argued, the relatively more equitable long period that characterized the middle of the 20th century was a historical anomaly, while the disparities of the Gilded Age (the late 19th century in the US history, from the 1870s to about 1900) and our own time are the norm. This becomes clearer during financial crises; the political system socializes losses but allows the banks to privatize profits, helping the victimizers but doing little to help the victims who lose their homes and jobs.

Hence, as widely recognized nowadays, a more egalitarian distribution of income is critical for the whole of society. For this it is necessary to reverse the actual level of wealth concentration and income inequality to help solve the inherent problems of capitalism.

Note

1 The Gini coefficient measures income inequality. A Gini coefficient of zero expresses perfect equality, where all values are the same (for example, where everyone has the same income). A Gini coefficient of 1 (or 100%) expresses maximal inequality among values (e.g., for a large number of people, where only one person has all the income or consumption, and all others have none, the Gini coefficient will be very nearly one.

5 The financial instability hypothesis

5.1 Introduction

It is widely regarded that the global crisis of 2007–2008 is a Minsky crisis. It has been thought that the processes identified by Minsky's financial instability hypothesis explain what happened during the run-up toward this global crisis. Hence no economist has been referred to as much as Hyman Minsky (1919–1996) concerning the financial crisis of 2007–2008.

The financial instability (or fragility) hypothesis is a theory of crises, in which the real and the financial sides of the economy interact and lead to a cyclical sequence of events. Hence by focusing more on the connection between real and finance, Minsky's views differentiate from the points that are elaborated by the arguments of financialization. And from his viewpoint, internal dynamics inherently tend to push capitalism toward an unstable state and severe depressions. Minsky argues that crises have a tendency to increase in size due to changes in the institutions of the monetary and financial markets that bring about an increasing sophistication, and due to the reactions of policy authorities.

In this chapter we will explore Minsky's financial instability hypothesis by floating his ideas, mainly about financial crises and their relevance to current and past crises. As we will see in the following sections, Minsky thinks of the economic functioning in capitalism as dynamic processes. This perspective differentiates him from mainstream economics. This explains why Minsky was widely ignored by the economists in the mainstream, who view economic issues as efficient market allocations. However, we observe that academic interest in Minsky's analysis has been growing significantly since the global crisis of 2007–2008.

5.2 Minsky's financial instability hypothesis (FIH)

Minsky wrote two important books, which are *John Maynard Keynes* in 1975 and *Stabilizing an Unstable Economy* in 1986. He defines his contribution to economics as an interpretation of Keynes's book *General Theory of Employment, Interest and Money*.

Minsky's theory has two key hypotheses. First, there are two financing regimes in a capitalist economy, which are mainly stable and unstable. Second, the economy can pass from one financing regime to another depending on economic dynamics. Hence, in Minsky's view, financial instabilities are not external; on the contrary they are endogenous and inherent characteristics of capitalist production.

In Minsky's financial instability hypothesis (FIH), the starting point is how financial commitments change the economic actors in the economy. He categorizes the economic agents (households, firms, and the government) with respect to their cash flows. In line with this, there are three main cash flows: income, balance sheet, and portfolio. Income cash flows include wages, salaries, and profits. Balance sheet cash flows are the existing and inherited liabilities or debt instruments. And portfolio cash flows are those that result in transactions in which capital and financial assets change hand. Minsky notes that the soundness of a financial system depends on the relative weight of those cash flows.

The balance sheet and portfolio cash flows are based on income cash flows. If income cash flows (realized or expected) are sufficient to meet the payments required, this unit is called to do hedge financing. If expected income receipts are less than the balance sheet cash flows, and so the only way to make payments is to borrow, the unit in this case is called to do speculative financing. However, in the case where units increase debt to pay debt service, they are called to do Ponzi financing[1].

In this sense, both speculative and Ponzi financing units require engagement in portfolio transactions. That is, they need to make their payments either by selling their assets or by borrowing. But hedge finance units do not enter portfolio transactions to make their payments on liabilities. This means that they will not be badly affected by changes in financial conditions when paying their liabilities. However, this is not easy for speculative and Ponzi units when things go bad. For example, a rise in interest rates or a fall in their incomes will hurt these units and cause them to have difficulties with realizing their commitments. In these cases speculative financing units can turn out to be Ponzi units. But in the reverse case (a fall in interest rate and an increase in incomes), the Ponzi financing units can turn into speculative units. That is, any change in refinancing structure, which affects payments due, can modify the balance sheet position of a unit. Hence passage from one financing type to another can occur depending on the change in earnings.

Consequently, in Minsky's view, sustainability and stability of a financial system is defined as sound if small changes or commitments in cash flows will not affect adversely the abilities of actors to meet their financial commitments. Minsky stresses that the relative weight of the trends in cash flows in an economy determines the fragility of the financial system. If economic units can fulfill their balance sheet commitments, the financial system tends to be financially sound. But if units need to make portfolio transactions to pay their balance sheet commitments, the economy tends to be potentially financially fragile and evolves to be crisis prone. Moreover, when Ponzi finance becomes widespread, it is frequently associated with fraudulent financial practices that can also create further devastating effects on the economy.

In Minsky's theory, time and uncertainty are crucial in the dynamic process of finance. Under uncertainty, private ownership and the complicated financial practices of the economic system, an economy having even sound initial financial conditions is likely to evolve toward a more fragile structure as time elapses. The endogenous structure of a capitalist economy tends to have a momentum that increases the weight of speculative and Ponzi financing units. This in turn makes the economy vulnerable to external shocks.

These varying financing tendencies of the different units in the economy summarized above are crucial in order to understand real investment. This is because in Minsky's theory investment decisions are crucially determined in financial markets. To Minsky, this is simply a Keynesian view because Keynes mainly bases his analysis of investment on the changes in variables of financial markets. And the changes in investments in turn significantly determine the degree of cycles in the economy. In this sense, Minsky argues that investment demand is determined by the difference between the demand and supply price of capital goods, which is mainly related to Keynes's definition of MEI (marginal efficiency of investment) versus interest rate. While the demand price is simply discounted value (present value) of the profits in the future years produced by purchasing a new capital good, this capital good's production cost constitutes its supply price. This supply and demand price framework is a theory in which investment is conceptualized as the outcome of an interaction between two partially autonomous sectors of the economy—the real sector and the financial sector.

Even though the expectations of financial and real agents diverge from each other to some extent, since the financial actors determine the discount factor used to convert profit expectations into a demand price for capital goods, we do not have a case where the information and expectations of decision makers of the real sector are not fully known by the financial sector. This is because the real economy does not have a relative autonomy in Minsky's model. Thus, since the demand price of capital goods is primarily determined by interest rates charged in the real sector in predicting the present value of profits, the supply price of capital goods is mainly determined in financial markets. He mentions this as follows: *"the demand price of investment is derived from the [financial] market price of capital assets. The market price of capital assets depends on relations that Keynes identified under the rubric of liquidity preference"* (Minsky, 1982, p. 29). That is, the real and the financial are interconnected in Minsky's work, as in that of Keynes[2].

Based on these theoretical foundations, we can trace the main aspects of the Minskian hypothesis regarding how an economic system can move from financial stability to financial fragility, as defined below.

The boom and bust phase—from financial stability to instability

In the aftermath of a crisis experience, borrowers and lenders become very conservative regarding finance. Lenders become more concerned and thereby demand high margins of safety. Borrowers become more pessimistic about future profits and hence they become more cautious about their investments. This change in behavior that reflects more conservatism in taking and giving debts forces the system into a more stable state even though profit expectations and investments are low. At this stage, expectations are realized, and lending–borrowing connections become more stable. According to Minsky's behavioral assumptions, the phase of stability slowly leads to higher confidence. Borrowers become more confident and start to borrow more, thus lowering their margins of safety. Hence, the effective demand price for investment goods increases. Meanwhile lower defaults on credits in the markets, namely the improvement of credit histories of borrowers, also push up lenders' confidence. This allows them to lower their margins of safety further and they want to lend more at lower cost. This means more debt-financed investment in the economy (Minsky, 1986).

Along with gaining higher profits with increased investments, other feedback mechanisms start to operate (Figure 5.1). There are three feedback effects here. Firstly, borrowers obtain an opportunity to meet their past debt commitments. Fulfilling their debt commitments increases confidence further and allows borrowers and lenders to lower their margins of safety and use more debt in financing their investments. Secondly, the present value of expected profits PV(π) is realized and regarded as permanent; therefore it will shift financing from internal (F) to external sources. Thirdly, this raises positive expectations of higher cash flows in future investments. These three effects lead to more internally and externally financed investments (denoted by I_i and I_d respectively).

As seen in Figure 5.1, the feedback process leads to the fact that investment (I) accelerates further in the end. This process is described by De Antoni (2006) along with other mechanisms. They are related to Minsky's view on the determination of asset prices, the importance of liquidity and the process of endogenous money creation.

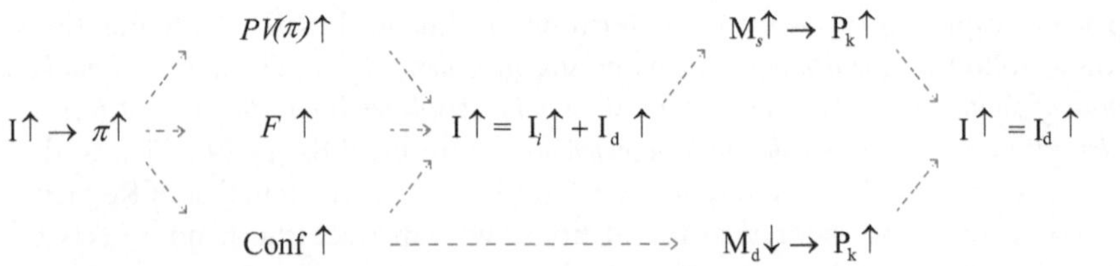

Figure 5.1 Feedback mechanisms of investment.
Source: Detzer and Herr (2014).
Notes: *Conf*= Confidence, I = Investment, I_i = Investment internally financed, I_d = Investment debt financed, M_s = Money supply, M_d = Money demand, π = Profits, P_k = Asset prices, PV(π) = Present value of expected profits, F= Internal funds.

In fact, all these mechanisms are ultimately associated with the view of Minsky on endogeneity of money creation. This means that credit expansions in the economy create the quantity of money (M_s). If the actors in the economy increase their demand for loans to finance their investments, this increases money supply and this in turn induces demand for assets to go up, as seen in Figure 5.1. Hence the market prices of assets (P_k) go up. This results in lower demand for money (M_d) due to increased confidence, higher profits, and validation of expectations. That is, confidence decreases the demand for money; on the contrary, people hold more money in a state of increased uncertainty. Therefore, in the environment in which confidence increases, the public turn to more illiquid assets, rather than liquid assets, changing the composition of their portfolio. This naturally leads to more investments financed by debt (I_d).

During this investment boom, since the actors in the economy reduce their margins of safety and expect more income than their liabilities, short-term lending accelerates. Eventually the relative number of speculative and Ponzi units goes up. Hence a slight deterioration in expectations triggers borrower defaults. So the system shifts from a stable financial structure to an unstable one. This describes an endogenous process that pushes the economy from a stable state to an unstable state. If the boom period is prolonged, the stability can be more detrimental. This is defined as "stability is destabilizing" as Minsky said.

As mentioned above, Minsky's theory of investment associates firms' investment decisions with their financing decisions and their lenders' decisions. This determines the level of economic activity and also explains the gradual move of the system towards instability. Minsky modeled the investment decision as the interrelation between current output prices (for new investment) and asset prices (the valuation of existing investment goods). This view is not same as that of Keynes, who used the marginal efficiency of capital and the money interest rate to explain investment. The difference between these views largely arises from Minsky's use of the concept of Tobin's *q* [3].

The supply price for new investment is defined as the current output price of investment, which is a function of labor cost, mark-up, interest rate and productivity. Its demand price is found from the discounted value of expected profits obtained from a new investment good, depending on uncertainty and the expected rate of return. The demand price is related to the returns in asset markets, namely financial markets. This analysis can be also seen in Tobin's *q*, which is simply equal to the ratio of demand price to supply price of new investment. If it is larger than 1, investors wish to maintain their investments until it does equal 1.

Investors make investments if the demand price, determined in the asset markets, is above the supply price. This investment process will continue until the demand price is equalized to the supply price when full capacity utilization is realized. After full capacity is enforced, the supply price will rise even if demand does not change. However, finance usually restricts investment demand before it reaches this point. This is because new investment needs more external finance. Along with more external financing, the borrower's commitments increase, but the profits obtained from the investments remain uncertain. This makes firms vulnerable to defaults when returns from investments become smaller than expected. This is also risky for the lender who may not get his money back if defaults occur because of the fact that the value of collateral is likely to be smaller than the loans given. Consequently, risk increases for both borrowers and lenders.

A crucial part of Minsky's financial instability hypothesis is the relation between profits and investment expenditures. This relation is to make financial fragility endogenous and create cumulative processes, thus more investment creating more profits, which in turn leads to more investment. Cash flows at the same time facilitate the fulfillment of debt commitments. In this way, this income generating process helps the maintenance of the financing of firms. However, when investments slow down and start to decline, the firms' incomes decline. The decline in cash flows risks firms not realizing their financial commitments. This eventually ends up with a crisis of overindebtedness.

When the economy is performing well during prosperous and stable periods, the problems accumulate. This prolonged expansion will transform investors' portfolios. They take on more risk, getting into more speculative and Ponzi financing. However, the rise in interest rates is generally the signal of danger that triggers the process from boom to bust. The central banks raise interest rates due to inflationary pressure during the boom. This is the beginning of downturn, and the feedback processes illustrated in Figure 5.1 work in reverse. Rising interest rates cause the net worth of Ponzi units to be negative. Over time, speculative and Ponzi-financed firms experience problems with paying their debts.

All the actors in the system including financial and non-financial firms need to raise new finance sources or sell their assets. Selling their assets (deleveraging) to meet their debt commitments will put pressure on the prices of assets. This in turn reduces investments and thereby profits. This leads to further decline in asset prices. The firms' cash flows decline and so this causes some hedge units to turn into speculative units. The risk perception of lenders and borrowers increases. They start to increase their margins of safety and reduce their debt ratios. Thus, cash flows are used to reduce their debt instead of making new investments. These developments will reduce demand for investment and consumption further, with accelerator and multiplier effects. This eventually leads to unemployment and depression (Minsky, 1986).

Here we have to recall some important issues about the pricing of goods and assets to better see the fluctuations in their prices during bust and boom. In goods markets, products are bought for consumption but in asset markets financial products are bought for their expected prices in the future. This shapes how buyers and sellers react to the changes in prices distinctively. In the goods market, when their prices rise, the demand for them declines. But this is not true in asset markets; thus when the prices of assets rise up, the demand for them goes up. Goods markets generally are prone to stable prices while financial markets tend to be volatile and have no balancing tendency in prices and are prone to boom-bust cycles. Financial assets are purchased for capital gains. If a person buys an asset, he/she expects a rise in its price. If it rises as expected, it creates confidence and an urge to keep it, because of expectations of further rises in the future, or to buy more of it. Hence investors do not sell their assets when their prices go up so their supply does not increase, unlike in the goods market. In the reverse case, namely where falling prices destroy confidence, investors sell the assets they have, hence increasing their supply and accelerating the fall in assets further. This is a fundamentally unstable positive feedback characteristic. It is a self-reinforcing asset–debt cycle, which is a crucial part of Minskian analysis.

Such a financially fragile and destabilizing environment creates real effects on investments; thus financial markets accelerate the rate of descent in the economy. This deterioration in the economy is magnified via multiplier and accelerator effects. The deleveraging process, which leads to a collapse in asset prices, in turn reduces incentive to reduce investment. Minsky stresses that if the central bank does not do anything such as stabilizing asset prices during these downturns, the degree of recession will be worse. And he also suggests that the government should intervene, for example, by expansionary fiscal policy to dampen demand fluctuations in the economy. The effects of downturn depend on the policies of governmental institutions. The subject of the role of central bank and government will be discussed in the final sections of the chapter in more detail.

As seen, Minsky provides an explanation of financial fragility that is fully endogenous and that is extremely useful to understanding the occurrence of financial instability. But here we have to stress that Minsky's endogenous analysis is not an information-based approach to financial fragility. His approach is not based on asymmetric information even though he makes use of it to describe the behavior of agents. Economic agents in his analysis are not totally rational, but bubbles, information, and other imperfections are not at the core of his analysis. Minsky thus explicitly dismisses approaches based on asymmetric information as the basis for his analysis: "*[T]he asymmetric information approach to constructing a meaningful macroeconomics is logically flawed*". (Minsky 1992a, p.9). He implies that even though informational imperfections are an important aspect of institutional design, it is only one dimension of financial institutions. There are other important integrated mechanisms in an economic environment where real and finance are highly connected. To me, however, the behavioral dimension in Minskian analysis is not well constructed. It should not be ignored that the prolonged transformations in portfolios in Minskian analysis take place under euphoric conditions even though he stressed that the euphoric economy is a natural consequence of the economy doing well over a prolonged period.

Regulatory relaxation

As defined above, the incentive to take risk is a starting hypothesis of Minsky's approach. The accumulation of risk-taking creates perverse results spreading

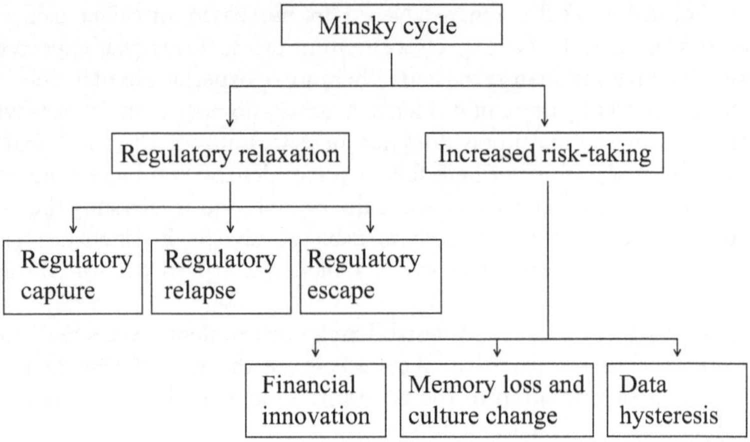

Figure 5.2 Minsky cycle mechanism.
Source: Transformed from Palley (2009).

economy-wide. There are several institutional factors that facilitate risk-taking such as financial innovations, term structure of interest rates etc. In addition to these, Minsky also draws attention to the degree of prudence among regulators and investors. The degree of prudence in the economy depends on the economic cycle, whether it is upward or downward. Prudence of all the actors in the economy declines during an upward cycle in the economy, while it increases sharply during a downward cycle.

This perspective is well elaborated in the notion called the Minsky cycle, which has two features: increased risk-taking and regulatory relaxation. This is shown in Figure 5.2. The increased risk-taking behavior of economic agents can be identified with increases in both their supply and demand for risk, while the process of regulatory relaxation can be characterized only as an increase in supply of risk.

In a Minskian cycle, there are important psychological effects, which are similar to several arguments of behavioral economics, which will be discussed in the seventh chapter of this book. These effects are particularly seen in the spreading of optimism of agents in the economy. During upturns, agents become progressively more optimistic. This optimism is seen in increasing prices of assets and optimistic expectations of flows of revenue. This in turn leads to more risk-taking behavior.

This process is accompanied by the process of regulatory relaxation. There are three dimensions of this regulatory relaxation. The first is regulatory capture. Minsky defines regulatory authorities as stabilizing or thwarting institutions which constrain the transactions of financial firms. Since these constraints mainly reduce the profit of financial firms, they aim to capture regulatory agencies to lighten regulations. This process is even acknowledged by mainstream economists. The second dimension is regulatory relapse. The regulators, as human beings, lose their awareness over time concerning the agents they regulate. The sensitivity of regulators falls due to increased optimism spreading to the whole economy. The third dimension is regulatory escape. Financial firms try to avert regulations by innovating new financial methods and products. By innovation they aim to get outside the domain of the thwarting institutions. Hence it is like a dynamic game played between regulators and financial agents. This partially explains the emergence of the shadow banking system and derivatives.

Each regulation, however well designed, creates incentives to be averted. This is the main foundation of the Minskian cycle. Despite these regulations, risk-taking behavior expands. Increased risk-taking behavior is composed of three dimensions. Financial innovation is the first dimension that produces new and risky financial instruments, including securitization and tranching of securities and complicated derivative contracts. These new financial products change the risk-taking behavior of the households and financial institutions in the economy.

As shown in the Figure 5.2, the second dimension is associated with memory loss and cultural change that induces people to take on more risk. People and institutions forget previous severe economic times over time. For example, in the aftermath of the Great Depression in 1929, people did not tend to buy shares because of the severe falls in company shares. However, later generations started to buy company shares again in more volumes. Cultural changes also contribute to changes in risk behavior. Current generations can be more prone to risk-taking due to their enthusiastic desire to become rich soon. The cultural environment is crucial in guiding risk behavior. And the third dimension is data hysteresis. In fact the data generating process is subject to continuous change, but people use past information and are likely to make wrong decisions based on past information. People do not abandon this method despite this.

5.3 The arguments of the FIH in the context of other approaches

Although Minsky began his research in the 1950s and continued to refine his theory until his death in 1996, his approach has been largely ignored by mainstream economics. This does not mean that his work was unknown, as it was long embraced by Post-Keynesian economists. The current financial crisis that began with the collapse of the subprime mortgage market in the US in 2007–2008 provides an important reason to show how his approach provides us with a grounding in the workings of financial capitalism.

Minsky's arguments have some crucial roots on which his arguments are based. The main argument of FIH is not only related to Keynes's financial theory of investment but also to Schumpeter's credit view, which emphasized the endogenous expansion of credit in the economy. Minsky integrated the intertemporal capitalist process of Schumpeter with Keynes's capitalist accumulation process, associated with fragile financial structures. Minsky (1993, p. 106) pointed out that:

> To understand the short-term dynamics of the business cycle and the longer-term evolution of economies it is necessary to understand the financing relations that rule, and how the profit-seeking activities of businessmen, bankers, and portfolio managers lead to the evolution of financial structures.

The capitalist dynamics that ended up in the global financial crisis of 2007–2008 manifest that Minsky's arguments can be a sound and relevant analytic tool to understand modern crises. It has become an important alternative to the mainstream approach based on the efficient market hypothesis, which disregards the imperfections in financial markets, which are on the contrary emphasized by Minsky[4]. In the mainstream approach, money is neutral, thus it does not have real effects, which implies that money cannot change relative prices, employment, and growth. Functionings of markets work to eliminate probable non-neutralities with their continuous tendency to clear equilibria.

In fact, there are some ways pointed out by mainstream macroeconomics in which money may affect the real economy in the short run. One of these is that for monetarists the increase in money supply creates excess money balances, which people try to eliminate by spending on consumer goods. Another is the effect of interest rates after an increase in money supply on the inducement of investment and consumption. However, in Minsky's views, these are not strong effects in terms of affecting real production. Firstly, Minsky stresses that the amount of money is endogenously determined and hence the quantity theory of money is not enough to explain what happens in modern economies. Then he says that interest rates are not that effective on consumption and investment, thus their interest rate elasticities are low and the effects of interest rates are counteracted by other variables. To him, what matters is finance rather than money.

Minsky considers that there are three channels in which finance affects the real. First, movements in the prices of assets affect expenditures on consumption and investment. Increases in the prices of assets create a wealth effect that induces those holding them to consume more. When asset prices rise, investors' incentive to purchase new capital goods goes up. In the opposite case, that is, when asset prices fall, people start to sell their assets to meet their financial commitments, and this also reduces the demand for investment goods.

The second channel is the expectation channel, through which agents revise their positions. Minsky does not believe in the rational expectations of the New Classical school[5]. Instead he believes in cyclical expectations that push the economy into an unstable state so that the financing regime shifts from speculative financing to Ponzi financing and after the collapse, it again turns into hedge financing. Financial actors are forward-looking, that is, they do not remember past mistakes in the optimistic phase of expansion.

Credit rationing is the third channel in which finance affects the real economy. During a boom, almost everybody asks for a loan. However, when the bubble bursts, even the most creditworthy borrowers are denied their demand for loans and are even forced to sell their existing assets. They are subject to credit rationing, which limits their expenditure on consumption and investment. This will have adverse effects on real production and employment levels.

As seen, financial connections are at the core of Minsky's hypothesis. Other relations in the economy, namely those in the areas of labor, industry, and production, are of secondary importance. He stresses that the critical connection is between banker and customer, not factory-owner and worker. He focuses on a representative agent, who is a financial capitalist, instead of an industrial capitalist in the Marxian approach or an individual consumer who does not have any class status as in the mainstream approach.

In Minsky's framework economic agents behave in a herd-like way. They imitate each other both in upturns and downturns. During upturns, they become more enthusiastic and exuberant, while they become cautious during downturns, triggering many complications in the economy. That is, during downturns, one default can generate cascades of defaults due to a fragile financing structure. As defaults become widespread, the value of financial assets declines. This can lead to what Irving Fisher called a debt deflation, deepening recession. This process aggravated the great crisis in 1929, as mentioned by both Fisher and Minsky.

However, mainstream theory denies such processes and proposes that debt deflation never occurs, thereby declines in prices of assets will not create payment difficulties because people act rationally and markets allocate efficiently. But Minsky argues that it is exactly this fact that made the Great Depression so severe. The main argument of mainstream economists is that crises may originate from policy mistakes, not from fundamental functionings of capitalism. Hence Minsky believed that mainstream theory is not enough to understand the world in which we actually live.

It is a well-known fact that Minsky's crisis theory is mainly based on Keynes's thoughts[6]. Hence here we should first talk about the main arguments of Keynes. This will help us understand Minsky better. For Fisher, the cycle starts with rising profits realized through new real or financial innovations. They make people more optimistic and urge them to make more investments. This eventually leads people to take on more debts. And new investors participate in this process and overall debt accumulates. This is where Keynes makes an essential contribution. Keynes is concerned with this overoptimism. He draws attention to fundamental uncertainty spreading all over the economy. He points out that

> By "uncertain" knowledge, let me explain, I do not mean merely to distinguish what is known for certain from what is only probable . . . The sense in which I am using the term is that in which . . . there is no scientific basis on which to form any calculable probability whatever.
>
> (Keynes, 1937, pp. 113–114)

In this sense, Minsky stresses that there are two crucial deficiencies of neoclassical theory: the lack of connection between real and finance and the ignorance of financial instability. The former is the extension of Keynes's views. It is associated with financial theory of investment. According to this, finance and money have real effects on the economy. The quantity theory of money is rejected because Minsky believes that the prices of assets are affected by increasing supply of money, not just general price level as asserted by the quantity theory of money. Moreover the changes in demand for money will influence not only prices but also the interest rate. This in turn affects the prices of assets and thus investments that create a real impact on production and employment. Hence volatility in expectations on asset prices will affect investments. In an economy where investment demand is determined by a combination of the valuation of the existing capital stock, the cost of external financing, and the supply price of investment output, a plunge of asset values leads to a collapse in investment. Minsky located the causes of asset price deflation and of investment fluctuations in the debt structure and in the financial system. As analyzed above, he does this by identifying three income–debt relations for economic units—hedge, speculative, and Ponzi finance.

In Minsky's view, Keynes's instability approach cannot be reduced just to changes in liquidity preference. The notion of instability in Keynes was more pervasive. This uncertainty became more critical when the capitalist economy became a complex financial economy. Investment that is the main component of aggregate demand is a flow deeply influenced by expectations of future financial variables. Changes in expectations can generate severe swings in investments, and thereby production. This implies that Minsky's argument is not associated with conventional dynamic macroeconomic instability in the mainstream economics, but rather with fundamental instability.

To Minsky, capitalism is by its nature unstable. He is a non-equilibrium economist, which is different from disequilibrium. Disequilibrium is defined as a reference to equilibrium, in which the economy sometimes deviates from this reference point. Disequilibrium turns out to occur if some conditions are not provided such as perfect competition, complete information and so on. They are only market failures and not inherent to markets. However, in contrast, from a non-equilibrium perspective there is no tendency toward equilibrium. That is, there are no mechanisms that allocate resources efficiently as argued by mainstream economists.

The inherent instability of capitalism is based on an external financing structure and accumulation structure. Hence, according to Minsky, there is a persistent business cycle moving from a robust state to a fragile state, activated by financing regimes in the capitalist economy. In this sense, Minsky's approach is more general than the mainstream approach because it does not accept the assumption of structural stability of the economic system and focuses on the evolutionary aspects of economic cycles. Mainstream economics sees cycles around an independent trend. However, Minsky sees cycles as spirals where the irreversible shifts of the trend are significantly affected by the cycle itself.

In this view there is no a stationary mechanism. These cycles are results of moves and counter-moves in the system, which are determined by changes, innovations and counter-actions in the behavior of households, regulators, policy-makers and institutions. This also implies the characteristics of economic policies because the economy is always in continuous evolution so there are no predictable results of economic policies. The policies to counteract crises can be different, depending on circumstances determined by space, time, and the actors involved.

Keynes (1936) believed that it was necessary to truncate the financial motives spreading in the economy. This can generate a state Keynes called "euthanasia of the rentier", who gained his income from interest and rent without engaging in productive activities. By contrast, Minsky thinks that the rentier aspect of capitalism is a transitional phase. There are deeper processes behind a rentier-driven economy. The economic system incorporating financial markets always has potential to produce financial crises of varying size. He was expecting the next Great Depression.

While advancing his thoughts, Minsky tried to show that Keynes's main ideas had been distorted by Hicks, Samuelson, and other proponents of traditional Keynesianism. According to Minsky, the main concepts of Keynes's theory such as the uncertainty component in the decision-making process, the unstable nature of capitalism and the role of finance, are lost in mainstream Keynesianism. The links between these notions can be described as follows. Transactions in economics or in any area of life occur at a historical time. This means that the past cannot be reversed and the future is unknown. Hence we are not able to go from the unknown future to the known past, unlike in logical time. People want to protect themselves from the uncertainty inherent in this historical time. For this they hold money which is a totally liquid and reliable asset. However, as Keynes mentioned, money cannot be readily produced. Hence demand for money determines the demand for other risky assets, which in turn determines national income and employment through changes in interest rates. This will lead to recession or booms. This is the basis of the cyclical nature of a capitalist economy. This cyclicity gets worse along with more complicated financial contracts that develop during the booms, leading to more accumulation of debt that is likely to generate heavy burden during recessions.

Minsky argues that these points of Keynes were disregarded in conventional macroeconomics. These circumstances encouraged Minsky to assert an inherent relationship between traditional Keynesianism and neoclassical theory. Minsky pointed out that both perspectives were *"based upon a barter paradigm—the image is of a yeoman or craftsman trading in a village market"* (Minsky, 1975, p. 57).

New Keynesians have also tried to incorporate Minsky's thinking into their models through the notion of a financial accelerator[7]. The main idea of this notion is that positive (or negative) cascades occur in financial asset prices. For example, increased asset prices lead to an increase in the value of collateral, which in turn increases borrowing and inflates balance sheets.

After this expansion, downturns eventually emerge. During downturns, the feedback mechanism works in reverse order; thus the decline in production and employment causes further declines in asset prices, deteriorating balance sheets, worsening expectations, and all variables reduce in the cumulative causation reasoning. This cycle is called a financial accelerator. It begins with a small change in the prices of financial assets but leads to greater effects economy-wide. This view reflects the New Keynesian business cycle view based on a financial accelerator. However, this view is in fact different from Minsky's instability hypothesis. This is because New Keynesian economists use stable equilibrium models, which is completely opposed to Minsky's inherent unstable model.

Notice that cycles are crucial part of Minsky but it is more than this. In fact cycles can result from several factors such as the financial accelerator or instabilities that can be produced by incorporating stochastic disturbances into the analysis. But these are completely in contrast to Minsky's instability based on the evolutionary process. In neoclassical economics, crises occur as the result of exogenous shocks such changes in economic policies, natural disasters or technological shocks. Hence they focus on the probability of the occurrence of these events, looking at their probability distributions. Thus they emphasize fat-tailed probability distributions, black swans and other metaphors of chance. Hence their approach is totally different from that of Minsky, who focuses on the endogenous character of crises.

Minsky is often praised for having systematically developed the notion elaborated by Marx in the third volume of Capital, which is the role of money and credit in the process of capitalistic accumulation. Marx describes the banks as the main agent of overproduction and overspeculation. According to Marx, accumulation financed by credit pushes the reproduction process to its absolute limits, hence it bears the potential of downfall. Marx argues that credit accelerates the emergence of crises, and hence the elements that bring about downfall of the old mode of production. Without money and credit, the accumulation process cannot work. During the crisis, it becomes the most essential component and means of accumulation.

However, we have to mention that Marx did not base his thoughts on crises on financial actors' behavior. He mentioned that financial speculation or recklessness of financial actors or panic can trigger crises, but they are not cause factors; triggering does not mean causing. The crisis, in Marx's view, occurs in the production and exchange sphere. But he is aware that crises are somehow related to the nature of money, which separates purchase and sale from each other in terms of temporal and spatial. Thus the realization problem is a kind of transformation into the money problem. This is why crises manifest themselves in the form of monetary panic.

Compared to the Marxian perspective, there is an important distinction of Minsky's financial instability hypothesis, which is that in Minsky's model there are no real-sector sources of instability. The problems start in the financial sector and then spread to the whole economy. The real sector is a kind of semi-autonomous sphere of economic activity and decision making in the real sector is not much emphasized. Hence this analytical framework of Minsky is one-sided and thereby is not sufficient to explain the crises of the 1970s and 1980s. The crises during these periods are mainly explained by the traditional Marxian arguments that emphasize developments in the real sector such as falling profits or profit squeeze rather than the financial phenomenon of speculation of financial actors.

Moreover, in Minsky's economic reasoning, real investments will continue until the expected profit of investment is higher than the cost of financial capital. Hence excessive investment is never the source of crises in Minsky. High investment levels will not start real chain effects (such as rising input costs, increasing wages, declining productivities or market saturation) which in turn will reduce investments. But, on the contrary, the adverse effects of increasing investments are more visible in Keynes. He argues that increasing investments eventually lead to a decline in the marginal efficiency of investment. The working mechanisms of the real economy do not exist in Minsky's arguments in this sense. In short, in contrast to Keynes, who argued that capital accumulation led to a short-run and long-run decline in the marginal efficiency of investment, Minsky can find no impediment to perpetual balanced growth in the real sector of the economy.

However, the new Marxist interpretation as carried out by Magdoff and Sweezy focuses on both the real and financial factors, hence being in between. This approach is not too much concerned with the financial system's ability to expand credits and does not take into account the financing methods of the FIH. But these views are synthesized by a new approach called structural Keynesianism[8]. First, it draws attention to the real factors that lead to wage squeeze and increasing income inequality. Second, it emphasizes the role of finance in maintaining the neoliberal regime by increasing borrowing and asset prices. This mitigates the effective demand problem by wage squeeze. This perspective leads them to incorporate Minsky's financial instability hypothesis into their analysis; in this way financial excesses are fueled by neoliberalism to counteract its stagnationist tendency.

In this sense, debt allows households to keep up their consumption levels despite their stagnant wages and their drop down the income ladder (increasing inequality). The financial structure provides their need for debt. Financial corporations fuel financial boom through securitization and increasing their credits. Non-financial corporations also induce financial boom through stock buy-backs and leveraged buyouts. This increased indebtedness explains the increasing weight of the financial sector; profits are shifting toward the financial sector. This view helps understand the connection between Minsky's financial instability hypothesis and the new Marxist view of crisis.

Minsky's thinking about human behavior in the dynamic economic process also fits the arguments of behavioral economics. In this sense, his emphasis on the role of changing psychology and expectations in financing behavior is critical. For instance, individuals in Minskian structure, depending on their expectations, switch from hedge to speculative or from speculative to Ponzi finance.

In fact, Minsky's analysis is based on the behavioral insights emphasized by Keynes. In Keynes's world, the notion of "animal spirit" plays a critical part in order to understand the decision-making process of people. This notion mainly defines the psychological factors that drive investors to take action under uncertainty. In this sense, firms' behavior is based on subjective decisions. Economic agents, in the decision-making process, want to verify their decisions, hence they look at each other and imitate each other. Investors' herd-like behavior starts upward and downward movements. This may lead to overoptimism or overpessimism. In the case of overoptimism, for example, the realization of expected profits induces people to purchase further assets, which increase their prices further. This leads to too much borrowing. Minsky views this dynamic process as endogenous as does Keynes.

According to Keynes, business investment was very volatile because it was very dependent on the expectations that derived from signals received from other agents in the economy. Keynes (1936, p. 156) compares investor behavior to a beauty contest having a game-theoretical reasoning. In this contest, contestants choose the most beautiful woman who was also mostly chosen by other contestants, and thus what is important here is to take into account other choices, rather than just their own choices. This is very similar to investor behavior. Thus, they will choose based on what they think others will do. This makes sense because their profitable opportunities depend on the general environment of the whole economy. When investors make more investments or hire more workers, this affects others as well. Because of these social and psychological reasons behind business investment, Keynes thought that the market was fragile.

In this sense, Minsky is very close to Keynes's thoughts. But here he diverges from Keynes from two important perspectives. First, Minsky thinks that the main source of instability is financial actors (Wall Street) rather than real actors. But Keynes rather focused on the real part, thus the decisions of business investors rather than those of financial actors. In Minsky's view, when banks get optimistic, they start to finance a large number of investments, leading to overborrowing in the economy. Second, Keynes believes that the government can solve or mitigate these problems via appropriate fiscal and monetary policies. But Minsky does not agree with this. He points out that governments attempts to prevent crises can be effective to a certain extent, but behavioral tendencies of people make it impossible to prevent a crisis. When optimism goes up, households and firms increase their borrowing. This is a kind of unavoidable process. Therefore, he is completely against deregulatory attempts.

However, here we have to mention something important in describing the behavior of agents from Minsky's perspective. Although he draws attention to behavioral insights such as optimism or overconfidence that trigger the boom, the source of the boom is not adequately explained; how the optimism of disparate actors turns into a system-wide effect should be better explained. Furthermore the shift from this micro behavior to the macroeconomic level is not well defined. That is, the micro and macro link is not that strong in Minsky.

Here we need more behavioral economic analysis. In fact, Minsky's analysis of the psychological and social causes of financial crises gets Minsky closer to behavioral finance. However, in general behavioral economists think that they can develop mechanisms to prevent behavioral biases leading to economic downturns, in contrast to Minsky.

Finally, to some scholars, there are also some commonalities between the views of Minsky and the Austrian school, in particular Hayek. For example, Flanders (2015, p. 89) makes such a comparison: "*In some respects Minsky's analysis is not unlike Hayek's*". In fact, at the core of their analysis of business cycles, there is intertemporal coordination failure. Thus, crises mainly occur when there is a serious mismatch between the plans of debt-financed investors. Both Minsky and Hayek argue that the banking system generally amplifies cyclical fluctuations in the economy. But, for Hayek, this is only one of several possible scenarios. Hayek focuses more on other arguments that emphasize external changes in monetary policies by central banks such as lowering interest rates. But Minsky's emphasis is more on the amplification role of commercial banking on fluctuations. He rejects the role of the financial system in coordinating intertemporal plans, a role that Hayek emphasized in his debate with Keynes. Moreover, in the contrast to the Austrians, Minsky ignores the role that money plays in initiating the cycle by distorting relative prices within the capital structure.

Austrian economists generally put forward two factors to explain the increased leverage of investment banks preceding the crisis of 2007–2008 in the US: (1) expansionary monetary policies that inflated the prices of house and other assets masked the total risk undertaken; and (2) lenders' and borrowers' increased morally hazardous behavior due to housing-finance policies. However, as Flanders (2015, pp. 100–101) mentions, even though Minsky is also concerned with the issue of moral hazard arising from too-big-to-fail policies, he does not emphasize the role of cheap money policy. Van Den Hauwe (2014, p. 21) also draws another connection between the two views. He points out that both Minsky and the Austrians are concerned with accumulation of risk during expansion in the economy. While for the Austrians the source of the accumulation of risk school is governmental failures, it is a non-governmental source for Minsky, and thus exactly the inherent structure of the financial system. In line with this, the Austrians consider that decentralized and competitive monetary and financial institutions will not cause crises unless they are misdirected by governmental authorities, but Minsky focuses on the positive role of the finance-related actors such as regulators and monetary/fiscal policymakers because they can prevent or delay crises or at least mitigate their destructive effects.

5.4 The financial fragility hypothesis and the global recession and past crises

As elaborated above, Minsky's financial instability hypothesis is mainly a theory to seek out the connection between finance and investment. In this way, it develops an endogenous model rather than a model that relies on exogenous shocks to the economy. As many economists argue, the endogenous structure of financial fragility until the crisis of 2007–2008 resembles what Minsky describes in his financial instability theory. The proliferation of new and risky financial instruments, securitization, overborrowing, increasing counterparty risks and loosening regulation constraints generated a great amount of risk in the US economic system until 2007. These developments resemble the main forecasts of the financial instability hypothesis of Minsky.

The US financial sector crisis spread to the entire world. Many economists have referred to the crisis as a "Minsky moment", questioning whether the US has become a "Ponzi nation". Even some mainstream economists recognized Minsky's main argument, which is "stability is destabilizing". This is in contrast to the neoclassical equilibrium concept, defined as the natural character of the market economy.

Minsky always drew attention to the point that modern financial capitalism with its complex financial linkages would experience periodically deep fluctuations. He defined this capitalism as "money manager capitalism", which developed post-war[9]. In this form of capitalism, financing regimes are a crucial part of understanding how it performs. Their cyclical behavior determines how an economy can end up with crises.

Before the global crisis of 2007–2008, starting in the early 2000s, there was a housing bubble. In the post-war history of the US, the longest boom in housing construction was observed until 2006. House prices saw historic records. The median home price increased approximately twofold between 2000 and 2006 (the home index increased from 100.74 in January 2000 to 226.8 in April 2006). The number of homes sold was on average 1.2 million per year in the period 2003–2006. This process seems to be a Minskian crisis, manifesting itself in the housing boom, which was accompanied by increasing debt, optimistic expectations, and financial innovation. Then this housing bubble exploded, triggering deleveraging, credit crunch and pessimistic expectations, and leading to a broader financial crisis. This shows the strong link between real investment related to housing and financial investment that can get out of control. Hence this is not just a financialization; rather the connection between financialization to real investment led to the crisis, just as housing in the case of the 2007–2008 crisis.

Here there is an important question asked by Dodd (2007). He asks how a relatively small number of delinquent subprime mortgages (about $34 billion in troubled loans) with respect to the large US financial market ($57 trillion in the US financial system) damaged the US economy that much. He answers this question. He stresses the fact that the increase in non-performing loans by lax lending policies created a more important impact than expected because it is about debt linking countless units in the economy. This implies that the potential losses originating from a breakdown in these links can be immense. The vast number of connections between financial and non-financial units makes any panic leading to asset sales or loan calls disrupt and lock all these connections.

In some academic circles, there are doubts on whether FIH is enough to explain the global crisis of 2007–2008. For example, Bellofiore and Halevi (2009) argue that some facts stated by Minsky may not be valid. For example, the increasing indebtedness of the real firms was not realistic because instead of borrowing, they lent to other sectors. Furthermore the financial actors also borrowed from each other too much. All these facts can be seen in the tables in Chapter 2 of the book.

Another criticism directed against Minsky is expressed by Kregel (2008). He argues that the notions of financial fragility, declining safety margins, Ponzi financing and debt deflation are crucial in understanding financial crises but these developments do not simply arise from an endogenous process as stated by Minsky. Kregel argues that they simply arise from structural changes, as happened in the US during the 2000s. The institutions and risk behavior developed by this structural change led to a Ponzi attitude to financing in the US. This implies that the widespread Ponzi financing was not random and expanding with upturns, but was very dependent on the structural rules determined by the institutions in the US. That is, this is not an endogenous process but rather a shift in regulation and environmental constraints. For example, the objective of financial units changed from interest payments to fee payments and investment banking operations (mainly underwriting operations) and switched from lending to off-balance sheet operations to avoid regulations. They shifted to the "originate to distribute model" that changed their risk evaluation perspective. Risk evaluation was not made directly by institutions themselves, but rather by rating agencies. This further changed the vectors of the risk space. Consequently, Kregel (2008) emphasizes the structure that financialization accelerated risk-taking behavior rather than the relationship between finance and real investment as suggested by Minsky.

Similarly, Palley (2010b) does not think that the Great Recession was a kind of Minsky crisis. He recognizes that the instability that emerged on the way to the crisis played an important role but it was just a part of a larger structure involving neoliberal economic model starting in the 1980s. Along with the neoliberal growth model, wage stagnation and widened income inequality became prevalent. Instead of increased wages, debt and asset price inflation became a source of demand. But this was not sustainable.

Moreover, Palley (2010b) stresses that in Minsky's arguments the crisis is interpreted as a purely financial crisis. If that is so, then the methods to fix this problem are just to fix the financial excesses. From this perspective, there is no need to be concerned with the problems of the real economy. Palley argues that, on the contrary, the problem is more serious than stated. Problems in the financial system need to be fixed because they generate various problems such as destabilizing speculation, overborrowing, regulator capture and excessive risk-taking. However, Palley points out that the source of the problem is not the financial sector. It is the neoliberal growth model.

5.5 Minskian economic policies to prevent crises

Minsky persistently elaborated that the Great Depression represented a failure of the small-government and laissez-faire economic model. Financial capitalism was tamed by the New Deal policies that expanded the power of the government. However, starting in late 1970s, New Deal policies were replaced with a new perspective that emphasized markets and deregulations, and relied on more personal responsibility and monetary and fiscal policies which were designed to provide full employment. In line with this reasoning, the global crisis of 2007–2008 also seems to be a result of the liberal government model that had promoted deregulation, privatization, and increased market power since the late 1970s.

In Minsky's view, macroeconomic policies cannot solve the inherent problems of capitalist economies that emerge endogenously and are biased toward instability. The government's stimulus gives rise to a sense of safety by corporates and banks. Successful investments make investors less cautious about the final results of their investments in the future. As Minsky (1985, p. 52) noted,

> once the doctrine of salvation through investment becomes deeply ingrained into our political and economic system, the constraints on foolish investments are relaxed. This is especially so if the government stands ready to guarantee particular investors or investment projects against losses.

Therefore, Minsky is completely aware that policy measures are effective only if they allow structural changes to happen and tame the financial structure of the economy.

But he also draws attention to the point that stabilizing measures can lead to destabilizing effects in the longer term. In this context, Minsky saw a problem in Keynes's arguments. He stresses that instability is not something that can be overcome as Keynes presumed. It is a natural extension of the modern financial system. Hence appropriate macroeconomic policies are not enough to remove instability. They change the behavior of agents in the way that promotes evolution toward a new kind of fragility. Therefore he rejects Keynesian macroeconomic policies that are used for fine-tuning of the economy. Successes of policies followed are not permanent and policies should always adapt to new circumstances.

Consequently, Minsky's analysis has a number of important implications for economic policy. First, it clearly appears that an economic policy cannot be reduced to short-period control of aggregate demand through monetary and fiscal policy tools. It is important to bring under control the financial fragility of the economy in order to limit the size and frequency of financial crises and their impact on the real economy. This implies that financial regulations should aim at constraining financial leverage, limiting the size of financial institutions to below "too big to fail" dimensions, strengthening surveillance authorities, and putting checks on speculative activities. Second, aggregate demand must be supported systematically. In this respect, Minsky interprets Keynes as proposing the "socialization of investment" and suggests that the government should pursue full employment as its main policy target. Third, monetary policy should attribute central importance to asset price movements, with the aim of avoiding the formation of speculative bubbles or, more generally, any situation in which Ponzi schemes appear to be profitable. Fourth, the remuneration of financial agents should be kept under control, keeping in mind that oligopolistic market forms dominate the financial sector where extra profits easily translate to managerial remunerations higher than those that prevail under competitive conditions. Lastly, it is necessary to reduce uncertainty which increases financial speculation, and acts as a disincentive to real investments. This implies the existence of adequate institutions, for instance, fixed or at least stable exchange rate regimes.

In order to implement these principles of economic policy, Minsky suggests various institutions. To him, in modern market economies there are several institutional mechanisms that shape economic fluctuations. Their role is to guide and correct the dynamic process. The aim is to shape the evolution of economic behavior and variables during prosperous and depressive cycles of the economy. In this way, economic mechanisms that are likely to get out of control are slowed down and reverted into a sound state. For this, in Minsky's view, institutional floors and ceilings should be placed into the system. Minsky argues that floors and ceilings primarily reflect the set of institutional mechanisms put in place by public authorities in order to confine the amplitude of economic fluctuations within reasonable limits. Minsky terms these institutional arrangements "thwarting systems".

These thwarting institutions and actors are (i) big bank: well-designed interventions by central banks as lender of last resort and to prevent or at least to reduce destructive debt deflation mechanisms; (ii) big government: appropriate structural policies by the government in order to maintain the soundness of the economy, especially in the spheres of production and employment. Now we will look at these in more detail below.

The Big Bank

Minsky (1982) argues that we should have "good financial society" to maintain the stability of economic structure. This is provided by constraining speculative tendencies in finance. Minsky points out that financial markets should be constructed in compliance with collective rules and regulations to prevent costly financial crises and ensure stable conditions of financial activities that provide a sound economic environment.

A Central Bank is one of these institutions to stabilize financial activities and manage crisis properly, which is called "Big Bank" by Minsky. Active economic policies of a Central Bank or Big Bank aim to create appropriate initial conditions to limit the inherent instability of the system. The economic system's long-run bias toward instability cannot be removed but can be mitigated or kept under control if well-designed institutions exist. To some extent, with timely and appropriate tools such as prompt refinancing and an adequate inflow of reserve, the Central Bank can constrain the destructive dynamics of the crisis that show themselves in the massive bankruptcies of financial firms.

Minsky proposes various important insights on the role of central banks in a world of sophisticated financial markets. In Minsky's view, the main objective of the central bank is not only to intervene in troubled times but also to provide resilient conditions for financial markets to perform in normal times. That is, the central bank should follow a policy to provide the conditions for financial markets to function efficiently. It should monitor secondary markets in a way that they should provide liquidity in normal and bad times.

The main concern of Minsky is not just to design the central bank as a unit to provide emergency loans during crises but also take measures during normal times. The central bank must be alert about market operations in normal times. For example the process of securitization carries a lot of potential problems within itself. This is because the central bank can no longer control the amount of money in the system after expansion of securitization, getting out of control. The danger that the securitization process poses to financial stability is expressed by Minsky as follows: *"Securitization lowers the weight of that part of the financing structure that the central bank (the Federal Reserve in the US) is committed to protect"* (Minsky, 2008, p. 3). This is what actually happened preceding the global crisis in 2007–2008.

Big Government

Although Minsky is regarded as a scholar studying only the financial instability hypothesis, he in fact has many studies on issues such as poverty, employment and development. In order to mitigate these problems, he advised policies such as unionization, high minimum wages and public provision of education and health services, and a full employment guarantee program in order to reduce economic insecurity.

Minsky was interested in several economic developmental issues. For these he had many suggestions to change bad economic institutions that created poverty, inequities and inefficiencies. Some of them are: medium-sized banks, creation of development banks, separation of banking activities, providing house loans to poor people, and implementing policies to increase employment. From these suggestions, it is understood that Minsky wishes to encourage local growth and employment, which in turn lead to a more sound economy. These institutions, in fact, are important not only in explaining the basis of financial fragility but also in limiting its costs. In this sense, Minsky noted that *"If amplified uncertainty and extremes in income maldistribution and social inequalities attenuate the economic underpinnings of democracy, then the market behavior that creates these conditions has to be constrained"* (Minsky, 1996, pp. 14–15).

During a crisis, the private sector is not only unit-building the debt, but the government budget deficit is also not in good shape because budget deficit expands during downturns due to falling taxes and increasing government expenditures. Despite that, Minsky supports a massive fiscal stimulus to get out of the crisis. In fact, he does not support the presence of big government just during crisis. Moreover, he stresses that without relying on private debt the government should exist in the economy with its large fiscal presence. In this sense, he argues that we should "definancialize" the economy by reducing the role of financial markets. For instance, we should keep healthcare and private pensions controlled by money managers away from all critical services for human beings such as healthcare.

It is well recognized that capitalist economies are not good at creating full employment. This mainly originates from the fact that the objectives of firms differ from those of workers. Firms aim to maximize their profits rather than employ each worker. In order to reduce unemployment and to create a secure workforce, Minsky proposed an employer of last resort (ELR) program. The main target of the ELR program is to provide for each individual who wants to work at decent wages (Minsky, 1986). To Minsky, the government should establish a decentralized job creation system whereby it can create an infinitely elastic demand for labor. The government will employ everyone wanting to work at a local level based on the social benefits to the community.

Therefore the government should create a buffer stock of employed labor to stabilize economic variables such as wages and inflation, in addition to providing minimum decent conditions that people can live. The ELR program also reduces income inequality and creates conditions for upward mobility on the social ladder. Moreover, such stable employment and income levels simultaneously facilitate home ownership and will prevent the financing of home-buying by risky financial innovations such as subprime borrowing.

Minsky also argues that employment policies should be consistent with the macro environment to reach desired results. Hence Minsky (1986, p. 343) mentions that: *"The policy problem is to develop a strategy for full employment that does not lead to instability, inflation, and unemployment"*.

Some researchers argue that the ELR program is too expensive to implement and it will create immense budget deficits that will get out of control. However, some reliable studies show that the probable cost of the ELR program in the US is about 1% of gross domestic product. The program is likely to reduce costs in other areas, making other social benefit programs redundant. Its cost is more likely to be lower than the money spent for bailing out bankrupt financial corporations. It also stabilizes expectations due to its creating a stable demand and a feeling of confidence.

5.6 Concluding remarks

Minsky constructs his theoretical framework on a dynamic economic process. This perspective is totally distinct from the mainstream approach using equilibrium notions that regard the economic problem as one of establishing efficient market allocations. Process issues are disregarded in this equilibrium perspective. In Minsky's view, the process is defined as "success breeds excess breeds failure". This implies evolutionary instability. The potentiality of instability is always present in modern financial capitalism. Thus the economic system is prone to financial crises.

As Minsky said, his aim is to reinterpret Keynes. In line with him, Minsky draws attention to various fundamental properties of monetary production in an uncertain environment. These are mainly: the crucial role of financial markets, non-neutrality of money, the cyclical nature of investments, and the decision-making process under fundamental uncertainty and bounded rationality. In this way, he extends Keynes by combining an investment theory of the business cycle with a financial theory of investment.

In order to prevent the inherent problems of capitalism, to some extent, Minsky proposes various thwarting institutions, which confine the amplitude of economic fluctuations within reasonable limits. The Central Banks and governments can alleviate the instabilities in capitalism by placing appropriate constraints on the dynamic behavior of the system. However this is not enough, as Minsky elaborates, to eliminate crises in capitalist economies. Instabilities are permanent. Hence constant attention should be given to the functioning of institutions in an economy. In calling for such reforms, Minsky clearly has a more positive view of the nature of government in a capitalist society, in contrast to Marx who sees the government as the executive body for managing the common affairs of the bourgeoisie.

To some critics of Minsky, there are faults in Minsky's reasoning. In order to mitigate these faults, they advise incorporation of various components into his analysis. One of these is to integrate income inequalities into the dynamics of financial markets. With this, the relations between borrowing and income inequality will be incorporated into the analysis. Another suggestion is to include global imbalances, which played a critical role in the development of the global crisis of 2007–2008. Here the relations between financial markets and global imbalances can be helpful in analyzing the crisis of 2007–2008. However, we have to admit that Minsky's model, elaborated in the 1970s, could not pay explicit attention to either of these factors. They were not then prominent problems that Minsky would take into account. Consequently integrating these perspectives into Minskian analysis will increase the potential to understand current issues in contemporary economies.

Notes

1 Ponzi finance is named after Charles Ponzi who became notorious for using the technique in the 1920s in the US.

2 The direction of macroeconomic activity is mainly initiated in one sector, then transmitted to the others. For Keynes and Minsky the initiating sector is the financial sector; for most Marxists, it is the real sector. Keynes criticized the neoclassical

dichotomy between a real and a monetary sphere. Instead of the dichotomy, he developed a model of a monetary production economy. In such an approach money plays a key role and penetrates all spheres of the economy. He recognizes that all disturbances happen in this monetary environment, despite Keynes not having developed a theory of crisis.

3 Tobin's *q*, or the *q* ratio, is the ratio of the market value of a company's assets (as measured by the market value of its outstanding stock and debt) divided by the replacement cost of the company's assets. Tobin's *q* ratio has been extensively used as a proxy for investment opportunities in the finance literature.

4 The Efficient Market Hypothesis is the idea that the next move in an asset's price must be entirely random and therefore uninfluenced by any previous price movement. It is this property that allows financial analysts to build estimates of probability distributions of future asset price movements. Since investors are rational and base their decisions on reliable information, mispricing is not permanent in this hypothesis.

5 The new classical macroeconomics is based on the rational expectations hypothesis. This means that people have rational expectations about economic variables. The implication is that people make intelligent use of available information in forecasting variables that affect their economic decisions. According to this hypothesis, forecasts are unbiased and based on all available information. The hypothesis holds that people make unbiased forecasts. Hence people do not make systematic errors in their expectations. And they are not affected by waves of optimism and pessimism.

6 In fact, it was Knut Wicksell (1851–1926), who first delivered a framework of cumulative processes which may lead to financial crises. Economists in the Keynesian and in the Neoclassical tradition followed his framework. Keynes and Minsky also followed his approach. In the Wicksellian approach dynamic economic processes are explained by the interaction of two rates of return—natural interest rate and money interest rate—which typically diverge or at least do not tend to equilibrium.

7 The New Keynesian approach developed in the 1980s in response to the criticisms directed at some of Keynes's thoughts. New Keynesians revised Keynes's views and constructed their hypothesis mainly on the inflexible adjustment of prices and wages to short-term economic fluctuations. This in turn leads to involuntary unemployment. Hence appropriate fiscal and monetary policies are required to correct their effects.

8 Structural Keynesian macroeconomic analysis focuses on the institutions and policy interventions needed for an economy to generate productive full employment with contained income inequality.

9 Minsky elaborates his analysis of the development of capitalism by studying the changing economic systems of the US between 1929 and the 1990s. This led him to identify five stages in the development of capitalism: (1) merchant capitalism, (2) industrial capitalism, (3) banker capitalism, (4) managerial capitalism and (5) money manager capitalism.

6 Tendency of rate of profit to fall

6.1 Introduction

The tendency of the rate of profit to fall is an important hypothesis in economics, most famously expressed by Karl Marx. Economists as diverse as classical political economists and contemporary economists elaborated it as an empirical phenomenon that needed to be explained. However, the explanations they presented in general vary from each other.

Marx called the tendency of the rate of profit to fall "the most important law of political economy". He described this tendency as "the mystery around which the whole of political economy since Adam Smith revolves" (Capital III, 1894, p. 319). Marx regarded the hypothesis of the falling rate of profits as proof that capitalist production could collapse in the end.

Marxian economic theory is based on a structural economic analysis. Its main structure is economic class in which the social relations of production are determined by the conflict between capital and labor. The capitalist tries to exploit labor to increase profit, leading to capital accumulation. The continuous expansion of capital is necessary for the reproduction of capitalist systems. For this reason, the structural conditions that are related to profitability determine the process of capital accumulation. Naturally breakdowns in capitalist accumulation are mainly shaped by developments in profitability.

Marxian theories of crisis have a long history and they have been debated in many places and diverse contexts. The recent crisis of 2007–2008 has renewed Marxian debate on crisis theory. Some scholars have focused on the role of the falling rate of profit in the global crisis of 2007–2008.

There are mainly three Marxian theories related to the tendency of falling profit rate, which are i) The hypothesis called tendency of the rate of profit to fall focuses on capitalization and mechanization driven by the unintended consequences of competition. This process drives value-creating labor out of the production process due to improvements in labor-saving technologies. This results in declining profits across the whole economy and hence the occurrence of crises. ii) Another version of Marxian theory in the context of falling profits is the profit squeeze theory, which mainly points out that the workers who struggle against capitalist exploitation put pressure on profits. This leads to a fall in the rate of exploitation and a decline in profits, eventually causing a crisis, and iii) Social accumulation of capital (SSA) theory also has Marxian roots. It aims to understand the persistent cycles in capitalism. SSA theory is concerned with the accumulation structures that sustain the profitability of firms. The fluctuations in profits of firms occur along with changing accumulation structures. This creates cycles in the economy.

In this part of the book, we elaborate these Marxian theories and their empirical relevance to crises. In fact, these theories are not mutually exclusive, and therefore it is hard to compartmentalize them within their own domain. This will naturally lead us to discuss them in an overlapping manner.

6.2 The "tendency of the rate of profit to fall" hypothesis

Classical political economists such as Adam Smith and David Ricardo argued the importance of the tendency for the rate of profit to fall. They saw this fact as an impediment to the expansion of capitalist accumulation. Smith pointed out that capitalists compete with each other and this competition pushes down the rate of profit. However, from a different perspective, Ricardo stressed that competition can affect only redistribution of profits rather than determining the rate of profit. To him, instead of competition, the increasing rent in agriculture due to falling productivity in agricultural production along with new less fertile lands reduces the profits of capitalists. The upward tendency of prices of agricultural products forces wages of workers upward due to rising food prices and this in turn lowers the profits of capitalists. That is, Ricardo explained the fall in profits by falling marginal productivity of land, which had been proposed earlier by Malthus. Rising food prices benefit the landlord class and lead to rising rents particularly on the most fertile land. To Ricardo, this tendency eventually implies the end of industrial capitalism.

Ricardo's explanation is mainly based on natural causes, that is, expansion of new less fertile lands to feed an increasing population. Marx was obviously attracted to the idea of falling profits but his approach was not to attribute social changes to natural causes. In his view, the rate of profit does not fall because of technological and natural constraints. He tried to explain the falling rate of profits within the internal contradictions of capital. Thus, in his view, it is the ever-rising productivity of capital, stemming from a continuous competition for relative surplus value, which in turn causes the profit rate to fall. Moreover Marx argued that this would be the ultimate "grave-digger" of capitalism.

Marx pointed out that along with technological advancements, factors of production became more efficient. The natural result of this being that physical productivity would increase, and thus greater output would be produced. However, these developments in technology facilitated the substitution of machinery for workers. Since Marx thought that only labor could produce new additional value, more machines replacing workers would lead to lower surplus value. Hence, in the long run the average rate of profit would tend to fall. Note that Marx claims that the rate of profit declines in the long run not due to a decrease in productivity but instead due to its increase, with the aid of a bigger investment in physical capital. Technological development, in Marx's view, is a fundamentally labor-saving bias in the long run. This implies that more production is made with more machinery, and the rate of profit on capital will fall eventually.

However, as Marx mentioned, the fall in the rate of profit is a tendency rather than a strict law. There are other factors that counteract this tendency, thus raising the rate of profit upward. Marx listed six of these counteracting factors in *Capital*, Volume III (p. 339):

(i) more intense exploitation of labor (ii) reducing wages (iii) reducing the cost of constant capital (iv) increasing the reserve army of labor (the number of the unemployed) that presses downward on wages (v) increasing foreign trade that causes the cost of inputs and goods to fall and (vi) increase in the use of share capital by joint-stock companies, which passes part of the costs of using capital in production to others.

Despite these countervailing tendencies, Marx stressed that they would not change the falling direction of the rate of profit. Its tendency to fall was intrinsic to the capitalist mode of production. Therefore the counteracting factors could not create enough strong barriers to this tendency.

Presently we will explain the main arguments of Marx regarding the falling rate of profits in a more technical sense, which will help us to better understand the basic trends that move profits. For this, let us start with a fundamental argument of the Marxian view that surplus value (s) can be only created by workers (living labor or variable capital). However, it is clear that the rate of profits is not only dependent on labor cost but also all other costs such as capital costs.

Here, the notion of organic composition of capital is critical to understand the tendency of declining profits. This is mainly defined as the ratio of constant capital (mainly plant, equipment and materials) to variable capital (labor power)[1]. It is conceptually similar to capital deepening in neoclassical economics (capital per labor). Formally it is defined as

$$k = \frac{c}{v} \tag{6.1}$$

where c is constant capital and v is variable capital.

The rate of surplus value (also called the rate of exploitation), is another crucial concept used to understand the falling rate of profit. It is defined as the ratio of the unpaid to the paid parts of the working time; in other words it is simply the ratio of surplus value (s) to variable capital (v):

$$e = \frac{s}{v} \tag{6.2}$$

This ratio manifests what proportion of the workers' working time is given up to the capitalist with respect to the time spent on reproducing the value of labor power. Thus it describes allocation of a worker's time between the capitalist and worker. When the ratio s/v increases, workers' time is being more appropriated by the capitalist and workers work less time for themselves.

The capitalist's rate of profit is the ratio of surplus to total capital (constant plus variable capital). It is different from the rate of surplus value because it is the ratio of surplus to total variable including constant and variable capital, rather than just variable capital. Therefore the rate of profit (r) is

$$r = \frac{s}{c + v} \tag{6.3}$$

If the above equation is transformed as follows by dividing by the variable capital, v, we will obtain

$$r = \frac{s/v}{1 + (c/v)} \tag{6.4}$$

and hence

$$r = \frac{e}{1 + k} \tag{6.5}$$

Here while $e = s/v$ shows the rate of surplus value (the rate of exploitation), $k = c/v$ is the organic composition of capital.

Benefiting from the equations above, we derive various propositions regarding the tendency in the rate of profit:

1. The process of capital accumulation by its own nature increases the level of the organic composition of capital ($k = c/v$).
2. If the increase in the rate of exploitation ($e = s/v$), counteracts the increase in the organic composition of capital, the rate of profit will not fall.
3. The rate of exploitation is not able to compensate the persistent rise in the organic composition of capital. Therefore the rate of profit will fall in the long run.
4. Decline in the rate of profit will lead to an economic crisis. Along with the crisis, there occur widespread defaults and subsequently capitalists reduce their investments due to declining profit opportunities. The decline in aggregate demand (both investment and consumption) leads to overproduction.
5. The crisis creates new conditions for further capital accumulation over time. This is provided by the facts a) there will be a fall in unproductive capital, therefore the remaining capital will work more productively; b) bankruptcies put pressure on the prices of existing constant capital, reducing their prices. This in turn causes a fall in the organic composition of capital (thus in $k = c/v$, c falls), thus raising the rate of profit and c) after the crisis, many workers are laid off and as a result of this the reserve army of the unemployed increases. This in turn causes a downward pressure on wages, thus increasing the rate of exploitation. All these developments facilitate restoration of the rate of profit, and hence the accumulation process begins again.

6. Crises in the capitalist system take on a periodic character. And each new crisis becomes more severe because they occur at higher capital levels (thus at a higher organic composition of capital), and creating new conditions for further capital accumulation over time becomes more difficult. Hence exit from successive crises will be harder.

The first three premises are critical to the tendency of the rate of profit to fall. The second and third premises can be understood formally in terms of equation 6.5. The equation indicates that the rate of profit is the inverse function of organic composition of capital (k). That is, if k rises for any given value of e, the rate of profit eventually falls.

However, the validity of the third premise is less obvious. In order to better understand this problem, we can begin by asking to what extent the rate of exploitation can offset the fall in the rate of profit. While the organic composition of capital goes up, the power of the rate of exploitation on the rate of profit becomes less. That is, along with higher organic composition of capital, increasing rate of exploitation will not offset the decline in the rate of profit. Moreover, as the rate of exploitation gets higher, a lower margin remains for exploitation to be used to increase the rate of profit; thus its power to completely counteract the rising organic composition of capital diminishes over time.

The development described by the first premise above, which is the increasing organic composition of capital, is the most controversial among all the premises. This is because neither the empirical evidence nor the theoretical arguments used for it are convincing. Even though it is clearly observed that the physical amount of capital per worker has immensely increased along with accumulation, the concept of capital contains a value definition rather than a physical definition. Hence, in this sense, it is not apparent that the value of capital per worker has gone up over time.

In fact, for the value of capital per worker to rise, the intensity of labor-saving technologies must be much more than that of capital-saving technologies. That is, machinery should substitute for labor more than the substitution of cheap machines for expensive ones. In the 19th century, increasing replacement of machinery for labor was a prominent fact. Despite that, Marx was aware of the fact that constant capital could be cheapened by increased productivity in the production of capital goods. But he thought that it was not a persistent development that would affect the organic composition of capital. Instead, Marx emphasized incessant labor-saving technological improvements in the accumulation process.

As pointed out by many scholars, there are various reasonable arguments which suggest that there are tendencies that capital saving can relatively dominate labor-saving innovations in advanced capitalist economies. In the earliest stages of capital accumulation, the introduction of machinery replaced labor power at a higher level. However, following this development, new technological innovations have been in the form of facilitating substitution of machines for machines mostly even though the substitution of machines for labor has continued. Competition between producers of machines makes their production cheaper and more productive. And it is expected that capitalists emphasize capital-saving technologies if constant capital appears more in the total cost (in the case of higher values of c/v). Furthermore, there can be an increase in the organic composition of capital but this does not guarantee the constantly rising trend in aggregate level of the organic composition of capital due to developments in other sectors. This can originate from, for example, an expanding labor-intensive service sector. Hence it is hard to mention a priori that labor-saving technologies will predominate within the production process.

Consequently, Marxians argue that when unsustainable levels of rate of profits emerge, the economic mechanism collapses, resulting in a crisis. Firms go bankrupt and investors do not make new investments due to lack of profitable opportunities. But this is also the starting point of new accumulation because the destruction of economic values and serious falls in the organic composition of capital allow the revival of new accumulation process and exit from the crisis.

6.3 The profit squeeze argument

A cousin concept directly related to the tendency of the rate of profit to fall is profit squeeze. Some economists such as Andrew Glyn, Bob Sutcliffe and Thomas Weisskopf, propose a "wage-push profit squeeze" theory to explain the decline in the rate of profit. The theory constructs its argument in this way: class struggle between workers and capitalists determines their relative income. The labor unions representing workers struggle to obtain higher wages from capitalists. In this sense, the proponents of this view stress that when the bargaining power of labor increases, higher wage demands rise and this in turn lowers the profits of firms (their profits are "squeezed") and naturally their investments. This is likely to end up in a crisis. However, the profits of firms can be recovered to the extent that the increased unemployment due to falling investments places a downward pressure on wages, because the working class's bargaining power declines. Consequently firms start to make high profit again, and thus profit squeeze is relaxed.

According to the profit squeeze hypothesis, economies during a boom employ more labor. This increases real wages, and thereby profits fall. This in turn leads to an interruption in the normal circuit of capital. At this point, a higher level of unemployment becomes an objective necessity for capital in order to reestablish normal profitability; this inevitably drives down real wages.

The profit squeeze argument is mainly built on Marx's view that crises could not be avoided by pushing up effective demand by increasing wages. This is seen in his following remarks:

> if one were to attempt to clothe this tautology with a profounder justification by saying that the working class receives too small a portion of their own product, and the evil would be remedied by giving them

> a larger share of it, or raising their wages, we should reply that crises are precisely always preceded by a period in which wages rise generally and the working class actually gets a larger share of the annual production intended for consumption.
>
> (Marx, 1894, pp. 475–476)

Some scholars such as Bowles et al. (1984) used this reasoning to explain the stagflation of the 1970s, because they argued that the increases in wages in the 1970s could not prevent the crisis in the 1970s.

However, some scholars such as Shaikh (1987) criticize the profit squeeze hypothesis and reject the hypothesis as theoretically invalid. A fall in profitability can appear in only two forms: failure to sell what is produced, or failure to sell it at a sufficient profit rate. The latter has to involve a rise in costs relative to price. The profit squeeze hypothesis is merely the generalization of this perception to capital as a whole. To demonstrate the error of this reasoning, Shaikh elaborates the relationship between the abstract concepts of surplus value and variable capital, on the one hand, and the empirical concepts of corporate profit and wage income. He argues that the profit squeeze theorists equate s/v with π/w, where π is total profit and w is total wage payments. By doing so they confuse the manifestation of the underlying causal variables with those variables themselves.

The profit squeeze argument, in fact, is not widely utilized to analyze recent crises any more. However, Wallerstein (2003) has recently developed a global perspective on profit squeeze. In his view, there are three main factors behind this: higher wages from deruralization (that is, deruralization of the world is reducing the global pool of low wage labor), increasing taxes to meet social services, and higher prices of raw materials because of their increasing exhaustion. These factors, initially, are at work in creating a profit squeeze at the level of the global system. That is, from this viewpoint, profit squeeze arises from contradictions created at a certain stage of world capitalist development.

Meanwhile here we want to draw attention to a critical point regarding the relationship between underconsumption theory and profit squeeze theory. As elaborated in the previous chapter of this book, the main argument of underconsumption theory is that there is not enough effective demand to meet the products generated by the increasing production capacity of the modern economies. Thereby developed capitalist economies will eventually enter a chronic stagnation process unless there is intervention by other demand-generating mechanisms. These arguments are apparently against what profit squeeze theory says. Profit squeeze theory basically argues that increasing wages are the cause of crises rather than falling wages as claimed by underconsumptionists. Profit squeeze theory focuses on the motivation of capitalists rather than the realization problem.

6.4 Social structure of accumulation theory

Social structure of accumulation (SSA) theory uses an evolutionary perspective that defines capitalistic development as successive stages. SSA theory, in fact, can be regarded as the generalized form of profit squeeze theory. Its main arguments derive from Marxian analysis, with more emphasis on institutional structures. The main argument of SSA is that the institutional strength of economies performs well over a certain period but after that it stops functioning well. This results in a period of stagnation and crisis. This in turn prepares the conditions for a new SSA.

SSA theory emphasizes the stability provided by an institutional structure. Without the sound external and internal environment that form the stability of institutions of an economic system, no economic system can function well. The social structure of accumulation takes into account all the institutions in the production process. The institutional structure provides the continuation of capitalist production and growth. But during the passage of time, institutions are not able to sustain this accumulation process permanently. Either the structure of economic growth leads to dysfunction of the institutions or the institutions themselves prevent the economic system from developing further. If the existing SSA does not function properly anymore, it is defined as a crisis of the old SSA. Hence the existing institutions of the old SSA should be redesigned to overcome the crisis. Each SSA collapse opens up a new stage in capitalism.

Since the Second World War, there have been two distinct SSAs at the global level. The first one is the post-war SSA, which is called the "regulated capitalist SSA". The second one is the "neoliberal SSA" which took shape in the late 1970s. The first SSA was constructed in the late 1940s and performed well until the mid-1970s. Its basic character was the dominant role of state intervention at national and international level. This was provided by welfare states, co-respective competition among large corporations and significant capital–labor cooperation[2]. This SSA is called regulated capitalism, which expresses a divergence from the past where the state had a minor effect.

During the late 1970s, due to the enduring fall in the rate of profit, business investments declined and thereby unemployment went up. Governments tried to contain this adversity by using Keynesian expansionary fiscal policies. However, these policies led to a new and significant problem, which was high levels of inflation because governments' expansionary policies—such as increasing fiscal expenditures and lowering interest rates—stimulated demand further. However, since inflation hurt financial actors, they began to push governments towards less expansionary policies and higher interest rates in the 1980s. Along with a shift to these policies, this resulted in lower inflation, but also higher unemployment. This in turn reduced the welfare of people. This negative environment led to a new SSA, which took shape in the 1980s.

According to Kotz (2013), there are five important properties of regulated capitalism. First, there was an important compromise between capital and labor, which was in favor of the unions that represented the workers. Second, there was an important role of the government in the sense of promoting growth, employment, regulative policies on finance and business and welfare policies. Third, there was no unrestrained competition; on the contrary, co-respective forms of competition were widespread among firms. Fourth, the main business of financial corporations was to finance the productive activities of non-financial corporations. Fifth and lastly, the economic system was a "mixed economy", where prominence of a market economy is recognized but this is realized via a regulative state and strong trade unions, to ensure the smooth functioning of markets in order not to undergo another crisis similar to the Great Depression.

This indicates that there was a great degree of coherence between institutions in the post-war regulated capitalist SSA. They complemented and reinforced each other and facilitated capital accumulation. Compromise between capital and labor was the main character of this SSA, in addition to other critical features such as active regulation of economic relations and market forces.

During the mid-1970s, the post-war SSA entered a period of crisis. A new stage was beginning in the US and UK during the late 1970s. This new stage, namely a new SSA, emerged alongside the prominence of market forces, which is called neoliberalism. The neoliberal SSA took shape by the early 1980s. This SSA was totally distinct from the regulated SSA. Kotz and McDonough (2010) define the main changes: the relaxation of constraints on the movements of goods, services and money; deregulation in many areas; privatization of state enterprises and public services; the shrinkage of the welfare state; a shift from cooperation between capital and labor to a relationship in which capital dominates labor; and shift from co-respective behavior by large corporations to unrestrained competition among them.

Neoliberalism promoted the idea of a free market that did not give the state any positive role in the functioning of markets, apart from some enforcement and judiciary roles. The neoliberal SSA brought transformations of global and domestic institutions in the countries that redesigned the global economic system. In fact as Kotz and McDonough (2010) noted, this development spread to all regions of the world. However, the Nordic countries and Japan tried to avert this wave that spread the hegemony of markets.

Like the regulated SSA, Kotz (2013) says that there are five important properties of the neoliberal SSA. They are almost the opposite of the properties of the regulated SSA. First, labor has been dominated by capital in this new SSA. Second, markets have dominated state, thus the withdrawal of state from all spheres of economic and social life such as decline in social expenditure, deregulations in all markets, privatization, etc. Third, unrestrained competition has become prevalent among large firms. Fourth, financial firms have shifted to other speculative areas instead of financing non-financial firms. Fifth, liberal values have dominated, emphasizing markets and efficiency. Market relations have permeated into each domain of economic life, from health to education.

There are some differences in liberal and regulated SSAs in terms of various contradictions within capital. One of these is regarding the form and intensity of competition among capitalists. While the competition in the regulated SSA is more restrained, co-respective and regulated, competition in the liberal SSA is more harsh and destructive. In the regulated SSA, co-respective competition does not show only the regulative constraints imposed by the government but also the competition tradition and co-respective behavior between capitalists. These differences in the competition stance of capitalists also shape their treatment toward workers. Under harsh and cutthroat competition, capitalists always pursue measures to cut labor costs. But in the other case, namely in the regulated SSA, the limited competition due to co-respective behavior and regulations looks for compromises with labor. In another domain contradiction in capital emerges in the relationship between financial and industrial capital. In the regulated SSA, the links between financial and non-financial agents are tighter, but in contrast this link is weaker in a liberal SSA. This shows that financial institutions pursue lucrative gains in more speculative areas rather than financing the productive activities of non-financial corporations.

Now the question is how the regulated capitalist SSA fell apart. Proponents of the SSA argue that the crisis in the regulated SSA started with fall in profitability. In the boom years of the late 1960s, there were low unemployment rates. Organized labor emerged as a powerful agent of capital accumulation. Falling unemployment and the increased power of unions led to rising wages, reducing the profits of firms. This prepared the conditions of instability in capital and labor relations.

There was an important conflict in income distribution between firms and unions in the 1970s. Income distribution developed in favor of workers, hence income distribution improved. This reduced the profits of firms. And along with increasing inflation, the profits of financial firms also declined. By the 1970s, some of the institutions of the post-war structure had already eroded, and those that remained did not perform well in sustaining the soundness of the economy in terms of economic growth, profitability and stability. Although there was not a surplus realization problem due to high wages and social transfers, the production of surplus value was not sustainable. For this reason, the sustainability of profits presents a critical perspective in order to understand the root of the crisis toward the end of the period of the regulated capitalist SSA.

The problems in the regulated SSA can also be defined as "profit squeeze" crises. That is, they are compatible with the main argument of the profit squeeze approach; the pressure on wages due to low unemployment and the power of organized labor led to a fall in profits and eventually resulted in a crisis. Some empirical studies evidence this. For example, Kotz (2013) stresses that during the regulated SSA period, the main reason behind all short-run economic crises (recessions) was profit squeeze because of increased wages.

The neoliberal SSA was a distinct capital accumulation process. Its institutions aimed to sustain profitability, and thus the production of surplus value was at the center of the accumulation process. However, this generated a different problem, which was the realization of surplus value. This mainly stemmed

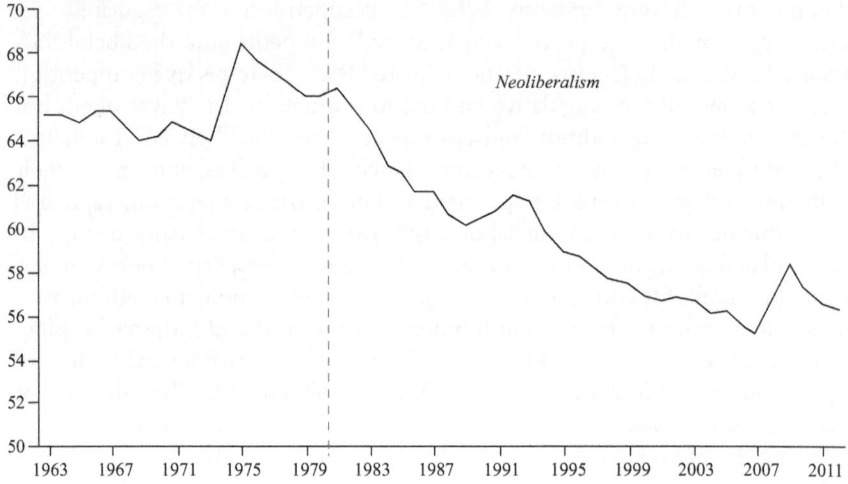

Figure 6.1 Wage share of national income in Eurozone countries.
Source: Kotz (2013).

from declining wages despite rising productivity. As Kotz (2013) argues, total real profit rose at 4.6% per year while total real employee compensation rose by 2.0% per year over the period 1979–2007. The divergence between profits and wages originated from several factors such as the declining power of unions, technological improvements and employment flexibility through international outsourcing and offshoring. Figure 6.1 represents the wage share of national income in the Eurozone countries during neoliberalism. It is seen that wage share fell drastically.

The economic growth rate during the liberal SSA period was lower compared to the regulated SSA period. There are several reasons for this. Wolfson and Kotz (2010) enumerate them as follows. First, there was a realization problem during the liberal period because wages and public expenditures declined. Second, due to the weakening role of the government, the effectiveness of counter-cyclical public expenditures and the regulating power of automatic stabilizers through shrinking social welfare programs declined. The prominence of financial agents because of deregulations exposed the economy to vulnerable shocks. Third, the scope of corporate managers became more short-sighted, focusing on the interests of shareholders rather than the long-term sustainability of the corporation in terms of maintaining business investment. Fourth, financial institutions were not concerned with the long-term production potential of the economy, transferring their funds to speculative financial areas.

The question we now have to ask here is how this liberal SSA has continued despite this deep realization problem. Scholars using the methodology of SSA argue that the realization problem was resolved or rather delayed mainly by increased debt financed by financial agents and asset bubbles that manifested a welfare effect on households. As explained in the debt accumulation section of this book, debt-financed consumption increased tremendously during this period. This kept effective demand stable. As is well known, during the liberal SSA period income distribution also became worse. To an increasing extent, more funds remained in the hands of the rich. With these, they purchased more financial assets, leading to asset bubbles. The stock market and real estate bubbles in the 1990s and 2000s in the US respectively can be counted as examples of this.

The realization problem of the neoliberal period seems similar to the underconsumption argument asserted by Marxists, which mainly argues that consumer demand falls due to stagnation of wages and rising profits. But in fact the neoliberal SSA did not have a crisis such as underconsumption because the consumption demands of households were met by rising debt despite stagnation of their wages. The maintenance of consumption allowed firms to increase their production capacity. Also with the stimulation of increased prices of assets, firms' production capacity increased further due to the wealth effect of asset prices inducing further demand, thus resulting in larger excess capacity.

According to the proponents of the SSA theory, the global crisis of 2007–2008 is essentially a structural crisis of neoliberal capitalism. Two important shortcomings of neoliberal capitalism led to this. First, the general rate of profit was persistently declining. Although there was a moderate recovery of profits generated by information and communication technologies, these vaporized during crises such as the dot.com bubble. Second, the accumulation process has a structural weakness, which is not just its inability to create a stable path but its own nature that does not facilitate productive investment due to its neoliberal financial and anti-labor bias. These scholars argue that if these shortcomings of the neoliberal capitalism cannot be solved appropriately, it always retains a potential to create new crises. In this sense, primarily abolition of the financial speculative hegemony and reducing inequality in favor of working people are critical issues that should be considered thoroughly.

However, as Kotz (2013) mentions, the arguments of the SSA cannot be tested empirically because we have only had a limited number of SSAs in the history of capitalism. We have had only one regulated SSA in the US, and hence deriving general results from a single example is problematic. And we have had two liberal SSA periods. One is the 1920s in the US and the other is the period starting in the 1980s until now in the USA. They resemble each other significantly. Both ended with deep collapses. However, Kotz (2013) mentions that it is still too early to construct a firm basis for generalizations, as it does not have strong empirical support.

6.5 A theoretical debate on the validity of the tendency of the rate of profit to fall

Marxian theory on the falling rate of profit has been always on the agenda within academic and non-academic spheres. Even though it is supported by many Marxians, it is also intensely criticized by other Marxians and non-Marxians.

As an important and well-known Marxian scholar, Harvey (2015) opposes the idea of falling rate of profits with a simple reasoning. In his view, the falling rate of profits and theory of crisis based on it are mono-causal. This means that such a view disregards the other causes of crises and counteracting forces, thus excluding other factors at issue. He argues that Marx's law of the falling rate of profits is based on various simple assumptions. This law applies only if the conditions assumed are realized in the real world.

Harvey stresses that these assumptions disregard all the other factors that counteract the fall in the rate of profit that is merely driven by labor-saving technologies. Harvey (2015) provides a statistical number regarding the tendency in the global labor force in order to support his argument. He stresses that there has been large enough growth in the world's labor force, which is around 1.1 billion between 1980 and 2005. This evidence alone, in Harvey's view, contradicts the tendency in the rate of profits at the global level. This implies the existence of a huge increase in surplus value production. In fact, Harvey does not show whether the rate of profit falls or not by looking at the trends in the numerator—profit—and denominator, invested capital. Harvey just elaborates that increase in employment is important evidence that Marx's falling rate of profit view has not been valid since the early 1980s. Hence, in his view, if the general theory of the tendency for profit rates to fall was correct, then the spread of labor-saving technological changes would mean a tendency for the number of waged workers employed by capital to decrease. But this is not the case; on the contrary, he points out that employment rises at the global level.

According to Marx, as mentioned previously, labor is the only source of value and surplus value derives from use of labor. If the expansion of constant capital, that is, new investments, increases more than the labor force, it also increases more than profits. Thus this leads to a downward pressure on the ratio of profit to investment and hence the rate of profits goes down. There are two objections to this view. First, technological improvements do not always lead to labor-saving (in other words, capital-intensive). They can also be capital-saving technologies. Thus new technologies may use less machinery per worker than old technologies. So the ratio of investment to labor may not increase.

However, proponents of the Marxian view oppose this objection. They argue that a greater number of "capital-intensive" innovations can be more than "capital-saving" innovations. Thus, they accept that technological innovations can also be capital saving, which counteracts the rise in the organic composition of capital (the ratio of capital to labor). However, despite this, competition among capitalists generates a pressure on them to reach the most advanced technological change by making more investments for new innovations. Capitalists are ready to pay more to grasp new technological improvements. So both technical composition of capital (average machinery per labor) and organic composition of capital increase. This implies that both capital intensiveness and capital saving can occur at the same time.

The second objection is that technological advances might not lead to a fall in the rate of profit because firms will choose technology that makes their profit higher. This will spread to the whole industry due to competition and the average rate of profit of all the firms in the industry will be higher after the introduction of these new technologies. This view has been shared by various Marxian economists, for instance by Nobuo Okishio, Andrew Glyn, Robert Brenner and Gerard Duménil and Dominique Lévy. Their main point is that capitalists will only adopt capital-intensive techniques that seem to reduce their rate of profit if that rate is already being squeezed either by a rise in real wages or by external competition. These things, not the organic composition of capital, reduce the rate of profit.

Using mathematical equations provided by Okishio (1961), critics stress that technological innovations reduce production cost, so goods are always being produced more cheaply than in the past[3]. If a rise in the ratio of capital to labor in a certain industry increases productivity, the price of its output will fall compared to the output of other industries. However, that in turn will reduce the cost of investment in these industries and its ratio to labor. Lower investment costs will lower the organic composition of capital and raise the rate of profit. That is, as Okishio's (1961) theorem pointed out, in contrast to Marx, capitalists will not adopt any labor-saving technological innovation that will lower their profits. Thus technical changes are made to raise firms' rates of profit.

In fact, Marx was aware of this argument. Hence he said that competition between capitalists triggers the process. That is, the first capitalist who develops new technology gets dominance in the market over the other capitalists. He will gain higher profits compared to other capitalists. But other capitalists are ready to adapt this new technology in order not to lag behind. When they adapt this new technology, increased production in the market puts downward pressure on prices of the good. This reduces profits and if firms try further to innovate new technologies, the rate of profit falls again.

In this sense, Marx implies something more comprehensive. Harman (2010, p.72) argues that

> the success of capitalism at accumulating leads to problems for further accumulation. Eventually the competitive drive of capitalists to keep ahead of other capitalists results in a massive scale of new investment which cannot be sustained by the rate of profit. If some capitalists are to make an adequate profit it can only be at the expense of other capitalists who are driven out of business. The drive to accumulate leads inevitably to crises. And the greater the scale of past accumulation, the deeper the crises will be.

Although Marx associates falling rate of profit with the internal dynamics of capitalism, its relation to the breakout of crises is not explicit. He argues that the tendency of the rate of profit to fall makes capital accumulation vulnerable to crises. However, Marx does not formulate a direct link between the tendency for the rate of profit to fall and the necessity for crisis, because the tendency for the rate of profit to fall is defined only at the most abstract level of internal relations of capital, while the tendency to crisis is only realized in concrete relationships between particular capitals expressed in the sphere of competition. Thus he does not elaborate how and under what concrete conditions crisis can break out during this process.

However, Marx recognized that just a fall in the rate of profit is not enough to trigger a crisis because it is still worth reinvesting capital, rather than leaving it to lie idle, even if the rate of profit has fallen, as long as the rate of profit is still positive. Thus the link between a fall in the rate of profit and the tendency to crisis is not direct. Some authors, for example, relate this link to the emergence of disproportionalities. There can be two tendencies in the change of disproportionalities during the process of falling rate of profit. First, new technological innovations can disrupt the connection between branches of production, namely the connection between the branch of means of production and branch of means of subsistence. For example there can be a relative increase in the demand for means of production and a relative fall in the demand for means of subsistence. Second, a fall in the rate of profit will itself induce disproportionalities as capital shifts into speculative channels, inflating the demand for particular commodities. This eventually ends up with a collapse. Hence the key link between falling profitability and economic crisis seems to be finance. In recent years, more intensively, Marxians have started to emphasize the role of financialization in recent crises. In fact, the credit market plays a crucial role in Marx's crisis theory because it is the credit system that forces overproduction and speculation to their extreme limits.

Therefore it is argued that Marx's interest in the credit system shows that his crisis theory is not a shortcut relation between a fall in the rate of profit and the emergence of a crisis. He argues that the rate of accumulation falls together with the rate of profit, but he does not assert that the fall in the rate of accumulation is a direct cause of an economic crisis. This mainly originates from his distinction between crisis (a rupture in the process of capital accumulation) and stagnation (continuing low or negative growth states of any economy). The business cycle consists of periods of moderate activity, prosperity, overproduction, crisis and stagnation, or periods of average activity, production at high pressure, crisis, and stagnation. A fall in the rate of accumulation can directly cause a fall in the rate of growth of output, but the fall in the rate of accumulation must be mediated by other factors in order to result in a crisis. Thus, Marx argued that a decline in the rate of profit leads indirectly to a crisis by encouraging speculation and overproduction.

As a mainstream economist Keynes expressed similar thoughts on falling profits. He argued that marginal efficiency of capital would eventually fall over time. His explanation for this is simply based on his overall marginalist approach. An increasing amount of capital will create less marginal return, and thus marginal contribution of each extra unit of capital falls. This continues until the marginal cost of capital equals its marginal contribution. This results in abundance of capital. Keynes does not complain about that because he thinks that the abundance of capital will lead to what he called the euthanasia of the rentier. They will not get unearned profit in excess of costs due to the abundance of capital, that is, capital is no longer scarce.

Post-Keynesian economics, represented mainly by Michał Kalecki, Joan Robinson and Nicholas Kaldor, also emphasized the tendencies in the rate of profits. However, their approach diverged from Marx's version of the declining profits hypothesis. They drew attention to stagnation (including falling profits) in the overall economies due to the concentration and centralization of capital, and thus industries were dominated by oligopolies. Hence there would not be harsh competition that drew the profits of capitalists downward as Marx assumed.

6.6 Empirical evidence on the falling rate of profit

As we mentioned earlier, Marx's theory on the falling rate of profit is an abstract explanation of general trends in the capitalist system. Therefore it is difficult to observe their apparent and concrete results in the real world because other factors are likely to be involved in this process. In fact, Marx does not claim that there is an inevitable secular trend of profits. He talks about counteracting effects. The rate of profit is not only affected by technology but also by the result of the class struggle over surplus value. Capitalists try to prevent fall in profits using various methods such as lowering wages, reducing cost of constant capital (capital-saving technologies) and increasing productivity of labor (labor-saving technologies). Nevertheless, the theory of crisis rooted in the tendency of the rate of profit to fall suggests that such policies cannot ultimately be successful.

Now our concern here is how these diverging explanations in the falling rate of profit debate have been compatible with the empirical data. The question is: Did the rate of profit indeed fall, or was it restored? The results of empirical studies mainly depend on the definitions and statistics that economists use. For instance, estimation of profits for diverse firms such as non-financial and financial firms will be different; how do we estimate the value of capital, over a short-term or a historical period of time; do we use annual turnover or a longer period for estimation of profits; do we include only private firms or all firms including public firms in estimating profits? Hence narrowing or broadening content and time change profit levels.

There are several methods utilized to estimate long-term trends in profit rates. But these methods do not use the same measurement definitions; for instance, their measuring methods used for fixed capital vary. Information obtained from firms and governments is also problematic. For example, firms, due to paying less tax, understate their profits to officials or they overstate their profits because of their desire to increase the value of their shares or borrowing capacity.

Despite all the differences in these definitions and estimations mentioned above, some groups of economists who are mainly Marxian (such as Fred Moseley, Anwar Shaikh and Ahmet Tonak, Gerard Duménil and Dominique

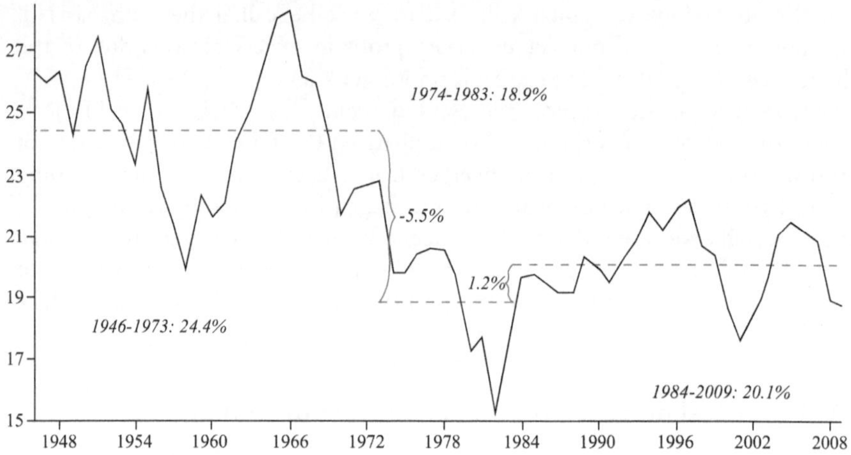

Figure 6.2 Long-term dynamics of the general profit rate. US, 1946–2009 (%). Source: Camara (2009).

Lévy, Robert Brenner, Edwin Wolff, and Duncan Foley) have all come to very similar conclusions, which show that there is a tendency for the rate of profit to fall. In fact, among many economists including non-Marxians, there is consensus that the rate of profit declined during the period from late 1960 to early 1980 but it recovered after the early 1980s.

In this sense we have two important periods that had different trends in profits. The first period runs from the end of Second World War until the 1970s crisis. This period is also called the Keynesian period. The second period includes the period from the 1970s crisis to the present, namely the neoliberal period. Camara (2009), using the definition of rate of profits—the ratio of total surplus value of the economy in total capital used in production—estimates that during the period 1950–1973, which is the first period, the profit rate in the US was high, averaging 24% (Figure 6.2). However, the rate of profits fell in the second half of the 1960s and the 1970s. Furthermore, in the early 1980s, the rate of profit fell to a value of 15%. During the period 1974–1983, the average rate of profit was about 19%. This means a fall of approximately 5% in comparison to the period from the Second World War until 1974.

During the second period, spanning from the 1970s until the present, the average profit rate improved, increasing to around 20%. This average rate is 1.2% higher than the one in the 1970s. However, compared with the first period, the average profit during the liberal period, starting in the 1980s until now, was lower, about 4.3%. Hence it can be described as a lower profitability period than the Keynesian period.

Camara (2009) also shows that as seen in Figure 6.3, there is a similar trend between the general rate of profit and the productivity of capital although the productivity of capital (output/capital) is less volatile than the rate of profit

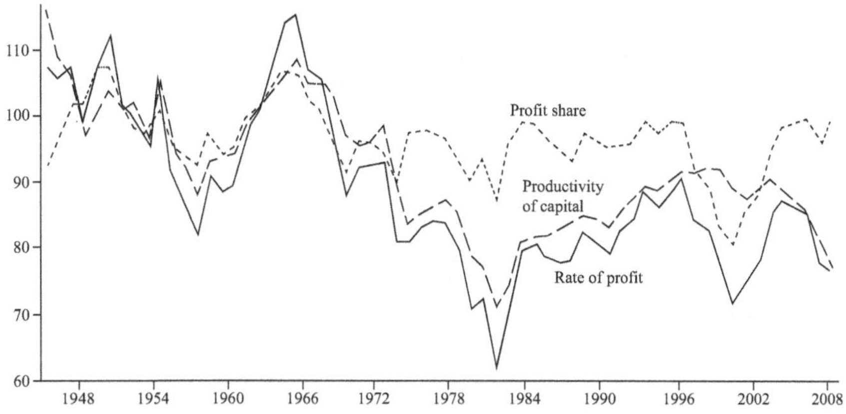

Figure 6.3 The general rate of profit, productivity of capital, and profit share.
Source: Camara (2009).

(profit/capital). This implies that productivity of capital mainly shaped the rate of profits even though there was an impact by short-term fluctuations in the profit share on the rate of profit[4].

In calculations by Camara (2009), when two periods are compared, namely the periods 1946–1973 and 1974–1983, the decline in the rate of profit between the two periods is explained mainly by the fall in the productivity of capital, about 78%. The remaining part of the decline, which is 22%, originates from the fall in profit share. Hence the largest component in explaining the fall in the rate of profit is the technological component, as suggested by the argument of the tendency of the rate of profit to fall. The recovery of the general rate of profit during the neoliberal period was also generated by the productivity of capital, accounting for 84% of the increase in profits. Profit share explains just 16% of the increase in profits.

In a study by Duménil and Lévy (2011), they examined the data in the US and concluded that the trend of profits, thus its rising or falling, depends on how it is defined and measured. According to them, if dividends are not included in profits, profit rate declined. In contrast, if it is added, profit rate shows a rise since the 1980s, even though not at the levels of the 1950s and 1960s. But if profits are calculated by subtracting corporate taxes, their levels were restored even to the levels of the 1950s and 1960s. Hence the fall in rate of profit is largely related to the fact that corporations paid more of their profits as dividends to shareholders. Various more recent calculations by scholars such as Moseley, Shaikh, Tonak and Wolff all reached the same result that rate of profits declined. But they argue that this mainly originated from an increased capital–labor ratio. This is compatible with Marx's view that increasing capital–labor ratio lowers profits (Harman, 2010).

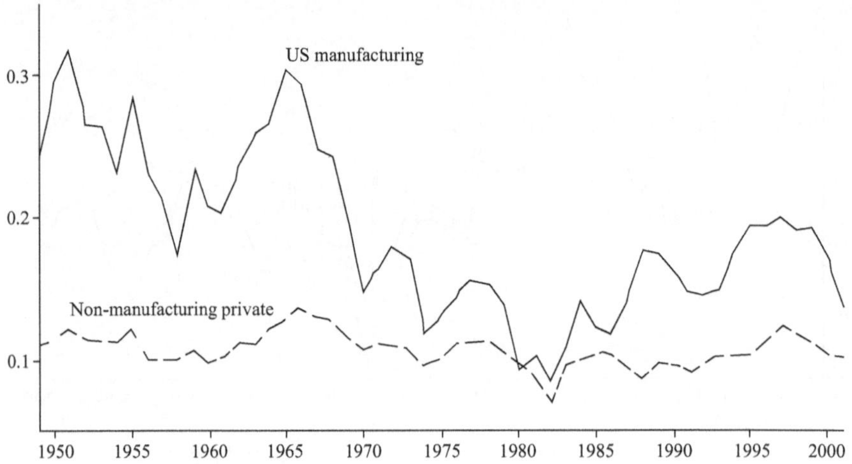

Figure 6.4 US manufacturing and non-manufacturing private net profit rates.
Source: Brenner (2006).

There were other attempts to explain the decline in profitability in the 1970s resulting from a wave of workers' struggles internationally which had forced up workers' share of total income and had reduced the share going to capital. This view is in fact in parallel with profit squeeze theory. However, this explanation is not enough to understand why all the Western economies moved into crisis at the same point in the mid-1970s. There were improvements in the living conditions of workers in England, Italy and France in the late 1960s and early 1970s. But there were no such improvements, for example, in Germany.

According to Robert Brenner (2006), the trend in the general rate of profits is shaped by the weighted average rate of profits of all industries in an economy. Thus, the weighted average rate of profits of the manufacturing and non-manufacturing industries forms the general rate of profit. Their rates of profit are independent of the general rate of profit. Brenner primarily looks at the manufacturing sector. He explains the falling rate of profit in this sector with the entry of Japan and Germany to the US market that created significant competition in the 1960s. This caused excess capacity in the manufacturing sector worldwide, especially in the US. In other words, monopolistic profits in the US declined sharply. Figure 6.4 shows this.

Brenner also proposed explanations for why overcapacity in manufacturing has continued for decades even though firms in this sector could not recover their profits. He gives various reasons for this: (1) the existence of large fixed capital of these firms prevented them from exiting the market easily (2) these firms, in order to avert foreign competition, resorted to developing higher technology to reduce their costs. This in turn increased excess capacity further

(3) in the 1980s, and along with the entry of new Asian countries such as South Korea and Taiwan, the world's overcapacity in some manufacturing industries (like automobile and steel) expanded further.

However, according to Mosley, Brenner's view does not explain the association between the trends in the rate of profits in manufacturing and the whole economy. Moseley (1999, p.9) mentioned this as follows:

> Marx's theory, on the other hand, is based on essentially the opposite assumption regarding the order of determination between the general rate of profit and the individual sectoral rates of profit. Marx's theory assumes that the general rate of profit is determined prior to and independent of the sectoral rates of profit, and is determined by aggregate features of the economy as whole (mainly the total amount of surplus labor in the economy as a whole). The deviations of individual rates of profit (e.g. the manufacturing rate of profit) from the general rate of profit are then determined (according to Marx's theory) by the relative proportions of supply and demand.

Moseley (1999) sees the similarities between Brenner's theory and that of Baran and Sweezy. Both approaches assume that the level of competition in the economy determines tendencies in rate of profit. Baran and Sweezy proposed that since the monopolistic power of the firms in the early post-war period was high, the rate of profit was large. In line with this, Brenner elaborates that especially after the mid-1960s the rate of profit declined due to increasing competition in the US. Mosley says that these two approaches are in essence the same approach. Their main difference is associated with the fact that they look at different periods having different degrees of competition. Both approaches emphasize level of competition. However, Mosley stresses that the general rate of profit in an economy is not determined by the intensity of competition. It only accounts for the share of profits among firms, not the general rate of profits. As in Marx, the total surplus value with respect to total capital in the economy determines the general rate of profit in the economy.

Meanwhile we should mention that both Brenner and Moseley as Marxist economists criticized the use of the theory of profit squeeze to explain the fall in the rate of profit. According to them, the main shortcoming of this theory is that it is not adequate at explaining why the rate of profit remained low for so long. It is able to explain the fall in profits in 1960s and 1970s by the increased power of unions because of declining unemployment. But it is unable to explain the slow and partial recovery of profits since the 1970s despite the increasing unemployment that weakened the power of the unions.

When looking at the US economy in more detail, we can see some counter-tendencies against falling profits, especially after the mid-1980s. According to the US Bureau of Economic Analysis data, profit rate reached its highest level in 1950 (22%), but it fell drastically to 3% in 1986. It rose back

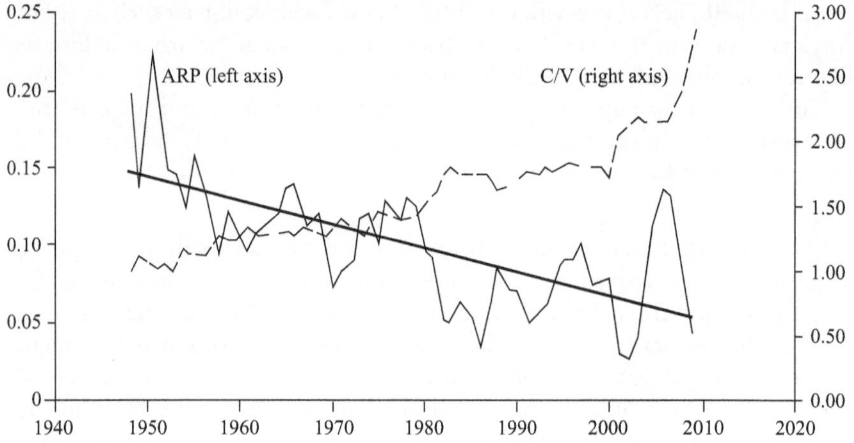

Figure 6.5 Average rate of profit (ARP) and composition of capital (C/V) of the US productive sectors, 1950–2009.
Source: Damen (2012).

to 14% in 2006 but again it fell back to its downward trend in 2009, to the level of 5% (Damen, 2012).

Damen (2012) shows that, as seen in Figure 6.5, average rate of profit declined in a downward trend while organic composition of capital went up. This is compatible with the hypothesis of tendency of rate of profit to fall. However, since the second trough of 1986 the rate of profit started to rise. Here it seems that some strong and longstanding counter-tendencies existed. Improvements in new technologies have been one of the important factors that created this counter-tendency. Rate of profit can be increased at least in the short run by lowering the values of constant and variable capital that lead to a fall in organic composition of capital. However, the effect of technology is transitory rather than permanent. That is, increased organic composition dominated rate of profit in a downward sense despite the positive impact of technology on profits.

Starting in the 1980s, there has been a stagnation of wages despite large increases in labor productivity. This helped firms to increase their profits. In addition to this development, firms have relocated their production via globalization since the 1980s. They shifted from places with higher capital intensity to those with lower capital intensity. This also implies a migration of production from places with higher labor cost to those with lower labor cost.

In addition to these developments, as mentioned previously in this book, productive capital had started to engage in speculative activities since 1980. This reached very excessive levels. Since non-financial firms have had some difficulties due to their declining profits, they have shifted to the financial sphere where profits have been more lucrative. This led both to the shift of productive capital to more speculative areas and to increasing financialization. As many studies show, profit rate and share of the financial sector have been rising in many countries since 1980 (for this see Chapter 3). This was the beginning of the financialization that kept increasing dramatically until 2007, when the economic system collapsed.

6.7 Concluding remarks

This chapter focuses on Marxian structural approaches that include the tendency of the rate of profit to fall, profit squeeze and the social structure of accumulation. Their main argument is that economic crises must be analyzed in the context of structural trends such as profitability and capital accumulation.

Marxian economic theory has some definite perspectives on the development of recessions and crises. Capitalist economies contain class conflicts, where capital's main objective is to maximize its profit and this occurs at the expense of labor. This is the source of capital accumulation. The reproduction of capitalism is provided by the incessant expansion of capital. Therefore, the structural foundations of profitability signal the soundness of the economy.

The tendency of the rate of profit to fall hypothesis is the most common perspective in the Marxist literature. From this perspective, economic crises are unavoidable because they are not caused by factors that are external. The falling rate of profit is instead rooted in the internal mechanisms of capitalism that incessantly induce firms to seek profit.

Marx and Marxists mostly consider crisis at the level of an abstract model of capitalism in which there can be inherent tendencies such as underconsumptionism, falling rate of profit, overproduction, disproportionality among different production departments, or profit squeeze. However, it is extremely hard to use empirical studies to search for the validity of arguments regarding these hypotheses due to measurement issues, diverse definitions and several counteracting tendencies in a dynamic economic structure.

Today most of the leading Marxists have, in contrast to Marx, seen crises as multidimensional and more complex. They cannot be reduced to one dimension as did the hypothesis of the rate of profit to fall. They argue that crises have gained a periodic character in the last two centuries along with evolution of capitalism. But their causes change depending on the changing dynamic of capitalist relationships. Hence they prefer to use a multi-causal approach to help them to understand deeper underlying causes, and the concrete manifestation of crises. For example, concerning the global crisis of 2007–2008, these Marxists mainly point out that the tendency of rate of profit to decline hypothesis is of little relevance. They draw attention instead to financialization and inequalities.

Notes

1 The distinction between constant and variable capital originates from the idea of Marx that asserts that only living labor (namely variable capital) creates new value, varying the value of the product. But constant capital (inputs, machineries used in

the production) do not by themselves add new value to output, or increase in value in the production process.

2 Co-respective competition was introduced by Joseph Schumpeter to capture the behavior by a company which avoids cutthroat competition in favor of competitors. This is a strategy to reduce corporate risk and is in direct conflict with the values of liberal ideology which emphasize competition.

3 The Japanese economist Nobuo Okishio (Okishio's theorem) argued that, if the newly introduced technique satisfies the cost criterion (i.e. if it reduces unit costs, given current prices) and the rate of real wage remains constant, then the rate of profit must increase. Assuming constant real wages, technical change would lower the production cost per unit, thereby raising the innovator's rate of profit.

4 The long-term dynamics of profitability can be further depicted by the decomposition of the general rate of profit (Π/K) between its distributive and technological components, the profit share (Π/Y) and the productivity of capital (Y/K), respectively, where Π is the surplus value, K is the capital in production, and Y is the new value created: $(\Pi/K) = (\Pi/Y)(Y/K)$.

7 Human behavior

7.1 Introduction

People act in an economic and social sphere by trying to understand the things around them. Their actions result from a combination of certain cognition, motives and emotions. In this sense, they prefer to cooperate or compete with each other, and trust or distrust each other.

Individual behavior is dynamic, endogenously influenced by the environment in which people participate. There is always an interactive connection between their sentiments and the outcomes realized in their economic or social environment. They behave differently from the typical "rational actors" depicted in economics.

Since the human factor is analyzed in mechanistic terms in mainstream economics, it does not contain much of a psychological element. The individuals in neoclassical economic models are abstract and primarily motivated by selfish motives. Behavioral economists regard this sort of modeling of human behavior as a significant failure. In fact, people have more complicated personalities. Their decision-making process is mostly under the influence of psychological factors rather than rationality. Therefore assumptions regarding behavioral biases should be incorporated into economic models to capture the tendencies in real human behavior. Nowadays many economists have started to assert that realistic economic analysis is beyond neoclassical reasoning, and thereby they integrate insights from behavioral economics that emphasize heuristic biases and cognitive issues.

Particularly with the global crisis of 2007–2008, many scholars recognized the importance of behavioral biases as a contributing factor to the crisis. Furthermore, they focused more on historic episodes of destabilizing speculation. They draw attention to the point that phrases used in the literature during previous crises can help us see the importance of psychology: manias, blind passion, financial frenzies, feverish speculation, insane land speculation, intoxicated investors, overtrading, overconfidence etc. All these expressions have been widely used across space and time during times of crises. And they imply the behavioral component of crises regardless of country and period.

In this chapter, I aim to search how psychology can be a contributing factor to financial crises using the methodology of behavioral economics and search for its relevance to crises in the past, especially the global recession of 2007–2008.

7.2 Behavioral economics

In this section, I will present a brief history of behavioral economics. The foundations of behavioral economics are based on the studies of Daniel Bernoulli (1738), who was concerned with the St. Petersburg paradox and relative utility notions[1]. Bernoulli developed the concept of utility that describes the fact that individuals can have different perceptions for the same amount of money. In line with the same behavioral insights, Herbert Simon (1955) developed the concept of "bounded rationality". With it he tried to show the boundaries of rationality and the prevalence of heuristics in the decision-making processes of individuals and also questioned the validity of optimizing behavior.

Oskar Morgenstern and John von Neumann in the 1940s had developed the notion of "expected utility" upon which rational agents base their decisions to maximize their utility under uncertainty. However, in the 1950s, Maurice Allais developed various arguments against the validity of expected utility theory. In this context he—with the help of experiments—tried to prove that individuals' behavior was not always rational, thus not performing consistently with the concept of expected utility.

In the 1970s, Daniel Kahneman and Amos Tversky evidenced similar results. Their approach is called "prospect theory". They focused on human behavior under uncertainty. The striking results they obtained made behavioral economics the new approach in economic thought. Both of these scholars recognize two approaches in economics: normative (rational) and descriptive (irrational, subjective). Using the descriptive approach, Kahneman and Tversky elaborated that economic behavior of individuals contains a non-rational way of thinking. George Akerlof (Nobel Prize in 2001) and Robert Shiller (Nobel Prize in 2013) wrote an important book titled *Animal Spirit* in 2009 to develop behavioral insights to analyze human behavior and its role in economic decision-making processes. In this sense they focus on behavioral trends that trigger or amplify crises, especially in the global crisis of 2007.

7.3 Neoclassical economics and behavioral economics

The neoclassical economic approach has dominated academic research on human interaction. The main argument of the neoclassical approach is that we as human beings are rational. In line with this assumption, we maximize our expected utility given a set of information. The first fundamental theorem of welfare economics asserts that decentralized competitive markets for current and future goods will ensure optimality given initial endowments. In these markets, the formation of prices occurs in line with the efficient market hypothesis, which suggests that people form unbiased and correct on-average expectations and so people do not make systematic errors and naturally excessive returns will not emerge.

Homo economicus as defined by neoclassical economics has some strange features. Equipped with immense computing abilities, they spends their time weighing different opportunities in an effort to maximize their utility, using wide knowledge of their environment in the process. To do this, homo economicus uses all available information to form beliefs regarding future states of affairs following different events or courses of actions, updating those beliefs in a Bayesian manner as new information emerges. This rational person uses their subjective probability distributions to evaluate the probability of the occurrence of events. They then follows a stable set of preferences to determine which alternative courses of action gives them the most satisfaction. Similar to this stability assumption (ergodicity), many researchers question why the market efficiency theory of neoclassical economics is widely used in economics. They think that one of the important reasons behind this is the ease of applying economic modeling. On the same lines, Herbert Simon mentions that otherwise the use of quasi-rational agents in these models would become very complicated. This is why mainstream economists have avoided modeling complicated and uncertain environments with more realistic agents.

Several features of the rational man are different from ordinary human beings. For example, their computing abilities go beyond that of ordinary humans. But it is hard to believe that people solve intricate optimization problems when they make decisions. Rather, actions appear to be motivated by customs, habits, rules of thumb, impulses, and emotional responses. The way that homo economicus deals with uncertainty is also problematic. The fact that he/she is able to form complete subjective probability distributions over future events implies that they essentially face a gamble, a lottery with different levels of risk, rather than actual uncertainty about the future. Hence, this representation implies that there exists an objective probability distribution that is in principle knowable. However, this assumption is very exaggerated given the complexity of the economy. In fact, agents in the economy are thus facing a future that is fundamentally uncertain and which prevents them from relying on objective probabilities to make judgments about the future. Due to this uncertainty, Keynes thought that people primarily make decisions taking into account past experience and rules of thumb, not objective probabilities that do not exist at all.

Behavioral economics presents a perspective for explaining human behavior in different contexts. In this way, behavioral economics provides a great deal of evidence regarding heuristics and biases in human behavior that systematically deviate from rationality. These sorts of violations mainly stem from various heuristic biases, faulty reasoning and complexity of making decisions. Mainstream economics interprets such actions as irrational and defines them as anomalies. However, since these sorts of actions are persistent and continuously verified by observations, it is hard to classify them as anomalies and ignore them.

These developments have increased interest in the subject of behavioral economics. Economists have begun to emphasize the anomalies seen persistently and commonly in the economic domain and tried to explain them with reference to psychological insights. They recognize that human behavior cannot be regarded as a "black box" that is not interested in the process of behavior but just outcomes. However, it becomes clearer that we need to understand the cognitive processes that drive human behavior, thus opening up the black box. This will provide us with more psychological insights to refine economic theory and this will facilitate our understanding of human behavior and individuals' choice behavior.

In this sense, in recent decades behavioral economics has more greatly benefited from the concepts and observations of psychologists, as compared to the past. One of these crucial notions is the cognitive modes regarding which psychologists have accumulated much evidence. These are the intuitive and the analytic modes. While the intuitive mode corresponds to the cases in which people make judgments and decisions fast, the analytic mode captures the cases in which people make judgments and decisions more slowly. Kahneman (2003) defines these modes as System 1 (intuition) and System 2 (reason) respectively. Behavioral economics and finance particularly focused on the functioning of System 1. This can help to understand some tendencies in individuals' choices. Research within this literature has evidenced and analyzed several behavioral phenomena that contradict economic rationality. However, it is in System 2 that neoclassical economics uses analytical or rational information processes due to its assumption of the rational economic actor.

7.4 Behavioral and psychological biases in economics

When human behavior in situations of choice or risk is studied, the picture that emerges is quite different from homo economicus. Rather than making use of complex optimization techniques, even implicitly, human beings appear to develop a whole set of habits and principles to process information in order to solve problems or formulate judgments, hereafter referred to as heuristics. People usually use heuristics to make their decisions because most of the time they do not have enough time and resources for this. They use mental shortcuts. However, in this case they can sometimes make mistakes or show cognitive biases. Some of the numerous heuristics defined in this chapter seem relevant to the study of financial markets and crises. Now we will explain them in short below.

(i) Loss aversion, disposition effect and endowment effect

An individual is called loss averse if he/she seems to dislike losing something more than they like gaining it. This phenomenon emerges in several contexts in real life. Prospect theory explains loss aversion in terms of an individual's value function for money that is concave for gains and convex for losses. This implies that individuals are more concerned with losses than gains of similar size. Figure 7.1 displays this case. As seen in the figure, there is a reference point, against which people assess their gains and losses. In this sense, the value function takes an asymmetric S-shape due to its declining sensitivity (marginal utility) when there is an increase in gains and losses.

The disposition effect is related to loss aversion. It describes the case in which people keep holding their assets even when their prices fall. That is, they are less willing to sell their assets in cases of adverse price movements in their assets with respect to positive movements. In other words, they are risk-averse in profit, risk-loving in loss. This is usually observed in the housing sector. During financial crises, when a housing bubble bursts, home owners are generally reluctant to sell their houses even if they expect that house prices will fall further. This is more likely to emerge from the fact that they take the purchase price of the home as a reference point and do not want to suffer a loss, that is, a feeling of loss.

In fact, for rational individuals, the current price and its trend would be critical rather than its purchase price. But, on the contrary, many experiments found that people do not act in this way; they mainly consider the purchase price as a reference point rather than the current price or its tendency. This explains why the prices of houses do not fall dramatically during crises. This is reason for price stickiness in housing markets. This seemingly irrational behavior constrains further falls in house prices. But during boom periods, the prices of houses can rise significantly via policies of low interest rates and little government intervention even if purchasers and mortgage lenders start to think that these prices are excessive. A similar behavior is also observed in financial markets. For example, when the prices of stocks fall, people wait for their prices to rise for a long time rather than cutting their losses, but during price increases they sell them more quickly.

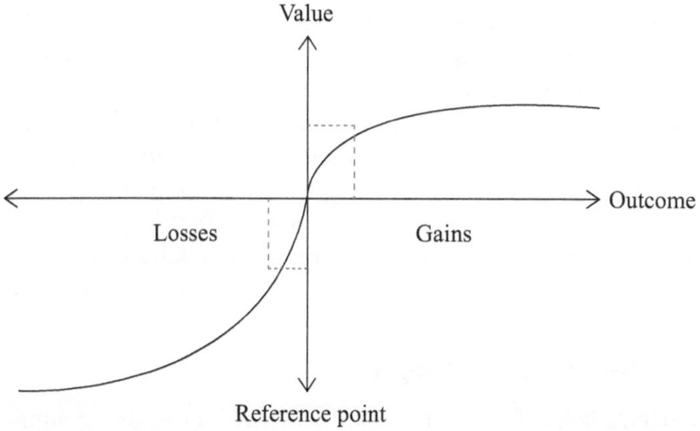

Figure 7.1 Value function.

Another state closely related to loss aversion is the endowment effect. The endowment effect addresses the tendency of individuals to offer higher prices for products (financial or non-financial) that they own than for products that they do not. This is not consistent with what mainstream economics says; namely that what people are willing to pay for a good should be equal to what they are willing to accept to be deprived of it. Empirical and experimental studies do not verify this argument. They show that people in general want a higher price to part with something they have.

(ii) Framing, anchoring and status quo effects

The way in which economic or non-economic options are presented is influential on what people choose. This is called the framing effect. Individual choices are significantly affected by how the relevant information is presented or framed. People change their responses depending on how the information is presented to them. For example, when something is offered to people in terms of rate of return as a percentage or absolute return, people respond differently even if they receive the same level of return in monetary terms.

A similar concept to the framing effect is the anchoring effect. This points to cases in which the way people appraise their options depends on the initial value, that is, the anchor. For instance, when realtors are asked to value the same property, their valuations change depending on the arbitrary anchor values presented to them. In financial markets we also observe this anchoring effect especially in the way investors in financial markets use statistics in evaluating the returns of assets. Investors generally are under the influence of past performance of financial assets even though statistics show that past performance is no guide to likely future returns. However, when such data that shows past performance is readily available, many investors cannot avoid using this information when investing.

We have another term related to anchoring, which is "status quo bias". It describes why people are present-biased, and thus why they do not change current choices too much. It seems that individuals keep up with current or status quo choices because it requires more mental effort to change them. Moreover in cases where people do not have a current choice, the default option becomes important in guiding choice. For example, when a free subscription for a definite period is offered to customers, they usually remain subscribed, not preferring to cancel. They stay with the default case. The default option is an important part of what has been termed "choice architecture", which encapsulates how choices are framed, or presented, to individuals. Choice architecture is used by firms or governments to direct and manipulate individual choices.

(iii) Cognitive dissonance and regret

Cognitive dissonance is another psychological bias that is crucial in guiding the behavior of individuals. It points to the case in which people face conflicting cases when their beliefs are not consistent with evidence. To handle this feeling of discomfort, they adopt irrational attitudes. For example, they disregard new information, or they look for new ways of convincing themselves regarding undesirable things that they keep doing, or they focus on the positive sides of what they do. New car buyers, for instance, look at advertisements or news about the car they bought rather than advertisements or news about other cars they did not purchase, selectively choosing to ignore them.

Behavioral finance defines this bias as a state of regret, explaining empirical research findings such as how investors often postpone selling stocks when prices fall in order to avoid feeling regret at having made errors. Thus investors do not want to sell their assets even if they make a loss, because they do not want to think that they made a bad investment.

(iv) Hyperbolic discounting tendency

People make intertemporal decisions on current and delayed outcomes. To do this, they use discounted values of future returns supported by a discounting rate that represents the time preference of individuals; namely the degree of willingness of immediate return versus delayed return. People generally prefer the sooner reward to the later reward for the same valued outcomes. People discount future rewards by a factor that increases with the length of delay. This is the conventionally used exponential discounting.

However, recent studies show that there are several deviations from exponential discounting. Individuals use alternative discounting methods. One of these is hyperbolic discounting. Hyperbolic discounting indicates that people's valuations fall relatively rapidly for earlier delay periods, but then fall more slowly for longer delay periods. For instance, "Would you prefer a dollar today or two dollars tomorrow?" or "Would you prefer a dollar in one year or two dollars in one year and one day?" Empirical studies show that a significant portion of people will take the lesser amount today, but will gladly wait one extra day in a year in order to receive the higher amount instead.

These individuals are defined as present-biased, and thus undervalue the future in comparison to the present. Now is more valuable than tomorrow. However, those biased with this feature frequently experience the sense of regret. They postpone currently undesirable actions and plan to do them in the future, but when the time comes to do them, it becomes difficult to actualize them. For example, when people received subprime mortgages, they initially preferred to benefit from teaser rates and intended to reduce their consumption and save more in the future. However, when the due date comes, it becomes hard to achieve that.

(v) Representativeness and availability effects

The representativeness heuristic is frequently employed in making judgments. People use the prototypes (representative figures in their minds) in assessing probabilities of events. These are taken as reference points to evaluate the events they face. Individuals overestimate the probabilities of events that are memorable. They disregard prior probability and sample size in favor of prototype, and moreover they neglect the phenomenon of regression to the mean. However, this creates a problem because people disregard base rates, and hence tend to extrapolate upward or downward. For example, representativeness can lead to lengthening upswings and downturns in financial markets due to a rapid change in expectations if some outcomes that deviate from the trend are regarded as representative. When people rely on representativeness to make judgments, they are likely to judge wrongly because the fact that something is more representative does not actually make it more likely. This heuristic is used because it is an easy computation. The problem is that people overestimate its ability to accurately predict the likelihood of an event. Thus it can result in neglect of relevant base rates and other cognitive biases.

These behavioral features are also reinforced by another class of heuristics, which is the availability effect. Subjective probability assessments are usually made with respect to events that come to mind easily. The salience of past events depends on their proximity such as spatially, chronologically, emotionally, etc. For instance, traumatic events are more easily remembered and new information is generally used to evaluate events. This heuristic is also valid among researchers when they make growth forecasts if they are biased to take into account just the current state of the economy or past traumatic crises.

(vi) Overconfidence and confirmation effects

The overconfidence effect is a well-documented psychological bias. People assess events with greater confidence than their objective accuracy. This is another case of a miscalculation of subjective probabilities. This case is widely emphasized in the prospect theory developed by Kahneman and Tversky.

Overconfidence can display itself in four forms: the above-average effect, the calibration effect, illusion of control, and unrealistic optimism. The above-average effect is about the fact that individuals usually think that they perform better than the average, thus overestimating their abilities. Overconfidence also stems from miscalibration—overestimating the probability that their judgments are correct. This can be observed in many professions. For example, financial analysts prefer to follow routine patterns even in more complicated and vague circumstances instead of processing the information and analyzing the case in a more refined manner.

Overconfidence also generates a sense of illusion in controlling surrounding factors. People often believe that their contribution to the occurrence of random events is too high. For example, when they win a lottery, they attribute this to their ability to choose the right ticket. This is, in fact, the self-attribution bias of people. That is, people attribute successes (even random ones) to their capabilities and ignore the effects of events they cannot control, like luck or errors made by other people. Economic agents, for example, assess their gains mostly as the result of their abilities rather than the conditions in the market.

Overconfidence also leads to ungrounded and unrealistic optimism. People usually cannot complete their plans as they program, and thus time to finish a project is improperly defined. Delays usually occur. This manifests itself both in large-scale investments such construction of buildings and infrastructure or in daily events such as shopping and car washing. Moreover people do not learn from previous mistakes. They still unrealistically believe that they will do better next time. As Montgomery (1997) showed, macroeconomic predictions by researchers were highly underestimated especially for unfavorable variables (unemployment, inflation) and highly overestimated for favorable variables (growth) when compared with their realized values.

The confirmation effect is to some extent related to overconfidence. People tend to confirm what they believe; they are more inclined to get information that verifies what they think. They disregard information or facts that contradict their beliefs. They stick to their wrong beliefs and even reinforce them, demonstrating overconfidence at the same time. For example, in the years preceding the 2007–2008 crisis, people underestimated risks and avoided signals that contradicted their beliefs due to unrealistic optimism. Confirmation bias prevented people from seeing certain warning signals that could have eroded investors' faith in the never-ending bull market. Along with the self-attribution effect, many market players attributed profits gained primarily to their own skills rather than to the general market situation. Investment successes intensified their confidence and encouraged them to take even higher risks.

(vii) Herding behavior

Social psychology evidences that social pressure forces individuals in the same way that others do. For example, if people see someone running toward a train, they feel a pressure to run as well. Social pressure is valid even in absurd cases, particularly in cases where sufficiently large groups act similarly. This conforming behavior to others is called herding behavior.

Herding behavior is employed in particular to understand movements in asset prices. This is because only mistakes in common at the macro level can affect the direction of asset prices. Individuals look at each other while making investments—that is, imitate each other—rather than looking at the fundamentals. They keep making investments by disregarding the fact that the assets were already mispriced. This resembles Keynes's animal spirit concept, which includes the spreading of irrational exuberance or pessimism in an economy.

In behavioral finance, for example, there is a common tendency to follow other people's actions, especially investment decisions. New investors follow a group of other investors whose number sufficiently increase, even when their predictions of the prices of stock exchanges or other assets clearly turn out to be wrong. People start to think that the prices of assets will go up because other people are participating in the market. Since prices become higher, this pushes prices to much higher values. Therefore it seems rational to follow others. This process works as a self-fulfilling prophecy. Into this frenzy, financial analysts also enter. They advise and publish reports to encourage other investors not to miss lucrative opportunities. Their motivation may be associated with the fear of loss of reputation if they make assessments against the general market consensus. This amplifies the investment spiral in the economy. For example, before the global crisis that broke out in 2007, almost nobody—including professionals and non-professionals—had doubts about risk models; but now it is widespread among everybody to doubt risk management practices.

(viii) Fear and greed

Two sentiments are also critical in determining and directing people's actions in economies and other areas. These are the fear and greed that have opposing effects on investors' behavior. The degree of risk aversion depends on which feeling becomes dominant. If fear dominates, people's risk aversion goes up; in contrast, if people become more greedy, their risk aversion declines sharply and they take on more risk. While fear dominates during crises, greed increases during booms. During times of panic in markets, assets are sold at fire-sale prices; that is, at lower prices than their values, generating a great deal of loss. These fire sales can also trigger various problems leading to widespread bankruptcies in the economy. During booms, greed motivates investors to take on more risk. This blinds investors, and the level of risk they take on is often forgotten in the middle of the frenzy. People focus on profits rather than loss. They ignore diversification of their investments. Risk is often forgotten in the midst of the chase after higher and higher rates of return.

7.5 Reinterpretation of financial crises: behavioral biases

It is generally accepted that a bubble is an episode in which irrational thinking or behavioral biases cause the price of an asset to rise to a level that is higher than it would be in the absence of the biases or the irrationality. The fact that a bubble may have played a critical role in recent global crises has led many observers to call for more research on why and how bubbles form. There are several behavioral explanations which try to explain why an asset has grown wildly.

However, as mentioned at different points within this book, the financial hypotheses of neoclassical economics are too focused on the actions of investors; one of these is the "efficient market hypothesis" (EMH). The main argument of this hypothesis is that all asset prices are rationally and efficiently valued and all prices reflect all relevant information about fundamentals. Therefore bubbles cannot occur. This hypothesis allowed economists and practitioners in the market to disregard the danger of inflated assets in the global crisis of 2007–2008. Moreover they were more concerned with profits from increases in house prices and underestimated the probability of a collapse in prices. They did not believe in the fact that there would eventually be a bubble. Therefore, to some extent, it can be said that belief in efficient markets led financial actors to overlook the real estate bubble.

In fact, there is a great deal of evidence that contradicts the efficient market hypothesis and this has been ever-increasing in recent years. These empirical observations are compatible with the main arguments of behavioral finance. It seems that even though there are some rational investors in the market their number or power are not enough to correct prices. Cumulative processes are natural market processes and bubbles in financial markets are likely to occur. As Krugman (2009) argues, *"many real-world investors bear little resemblance to the cool calculators of efficient market theory: they're all too subject to herd behavior, to bouts of irrational exuberance and unwarranted panic*". Hence behavioral economists stress that financial crises will always exist if humans behave like humans.

Behavioral economics develops a theory of asset price bubbles. One of the findings of behavioral economics is that asset prices do not reflect fundamentals. Furthermore, the change in the long-term trend of market prices does not reflect the change in the trend of fundamentals. Hence the role of fundamentals in pricing remains vague. People do not act compatibly with the assumptions of neoclassical economics. Even if rational actors act in parallel to these assumptions, prices may still not reflect the fundamentals due to restrictions on arbitrage processes. Furthermore it is difficult to calculate fundamental values because future cash flows of assets are very complicated to estimate under increased uncertainty.

Mainstream economists and practitioners in the market have understood markets by using the traditional assumptions of rationality, profit maximization, and the efficient market hypothesis. To do this, they used complicated quantitative methods. But this understanding and consistent methods in line with this have been put in doubt because they have not taken into account the role of behaviors, mistakes, biases, fear or greed in their complex methods. Moreover, the complex quantitative models (econometrics, mathematics, tables, statistics, charts, etc.) created an illusion that risk is under control. But the sentiments of people are a crucial component of the decision-making process. It is not easy to keep this component under control. It seems that financial markets always tend to be subject to behavioral biases such as herding, greed, anxiety etc. Nassim Taleb (2007) says that risk models used by financial analysts in Wall Street, no matter how mathematically sophisticated, are bogus. Furthermore, he claims that they have done more harm than good. The reason for this is that the greatest risks are not the ones you can see and measure, but the ones you can't see and therefore can never measure. Hence Taleb is more concerned with the risk of the 1% case event, the so-called "six sigma events", "fat tails", or "black swans". In his view, any system vulnerable to a black swan will eventually explode.

In this sense, many researchers have drawn attention to the shortcoming of the normal distribution model, which is often used in financial analysis. They notice that fat-tailed distributions are the more widespread distributions behind the movements of asset returns frequently found in finance, instead of stable distributions such as normal distribution. Fat-tail distributions of market return also take account of excessive results under excessive optimism and pessimism. In this case, for example, a 5- or 6-sigma event is much more likely than the normal distribution would predict. However, it is hard to model these risks mathematically as modeled in normal distributions because they take into account jumps in "real-world" events (such as a large corporate bankruptcy, or an abrupt change in a political situation). For example, the Black–Scholes option pricing model based on normal distribution is not good at predicting dramatic price movements.

During recent decades, there has been an immense development of the derivatives market, not only in the sense of their increasing volume but also their increasing degree of complexity. Since derivatives contracts are widely occurring over-the-counter markets, it is hard to observe their quantity and the risks burden on markets. The transparency of these financial transactions is very low. That is, it is not clear what affects the price and risk of derivatives. Since their operations are complicated, investors' abilities are not enough to evaluate their pricing. Hence even professional investors use various simplifications and heuristics in assessing financial assets. Even Nobel prize-winning economists have trouble understanding their economy's complex system. The collapse of Long-Term Capital Management (LTCM) in 1998 with two Nobel laureates in economics on its board (Robert Merton and Myron Scholes) serves as a good example[2]. Similarly, portfolio managers can never have complete knowledge of all the stocks and bonds available in the world. Since we face an information overload, we become very selective with the information we acquire. In the words of Henry Kaufman, "*there are two kinds of people who lose money: those who know nothing and those who know everything. With two Nobel prize winners in the house, LTCM clearly fits the second case*" (Forbes, October 19, 1998).

Particularly in the development of housing bubbles, inexperienced and financially unsophisticated individuals play a critical role. Most of them do not have enough financial knowledge to assess the probable risks involved. In people's lives, purchasing a house is their most significant financial transaction. And almost all house prices are bargained individually (rather than on a market system like the stock market); the low frequency of purchases in housing markets is likely to reveal inefficient allocations in these markets. Most people in a housing transaction are inexperienced amateurs and their purchases are based on limited information; for example, they are unable to predict payment difficulties in the future. In this context, the extent of the computational ability of individuals has been analyzed thoroughly. It shows that people have differing cognitive abilities. This situation is in line with the notion of bounded rationality.

The psychological basis of having distorted beliefs is that people rely too much on their ability to make predictions. This overconfidence, a feature commonly seen among investors, has the potential to create the formation and development of financial bubbles in the pre-crisis period. They overestimate their knowledge and abilities and disregard the probable risks and uncontrollable events. They forget the phenomenon that their peers may have the same beliefs in assessing their performance. Overconfidence can be reinforced by positive performances in the past, which increases the degree of recklessness in future decision making, becoming less risk-averse. A fall in risk aversion makes investors buy more assets with more enthusiasm.

When we become overconfident, we always believe, for some reason or another, that history no longer applies to the present situation. When asset prices rise, we try to explain this with fundamentals. When banks become too large in any economy, we explain this through globalization of finance. When countries live beyond their means (i.e. run a massive current-account deficit), we think the reason is higher growth potential (i.e. higher return). But when reality emerges, we come to realize that we have once again overestimated or underestimated. Unfortunately, as soon as the next boom starts rolling, historic lessons are forgotten again and similar arguments will be presented.

The speculative and complicated nature of financial markets also makes them particularly susceptible to overconfidence bias. This enables financial investors to attribute positive returns to their performance and blame other external and noisy factors for their losses. Psychologists argue that overconfidence strengthens psychological anchors, because people tend to believe strongly in stories or reasons. Similarly, Reinhart and Rogoff, in their book *This Time is Different* (2009) assert that individuals usually, with overconfidence, overestimate the possibility of markets to remain stable because of an "invisible balancing hand".

Another behavioral bias, the representativeness heuristic, is also utilized in explaining the emergence of a bubble. According to some economists, bubbles appear because investors explore past results in the future (for example, Greenwood and Hanson, 2010). This is mainly related to the representativeness heuristic. Representativeness, as defined previously, represents situations where people have a tendency to develop a belief about an event or someone depending on its characteristics. Such heuristics cause people to extrapolate the past when making predictions about the future. This was also observed during the global crisis of 2007–2008. When house buyers saw the current prices of houses increasing, they extrapolated the growth of the past and expected prices to rise and took out more loans. Hence this led them to delude themselves into thinking that their house purchases with risky loans were not risky, but rather, worth pursuing. Most of these houses were purchased mainly with external funding sources. People who borrowed money did not ask how long it might be until a disruption to the economy that would probably cause difficulties in repayment. In this way, this caused artificial economic growth (Roubini and Mihm, 2010) and resulted in a housing bubble in 2007–2008.

Behind this delusion there might be also cognitive dissonance. Cognitive dissonance, as defined previously, is the discomfort people feel when they experience a state in which the facts contradict what they know or do. People often try to remove the feeling of discomfort, and thus they manipulate their beliefs. For example, if a trader starts to be aware that the risk he is taking is rising, hence damaging the institution he works for or the society he is in, he will face a state of cognitive dissonance. That is, he does not want to have the feeling that while he risks others, he himself becomes richer. In order to overcome this dissonance, he makes himself believe that the business he is dealing in is not that risky.

A similar mechanism may have been at work in the credit-rating agencies. In the years preceding the crisis of 2007, credit-rating agencies rated financial firms and products more highly than they deserved. By rating the product high, the analyst would avoid losing the business to another rating agency. But the analyst would also want to be able to maintain a positive self-image, by thinking of himself as a responsible person providing a useful service to society. The analyst may have reacted to the uncomfortable feeling of dissonance by manipulating his beliefs, by telling himself that the product he was analyzing was perhaps not that risky, and therefore deserving of the high rating. For example, he may have told himself that, since house prices had been rising for years, they were likely to keep rising, thereby ensuring that subprime defaults would remain low (Barberis, 2011).

Behavioral trends of financial agents were much investigated by Shiller (2012). He looked at several crises in history including the global crisis of 2007–2008. From analysis of these crises, he aimed to reach a more general theory of asset bubbles. Benefiting from the thoughts of Charles Kindleberger on the spreading of perceptions leading to crises, Shiller defined a speculative bubble as

> a situation in which news of price increases spurs investors' enthusiasm, which spreads by psychological contagion from person to person, in the process amplifying stories that might justify the price increases and bringing in a larger and larger class of investors, who despite doubts about the real value of an investment, are drawn to it partly through envy of others' successes and partly through a gambler's excitement.
>
> (Shiller, 2012, p. 245)

In the process leading up to the crisis, Shiller particularly emphasized the role of news media, which determines public opinion and draws people's attention to particular stories. It reinforces feedback processes. These are likely to create attention cascades. Thus people will pay attention more to a definite fact. So the public's perception is directed to a certain point, and new stories are told to justify increases in prices. Hence new people will participate in the market. This is why narratives create bubbles. It is like a contagious disease spreading all around. People keep telling stories that convince other people. These stories are amplified by media such as television and newspapers. Positive story-telling arises mainly from the fact that the illusion of patterns makes us expect past price increases (even if for a very short period) to continue. Most people disregard past episodes ending up with collapses after a dramatic rise in asset prices.

Empirical studies usually indicate that collective judgments are usually more correct than individual judgments. That is, when people collectively decide on some subject, its results are more beneficial than decisions made by individuals. Maybe this is why people often use the argument of "wisdom of the crowd" when they make decisions. However, financial history shows that this may not be correct and the crowd can go in the wrong direction and following the crowd can end up in a collapse. The main reason behind this is information cascades. In financial markets, people usually make decisions in a sequence so that the second decision taker can observe the decision of the first, the third decision taker can observe the decision of the first and the second, etc. Hence usually an exchange of stories takes place rather than an exchange of fundamental information.

It also seems that herding behavior played a significant role in the global financial crisis of 2007–2008. Increasing subprime loans in particular give an indication of herding behavior. When financial institutions gave out cheap loans, then households—even those with low income—began to take these loans because they observed that all other households were taking these loans.

But herding behavior alone is not enough to explain a crisis because it is not able to explain why different groups display the same behavior at the same time. As Shiller (2005) mentions, imitating others was not the critical factor in the global crisis; in fact these actors were affected by a common environment, which was determined by seeing houses as a kind of cash machine and bonds as lucrative assets. Many people from diverse income groups shared this way of thinking.

In this herding behavior, social motives also incentivize people to buy what others buy. People compete with others at buying a house, which is encapsulated by the remark "keeping up with the Joneses". Even if people do not have enough income to purchase assets such house or cars, they will borrow to buy them. As Kindleberger and Aliber (2011) mention "*there is nothing as disturbing to one's well-being and judgment as to see a friend get rich.*" One important reason why we borrow more to increase spending is because credit use is widely recognized socially, as happened in the recent global crisis. For that matter, it is no longer shocking to see our neighbor stepping out of his mortgaged home to drive his leased car with credit-card gas.

This situation is, to some extent, associated with the concept of shared reality in social psychology. This concept originates from experiments of social psychology developed by Sherif's (1935) study on the so-called autokinetic effect. In an experiment, people are asked to look at a stationary light in a dark room and are asked what they see. After a while they say they observe a moving light. But they see the moving directions of light differently; some say it moves horizontally, some say vertically and so on. But when they start to talk to each other about what they see, their thoughts converge and they start to say they see the same movement. That is, the sharing of their thoughts leads to a convergence, and a shared reality emerges.

In fact, during normal times, people have different shared realities that balance each other. The net effect reflects a more accurate representation of reality. This is also true for actors in financial markets. Their shared realities about prices are likely to lead the prices to be economically sounder because buyers' and sellers' shared realities push prices to equilibrium levels. However, this is hard to achieve during boom periods because it is generally disregarded when asset prices inflate during the boom; sellers and buyers do not take into account fundamental values and focus on future values of assets that are incompatible with the fact of one-sided shared reality. Increasing prices create more optimistic expectations, which in turn feed new purchases of assets and lead to further divergence from fundamentals. This herding behavior was observed in the recent global crisis. This was accelerated by the introduction of complex financial products that support a feeling of security in the markets. Rating institutions also participated in the herd and were tempted to rate firms and financial products more highly than they deserved (Montgomery, 2011).

During crises, as observed, there is immense borrowing. Behavioral economists explain this immense and ungrounded borrowing through various behavioral biases. One of these is present-biasedness, which means that people prefer current rewards to delayed rewards. Hence people most of the time emphasize current than future. This tendency becomes more intense if they are optimistic. Present-bias preference can be better understood through the following example. Studies show that someone is much more likely to purchase a television with a loan if he has a present-bias preference. This is because the reward is immediate (the television) but the cost (payments at later dates) is undergone later. Experiments show that the cost of a product appears to be even smaller since periodic installments are rather low amounts (Garling et al., 2009).

Herd behavior is not only widespread among the irrational but also among the rational. Financial analysts, making decisions rationally in their own opinion, usually observe other analysts as well. They do not want to act differently from each other. This primarily arises from the fear of loss of reputation (reputational risk) that may occur if their decisions are opposed to the market consensus. Participation in a herd alleviates regret because imitating your peers' actions reduces responsibility and this makes the analysts feel comfortable. Furthermore, experts tend to imitate other experts more according to the degree of difficulty that a decision maker faces in processing information independently. As stated previously, within the complexity of financial systems, information cascades will be effective among the rational and professionals as well. This leads them to behave uniformly, which in turn provides amplifications of the economic and credit cycles.

Note that herd behavior plays a major role when markets shift from a period of euphoria towards periods of excessive skepticism. The shift from euphoria towards periods of excessive skepticism can be abrupt. As stated in the literature, when the bigger fool does not appear in the market, a panic will spread to everyone and prices will go down dramatically. Generally speaking, our panicky reaction (e.g. selling assets at fire-sale prices, withdrawing money from a bank or refusing to rollover debt) can ultimately result in greater losses than if we had just stayed put. The reason why we follow the herd when things turn sour is due to another factor; lack of coordination. Everyone is individually aware that taking action can lead to more losses than if they stayed inactive. But as Keynes noted in his beauty contest analogy, an individual's private information is less important than his/her evaluation of other peoples' expectations[3]. Given the uncertainty concerning the latter, sitting there and guessing what others will do is an inferior strategy to immediate action. So this triggers everybody to move, and when people start selling their stocks or bonds, others are also better off immediately following suit.

Such a physiological shift under uncertainty is also observed during bank runs. The prevalence of uncertainty makes people panicky. It is a kind of panic among nearly all depositors who are scared of losing their money if the bank fails. People lose their confidence in the stability of the bank because if other depositors are expected to withdraw in order to avoid losses, then every saver will run to the bank. That is the case with self-fulfilling prophecies: If people define situations to be real, then they are real in their consequences. The idea that an entire bank gets into serious trouble because of a false assumption combined with herding behavior of anxious savers gives reason to worry. Diamond and Dybvig (1983) characterize the bank run situation as a bad equilibrium (one of multiple equilibria) where everybody demands his deposit anticipating that the bank's asset value is lower than the deposit value. This process leads to a bad outcome for all participants due to its resulting in a bank failure that can interrupt real economic processes through loan callings and contagion effects.

Bank runs have occurred in many countries throughout history. They were common during the banking panics of the 1800s and in the early 1900s (especially during the Great Depression) in the United States. Governmental policies such as deposit insurance adopted in the 1930s largely reduced the likelihood of such events. However, runs are still a prominent phenomenon behind financial crises in cases where insurance is partial or does not exist. Widespread runs have also happened frequently in emerging markets and developing countries in recent decades, such as in Indonesia during the 1997 Asian financial crisis. Although runs occurred more rarely in other advanced countries, the case of Northern Rock—a bank specializing in housing finance in the UK—was an interesting case, where investors lined up in the street to withdraw money from their accounts in 2007.

In fact, widespread runs can also take place in non-bank financial markets. For example, in the US during the fall of 2008, net asset value of mutual funds fell below its par value. This triggered sharp outflows from individual investors and many other mutual funds collapsed. And other investment vehicles specializing in specific asset classes (such as emerging markets) also experienced sharp outflows as there was a run to safe assets such as advanced countries' government bonds. The run to currencies or run away from currencies is also a widespread phenomenon in the history of countries, especially emerging countries. Countless numbers of speculative attacks on foreign currency, mainly the dollar, in recent history have created drastic devaluations in many emerging countries.

The sentiments of greed and fear are also critical in the development and deepening of crises. Greed mainly makes people buy assets at a high price and prevents people from seeing the destructive effects of their risky behavior. They turn out to be risk lovers, focusing on gains rather than their probable negative effects. In contrast, the sentiment of fear leads people to sell at a low price. In a panic, people start to sell off their assets, which in turn lowers their prices further when everybody participates in the panic environment.

This was clearly observed in technology shares in the late 1990s. People started to buy primarily internet-related shares in large amounts. Investors became greedy to buy more and this caused prices to reach shocking levels. They got further away from fundamentals, leading to a stock bubble. But it soon burst in the early 2000s. In another example, in 2006 fully a third of new mortgages issued in the US were for second, third or even fourth properties. In the "bubble states"—Florida, Arizona, California—the percentage was as high as 45%. Obviously, these were not the fortunes being made on Wall Street or on the Gold Coast of Connecticut, but real estate speculation had become a mass sport. People wanted to be rich in a short time and that prevented them from considering the negative effects of this hustle in the midst of the frenzy, or the irrational exuberance as it was called by Alan Greenspan.

In a similar way to greed, fear can create devastating effects. Once the prices of financial assets fall sharply, all actors in the markets can become more fearful of sustaining further losses. They start to sell off their assets. This in turn leads to further declines. This is an amplification mechanism that aggravates the drops in the prices of assets. People deleverage to avoid further falls, selling off their assets to pay their debts and hence reducing prices further.

These psychological amplification mechanisms are primarily associated with the notions of risk aversion and ambiguity aversion. Along with investment losses in their risky assets, investors' degree of risk aversion and ambiguity aversion (increasing uncertainty makes people more cautious) increases dramatically[4]. They wish to protect their welfare in a hurry by reducing their holdings of risky assets, thereby pushing the prices of these assets down even further.

Some wonder why rational investors do not start to buy the currently cheap assets if the panic is not justified by fundamentals. The reason why they cannot is because of limited collateral. For example, when a stock of a company is purchased, the share price can continue to fall and stay low for a very long period. This can eventually force the investor to file for bankruptcy. This is why Keynes noted *"markets can remain irrational a lot longer than you and I can remain solvent*" (Lowenstein, 2000). So selling amid market panic is a rational response for everyone individually. The collective outcome is, unfortunately, far worse in comparison to the situation where everyone would have coordinated their actions by deciding to stay put, as mentioned above. This is a case of the prisoner's dilemma, which implies that what is rational for an individual is not rational for society.

It is also argued that the compensation and promotion systems of financial institutions are important in determining the primary motivation of executives in financial corporations. This mainly affects the level of risk they take on. Their payment structure can be contingent on performance or fixed salaries or a mixture of both. These different payment structures affect the risk-taking behavior of employees. For instance, in the case of high bonuses given to them depending on their success, it is evidenced that they emphasize more short-term profits. However, the studies also show that when hedgè fund managers invest their own funds in assets, their risk-taking behavior is much more moderate than when investing funds of other people rather than their own.

Finally, what about scholars, who have to have ethical and scientific responsibilities to warn the entire country of forthcoming crises. However, in this domain we have some biases as well. Researchers in this field are frequently not aware of developments that may result in crashes. For example, an important economist, Irving Fisher, a short time before the market collapse of 1929, said that *"stock prices have reached what looks like a permanently high plateau. I expect to see the stock market a good deal higher than it is today within a few months."* A similar example is that the World Bank, its publications, defined Asian countries' economies as a miracle right before the Asian crisis happened in 1997. Bernanke stated in testimony to the US Congress just before the global crisis (2005) that "*at a national level [house] price increases largely reflect strong economic fundamentals.*" There were even strong signs of drops in house prices in 2006 before the global crisis; many economists did not believe that it would lead a general collapse of house prices countrywide. Eugene Fama, who developed the efficient market hypothesis, for example, in an interview, said that

> the word bubble drives me nuts. ...housing markets are less liquid, but people are very careful when they buy houses. It's typically the biggest investment they're going to make, so they look around very carefully and they compare prices.
>
> (Fed of Minneapolis, 2007)

7.6 Empirical evidence: behavioral biases and crises

In this section, we talk in more detail about various diverse past empirical cases in which behavioral biases probably led to bubbles. This can open up our vision about the role of psychological reasons in causing financial crises or expanding the dimension of their economic cost.

Asset bubbles, which have a very long history, have been an interesting topic for behavioral economists. Bubbles are a result of a continuous rise in asset price triggered by an event or optimistic expectations. Once asset prices begin to rise, nobody can keep themselves from participating in this frenzy when they see their peers benefiting from this. Everybody desires a piece of the pie. This draws more investors who do not want to be left behind. Regardless of the original stimulus for the frenzy, everybody enters the market to buy with only the intent of selling at a profit. This process leads to an inflation in asset prices. For example, at the peak of the tulip bubble in 1637, a tulip was sold for 90,000 guilders. This was about 100 times a prosperous merchant's annual income at the time.

In the early 18th century, the shares of the South Sea company increased excessively, turning into a bubble. The stock of the South Sea company soared almost tenfold in a matter of months. The whole of England became involved in this bubble. Stock prices increased too much and huge fortunes were made. But later when prices of stocks collapsed, immense numbers of people were ruined. An anecdote in Benjamin Graham's book *Intelligent Investor* written in 2006 describes the general frenzy that even grasped the well-known scientist Isaac Newton during this time. In 1720 Newton bought stocks of the company and sold them after making a sizable profit. But just months later, Newton found himself in the wild enthusiasm of the market and jumped back in at a much higher price and lost a great deal of money. After this event, it is narrated that the great physicist said that he "*could calculate the motions of the heavenly bodies, but not the madness of the people*".

In a recent case, we see a similar process in the dot.com bubble of the 1990s in the US. During the period 1995–2000, excessive speculation in shares of internet companies occurred. The Nasdaq Composite stock market index reached its peak level in 2000. But, after a short time, it collapsed; that is, the companies turned out to be worthless because they either went bankrupt or their share prices fell dramatically, and trillions of dollars of investment vaporized.

The internet bubble was the result of a combination of factors such as low interest rate, easy access to credit, overconfidence in the market and an excessive speculation motive. Anxious investors searched for shares of companies with a ".com" after their names. Their valuations were not based on traditional fundamentals such as earnings and profits. That is, investors did not take those into account because they bought shares in companies that did not even generate any revenue at all. However, their share prices increased three- to fourfold in one day. For instance, Priceline.com, which was a travel agency selling airline tickets below their purchase price, went public in 1999 and saw its share price rise from $16 to $85 (an increase of 530%) in a single day. Its share price reached $120 a month later and this made it the most valuable firm in this sector (Rapp, 2009).

Similarly, there were excessive valuations that were also out of control in Japan during the 1980s. In 1989, the market value of company shares reached its maximum value (around $4 trillion), amounting to a value that was 1.5 times the market value of US companies even though the Japanese GDP was less than half of the US GDP at the time. The market capitalization in Japan was then about 40% of that of the world. Within this period of euphoria, the price/earnings (P/E) ratio jumped from under 25 to over 60 in 1989 (Kamalodin, 2011).

All these events show that we are not necessarily fools, but we get involved in bubbles when we see others become wealthier by the day. Thus, we do not want to miss the train to prosperity (herding behavior) even if we feel that there can be a problem. It indicates that all these bubbles in history, in different periods and countries, are to some extent related to story-telling arguments of behavioral economics supported by the heuristic biases mentioned above. Participation in bubbles is intensified by good stories (information cascades). Stories are an important part of human knowledge. This knowledge spreads through contagion and amplifies enthusiasm for a boom. As mentioned previously, at least as an amplification of crises, positive narratives—success stories—facilitated further financial investment. This was also observed in the 1920s; most publications fueled the purchase of shares, leading to a bubble and burst in 1929.

Positive story-telling shows itself especially among equity analysts. McKinsey's (2010) study points out that financial experts overoptimistically estimated earnings growth of the S&P 500 in a range of 10–12% in the past 25 years but actual earnings growth was just 6%. This implies that analysts' forecasts were on average almost 100% higher. This positive thinking is also visible if one looks at the number of buy and hold ratings in equity research departments, which usually far outnumber sell ratings.

The Asian crises in the late 1990s also give hints that are related to various behavioral biases, which enforced each other and led to the crash. The overconfidence bias was one of these biases. Investors overconfidently expected higher values in Southeast Asian markets and stability in the value of their currencies. For example, domestic banks used to borrow from foreign banks due to lower interest rates. But what is striking is that the foreign banks were too confident in lending despite the possibility of devaluations. They even underestimated the contagion effect after the currency crisis in Thailand, which spread to Indonesia (Ueno, 2001). This overconfidence was fed by past performance of Asian countries and the many studies and international institutions such those as by the World Bank and IMF that overpraised the success of the economies of the East Asian countries.

It seems that historical experiences do not help reduce the potential dangers of overconfidence. They do not create an additional awareness of its problems. For this we can give several examples. One of them is what happened in Japan in the 1980s. The Japanese banks experienced both a collapse of real estate and stock market bubbles at the same time. But they forgot this experience within a decade and were caught in the financial frenzy and inflation of asset prices in the Southeast Asian countries. The banks in these countries became less risk-averse and underestimated risks involved in these countries, as in their own crises in the 1980s. This recalls the bias that people usually propose reasons that this time is different.

Similarly the representativeness heuristic can also be employed to understand the Asian crises in the late 1990s. According to this heuristic, perceptions are constructed in a combined manner, and thus people extend the perceptions they have in one category to other categories. Foreign banks, for example, did not differentiate their lending policies with respect to the differences of the Asian countries. They saw "emerging markets" as one category. For example, Malaysia and Thailand were the same for them even though they had different economic structures. Foreign investors rushed to these countries. But the same heuristic bias was also observed during the crisis in these countries. Foreign investors acted in the same manner along with the emergence of the crisis in Thailand. Foreign banks abruptly withdrew all their investments from all the countries in the region even though they were affected by the crisis differently.

Anchoring bias can also explain, to some extent, the structure of perceptions of foreign investors in the East Asian crisis. Many observe that foreign investors did not change their positions after a deterioration emerged in the Asian countries because they still thought that their economies were within a sound framework. This mainly originated from the fact that they used their past performance as anchor. A similar anchoring was observed in Japan in the late 1980s and 1990s. US investors regarded stock price–earnings ratios in Japan in the 1980s as very high because they used US price–earnings ratios as an anchor. But in the 1990s they did not think that stock price–earnings ratios in Japan were high even though they were higher than those in the US, because they changed their anchor; thus they used values in Japan in the 1980s as their anchor.

Behavioral economists also use various arguments of heuristics to understand the recent behavior of the real estate market in the US and Spain in the late 2000s. As mentioned several times above, households over-extrapolated the past when making forecasts about the future; this also happened in these countries. However, we need to say here that over-extrapolating by households is not sufficient to create a real-estate bubble. This is because these houses were purchased by borrowing widely. Therefore it seems that over-extrapolation bias was also valid for lenders and rating agencies. Banks and other financial institutions provided an immense number of loans, including subprime loans, to home buyers. Loans continued to be given with the inducement of the securitization process. Rating agencies overrated these securities because they extrapolated the economic performance in the past into the future, especially due to rising house prices, and could not appreciate properly the probability of subprime defaults in the future (Barberis, 2011).

Moreover credit-rating agencies made several mistakes on behavioral grounds in the years preceding the global crisis of 2007. They could not evaluate risk structure completely. They focused on the individual borrower's diversification, that could reduce the probabilities of defaults. Through this, it was possible to eliminate unique non-systematic risks in the portfolio of individual borrowers. This is in fact mostly what Markowitz's portfolio theory in mainstream economics suggests. The result of this evaluation led to the fact that they regarded risky CDOs as safe and rated them highly. Rating agencies, thus, underestimated the systematic risk. They could not consider that systemic risks could devastate even well-diversified portfolios. The simultaneity of negative shocks that could cause a collective collapse was ignored and assessed as unlikely.

The US subprime crisis manifested another bias that facilitated the occurrence of a crisis. This is primarily associated with the question of why households bought houses despite having no income, no wealth, and no jobs. It seems that they were primarily convinced by financial firms of the fact that house prices would rise. Behavioral economists explain this by present-biasedness, that is, the fact that people most of the time emphasize current than future. For example teaser rates attracted people to take on more risk on the way to the crisis in 2007–2008, without thinking about probable payment difficulties in the future. It was because the reward was immediate (buying a house) but the cost (payments at later dates) was suffered later.

Compensation and promotion systems of financial institutions are another factor that influenced the risk-taking behavior of financial executives of the firms. In the years preceding the global crisis of 2007–2008 in the US, incentive mechanisms of the financial firms intensified risk-taking by their own financial executives. The badly designed payment structure within the financial sector, as the report by the European Commission (2009) evidenced, contributed to excessive risk-taking behavior and the shortening horizon of executives of financial corporations. This affected the long-term performance of economies in a negative sense. For example, the investment bank UBS assessed its losses (about $18.7 billion loss in subprime mortgages) in terms of its incentive structure presented to its employees. Its managers were involved in riskier activities due to its fee structure leading its employees to take more risk to gain more in a short time. They were paid a fee 3–4 times higher when they purchased risky CDOs, with respect to less risky and safer assets.

In contrast the French giant bank BNP Paribas followed a more cautious and conservative risk-taking policy in the run-up to the global crisis of 2007–2008. But this made it less competitive compared to other banks such as Deutsche Bank and Société Generale that were gaining too much. These banks used diverse incentive mechanisms such as contingent bonuses and stock options to induce their executives to seek short-term profits. These mechanisms were not concerned with the long-term consequences of the actions of their executives. In fact, the demands of their shareholders also pressured managers to get involved in obtaining more short-term profits. Hence BNP Paribas was criticized for its less risk-taking behavior, which led to stagnant stock prices and lower profits. Shareholders attempted to change the senior management of the bank. But during the crisis it was seen that BNP Paribas performed much better than these other two banks.

7.7 Concluding remarks

The main argument of the behavioral approach is that it is not possible to understand and make sound predictions using the rationality assumption. Economic models based on this assumption do not help us understand deviations in market results, especially during financial crises. The heuristics and biases that people have, which contradict rationality, are widespread and fit the real observations. Hence they are no longer disregarded and are not regarded as just aberrations.

Mainstream economic theory primarily presumes three features of the human way of thinking, which are: "unbounded rationality", "unbounded willpower", and "unbounded selfishness". However, it is widely recognized that these are not realistic. Behavioral economics constrains this unboundedness and ties it to reasonable boundaries of realism. This makes the behavioral perspective crucial to understanding the mechanisms behind financial crises, in addition to the functioning of economies in normal times.

In this sense, a psychological perspective can be used to complement the perspectives provided by economics. For this, three subjects may be listed. First, cognitive biases are pervasive and important in human behavior in a general sense, and in economics in particular. Second, cognitive biases can be mitigated by various cognitive or structural tools. Third, economic behavior is not only concerned with individual behavior but it occurs in a collective environment, such as herd behavior.

Policy implications of behavioral economies are valuable, especially in order to guide decentralized interactions among actors in any economy, which has the potential to lead to financial disruptions. Hence we have to mention that there should be an external constraint that will limit markets whose main concern is not to optimize social welfare. Markets can contain imperfections, inefficiencies, and psychological biases of their agents, such as greed, herd behavior, fear, ignorance, competition among people (jealousy), and many other biases mentioned above. Understanding them can help us to construct more resilient economic structures. However, if we reduce the reasons for crises to just behavioral biases, we cannot understand the other structural mechanisms playing critical roles in the development of crises that are discussed in the different chapters of this book. We have to think in a more holistic manner.

Notes

1 The Saint Petersburg paradox is a theoretical game used in economics, where people take into account only the expected value as the only decision criterion; the decision maker will be misled into an irrational decision.

2 Long-Term Capital Management (LTCM) was a large hedge fund led by Nobel Prize-winning economists and renowned Wall Street traders that nearly collapsed the global financial system in 1998. This was due to LTCM's high-risk arbitrage trading strategies.

3 Keynes described the behavior of rational stock market investors, using an analogy based on a fictional newspaper contest. This came to be known as the Keynesian Beauty Contest. It suggests that investors may guess what other investors are going to think as opposed to what they think themselves. Keynes believed that similar behavior was at work within the stock market. This would have people pricing shares not based on what they think their fundamental value is, but rather on what they think everyone else thinks their value is, or what everybody else would predict the average assessment of value to be.

4 Ambiguity aversion is also known as the Ellsberg paradox. The basic idea is that people usually prefer taking on risk in situations where they know specific odds rather than an alternative risk scenario in which the odds are completely ambiguous. They will always choose a known probability over an unknown probability. That is, people "prefer the devil they know" rather than assuming a risk where the outcomes are difficult or impossible to calculate.

8 Global imbalances and crises

8.1 Introduction

The issue of global imbalances was being debated frequently before the global crisis of 2007–2008. Since then, it has still been on the agenda of economists and practitioners. The term global imbalances is mainly used to describe external imbalances of large economies that lead to disruptions for the global economy, and even deep crises. Here we use the term external imbalances to imply not only current-account imbalances but also huge financial-capital flows at the global scale.

While the US economy has run a large amount of trade deficits in recent decades, several other large countries such as China, Japan, and Germany have had large trade surpluses. This coincidence reflects important problems. That is, this distinct trade structure among the global powers highlights many related problems such as different growth models of these countries, the direction of capital flows, and excessive consumption and borrowing.

Before the global crisis of 2007–2008, global imbalances were widely recognized, even by analysts of diverse ideological inclinations. For instance, even Costas Lapavitsas, from a Marxian perspective, mentions that capital flows to the US from savers in the emerging economies caused cheap money. The inflation of financial assets in the US bubble was sustained by capital flows from these countries. That is, an excess of saving over investment in emerging market countries—showing itself in the trade surplus—flowed to the trade deficit countries, especially to the US. This in turn led to lower interest rates and naturally more loans were given, which in turn drove more consumption, mainly in the US. This mechanism, triggered by global imbalances, planted the seeds of the global financial crisis. This is the main argument of the global imbalances view. In this chapter we argue the validity of approaches that suggest that financial crises historically and especially the global crisis of 2007–2008 were primarily generated by global imbalances.

8.2 Global imbalances

8.2.1 Historical trends in international trade and finance

International capital mobility showed diverse trends over the course of recent history. Starting in the 1870s until the First World War, international trade and finance were at very high levels and there were no economic and political impediments obstructing them. Technological improvements in communication and transportation also accelerated this process further. However, during the interwar period, and especially in the 1930s, countries implemented autarky policies, and this continued until the 1970s. Since the 1980s, a new globalization has emerged, resembling the state before the First World War, in such a way that a neoliberal environment for freer trade and financial capital developed intensively. Hence mobility of international capital took a U-shape during this long period. Figure 8.1 shows this trend of international capital flows over the last two centuries.

A similar historical pattern to capital mobility is observed in financial crisis events (Reinhart and Rogoff, 2009). Financial instability was a normal feature of all advanced economies in the late nineteenth century period; a feature that continued into the 1930s when the intensity of crises reached an all-time high during the Great Depression. But from the 1940s until the early 1970s, the world was virtually free of financial crises, with a few crises witnessed in emerging markets but none seen at all in advanced economies.

Global imbalances have existed ever since the period when international trade became widespread. Countries such as the UK, France, and Germany had

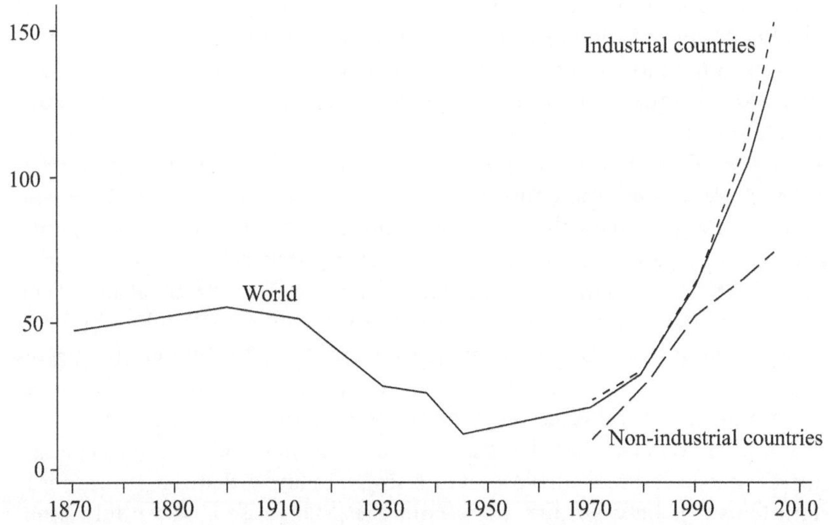

Figure 8.1 Capital mobility in the last two centuries (external assets as % of GDP). Source: Reinhart and Rogoff (2009).

Table 8.1 Creditor and debtor roles in international trade

Time period	*Creditor*	*Debtor*
Gold Standard	Advanced	Emerging
Bretton Woods	–	–
1970s	Emerging	Emerging
1980s	Advanced	Advanced
1990s	Advanced	Emerging
2000s	Emerging	Advanced

Source: Bracke et al. (2008).

run sizable trade deficits in the early 20th century. However, after the Second World War, these countries lost their supremacy in international trade to the US. The US became the world's largest creditor, mainly because of the Marshall Plan. This continued throughout the entire period of the Bretton Woods system and Germany and Japan also began to have current-account surpluses during the same period.

However, events such as the end of the Bretton Woods system, the oil crisis in the 1970s, the growing indebtedness of countries in South America in the 1980s, which was primarily financed by the banks in the US, tax cuts by the Reagan administration at the beginning of the 1980s, and increased capital flows to the US economy led to a change in the position of the US. Since 1982, the US has been in the position of debtor. Toward the end of the 20th century the Asian region was becoming important. China in particular emerged. The Asian crisis in the late 1990s and the policy shift of the countries in the region to increasing their exports further were a critical juncture for the Asian countries that had experienced the crisis. They became more cautious about their trade policies and aimed to accumulate greater current-account surpluses. Therefore, in the 2000s, countries changed their creditor and debtor roles in international trade. This can be seen in Table 8.1.

The trade balance before the global crisis of 2007–2008 is given in Figure 8.2. As seen, there is only one country that shows a huge deficit—the US—and there are a few countries that have large current-account surpluses—China, Germany, and Japan. This is the picture of global imbalance before the crisis of 2007–2008. It shows the distorted state of the world's trade imbalances. The deficit of the US is extremely large, reaching the value of $718 billion in 2007. The surpluses of China, Germany, and Japan were over $200 billion (the surplus of each country, not in total). After these countries, oil-exporting countries such as Saudi Arabia and Russia had the largest surpluses (Blecker, 2011). These figures imply that in fact global imbalance is a misnomer because there are a few countries that have huge surpluses and a single country that has an immense deficit. Thus it is between just a few countries. This case is also valid within the European Union (EU). Even though there are individual countries running relatively large surpluses or deficits, they balance each other out and there have

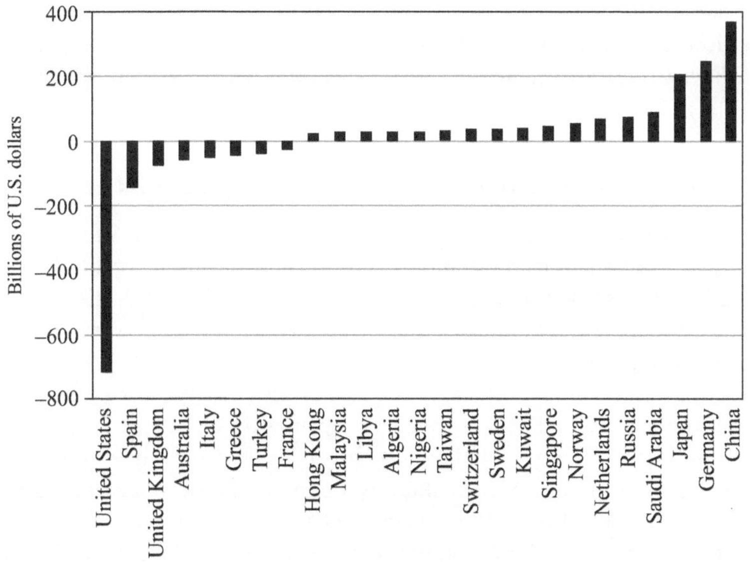

Figure 8.2 Countries with current account imbalances, 2007 (US $ billion).
Source: IMF (2010).

been no big trade imbalances within the EU during recent years. This implies that the notion of global imbalances is primarily associated with the case of the US versus East Asian countries (especially China), rather than with imbalances within the EU or resource rich and poor countries, which have much smaller imbalances.

To better see the recent dramatic developments in global imbalances, we can look at the period between 1996 and 2006. During the period between 1996—just before the Asian financial crisis—and 2006—just before the global crisis—global imbalances reached their peak, about five times the value of world production. During this period, in fact, three country categories that showed surpluses emerged: one is new emerging Asian countries such as China and other countries in the region, another is aging high-income, export-oriented countries such as Germany and Japan, and the last is oil-exporting countries such as the Gulf countries, Russia, and Norway. But on the other hand there emerged two categories of country that showed trade deficits, which were the US and the peripheral European countries.

The magnitude of trade imbalances increased significantly during this period: In 1996 the cumulative current-account surpluses of all countries with surpluses added up to $298 billion, of which the top ten countries contributed $228 billion. By 2006, the total had risen to $1,527 billion, of which the top ten contributed $1,037 billion. Japan was the largest surplus country, with just $66 billion in 1996, followed by Italy with $39 billion. However, in 2006 China was the largest surplus country, with $232 billion, followed by Germany with $182 billion and Japan with $171 billion. Current-account balances and thus net capital flows (the mirror image of current-account balances) were transformed (Wolf, 2014).

8.2.2 Global imbalances within the US and the rest of the world

The global imbalances in the 2000s were mainly related to the US trade deficit, which was almost equal to the trade surplus of the rest of the world. Table 8.2 gives the US goods trade deficit with respect to regions in 2007, the peak year before the global crisis. It indicates that the US run trade deficits with all large countries and regions.

There are a number of countries that run persistent large trade surpluses in their trade with the US. These countries are primarily Germany, Japan, China, Taiwan, and South Korea. Their main feature is that they have pursued an export-led growth model. Hence there is a connection between their growth strategy and features of the US economy. That is, the US economy provides the external demand of these countries and encourages them to make more investment.

Figure 8.3 shows that the global economy has primarily three different economic geographies: the US economy, balanced-trade economies, and export-led economies. The Pacific Rim (including China) and the euro area (especially Germany) are essentially export-led economies. They run trade surpluses with the US and with other balanced-trade countries. The US runs a trade deficit with both balanced-trade and export-led economies. The net position is that the US has a trade deficit, the export-led economies have a large trade surplus, and the balanced-trade economies have approximate trade balance.

Global imbalances mirror the difference between gross capital inflows and outflows. On the deficit side there is an excess of investment over domestic savings in the US, but on the surplus side there is excess of savings over investment in the emerging Asian countries, namely an accumulation of US

Table 8.2 A decomposition of the US goods trade deficit in 2007

	$ billion	*Percentage*
Total	–808.8	100
Pacific Rim	–372.3	46.0
China	–258.5	32.0
Canada & Mexico	–143.0	17.7
European Union	–110.2	13.6
OPEC	–117.2	14.5
Other	192.4	23.8

Source: IMF Stat.

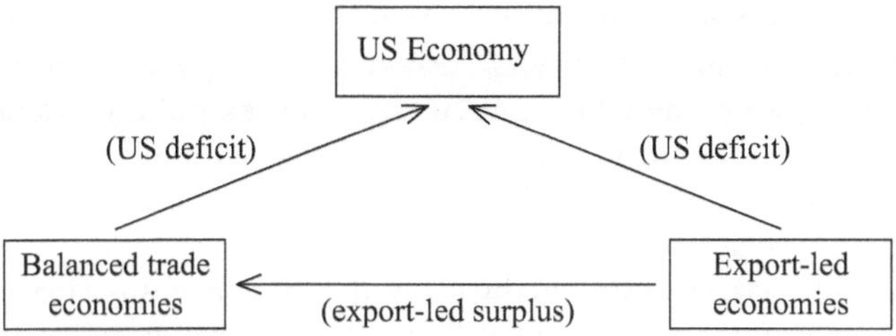

Figure 8.3 Structure of global imbalances.

assets in their hands. They therefore financed the US deficit. During the period between the 1980s and the early 1990s, these imbalances did not change greatly but did increase about twofold since the second half of the 1990s. Figure 8.4 shows the development of current-account deficit (in absolute terms), starting with the mid-1990s in the US. It is clear that it reached a highest value, which was 5%, in 2006.

According to Blanchard and Milesi-Ferretti (2009), the widening current-account deficit in the US until 2006 was the result of two distinct developments in different regions. One of these is what happened in the US, where investment in the US exceeded saving during strong economic growth in the 2000s until the crisis. Another is what developed in the Asian countries after the crisis of 1997. After the crisis, their investment motivation declined, and hence saving exceeded investment. Consequently the investments of the US were financed by saving in the Asian countries.

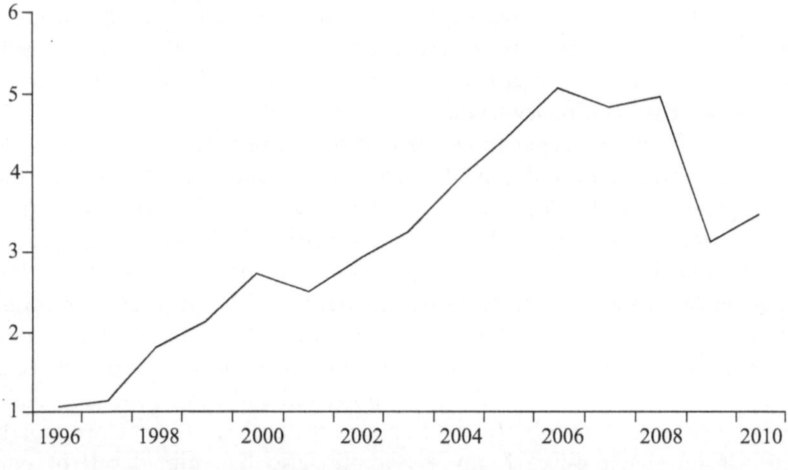

Figure 8.4 Current account/GDP in the US (absolute values).
Source: Dettmann (2014).

The saving and investment patterns in different countries provide us with information to trace the capital flows and current-account positions of these countries. Over the past decade while East Asian countries and oil producers as trade surplus countries have had high and rising savings with respect to their investments, primarily the US as a trade deficit country has had lower and falling savings with respect to its investments.

During the period between 2002 and the crisis in 2007, there was a boom in economic activity and international capital flows, with widening imbalances. The current-account deficit in the US deteriorated further. According to Blanchard and Milesi-Ferretti (2009), in the period spanning 2000 to 2004, this mainly originated from the fall in US public saving—while private saving was rather stable. However, starting in 2004, the household saving rate declined drastically and investment increased. Consequently, the US current-account deficit increased even further until 2005. In 2006, a further fall in the saving rate led the current-account deficit to reach its maximum.

The widening global imbalances before the crisis of 2007–2008 were different from former times of widening global imbalance (such as the interwar period or the time after the collapse of the Bretton Woods system). According to Bracke et al. (2008), there are three differences in the global imbalances before the crisis of 2007–2008 with respect to these. First, there are more countries running surplus in this case. New countries like China were added to traditional surplus countries like Japan and Germany. However, on the deficit side, there is less dispersion relative to earlier periods. A single country—the US—became the source of the expanding deficits. This means that the world economy has been more and more dependent on a single country's ability to absorb the excess savings of the world. Second, financial globalization has accelerated and capital flows have amounted to immense numbers during recent decades. Third, distinct developments in different regions concerning savings were important. While declining volatility with a strong growth trend in the US during the period of great moderation as defined by Bernanke (2004) led to a fall in precautionary saving, the Asian crisis in 1997 caused the Asian countries to increase their precautionary saving.

In fact, there are deeper forces behind these huge shifts in global patterns of saving, investment and capital flows. Three fundamental transformations can explain these developments. The first was the shift towards economic liberalization, namely the embracing of the market as the organizing principle in economic life. In the 1970s, regulations were prevalent in all developed countries on product, labor, and financial markets. Marginal tax rates on high incomes were above 70% in both the US and the UK. While the high-income countries had substantially liberalized trade in goods in the 1950s, 1960s, and 1970s, trade in services was still highly restricted and most countries retained foreign exchange controls. In developing economies, controls over markets were far more extensive. Many economies also had high levels of public ownership of industry. The developing countries and socialist countries also imposed comprehensive barriers to trade and capital flows.

Political and economic developments changed the closed and highly regulated economies and transformed them into liberalized economies. One of the most important changes was the opening-up policies followed by China after 1978, under the leadership of Deng Xiaoping. Margaret Thatcher and Ronald Reagan's coming to office in 1979 and 1980 respectively began a serious change in the high-income countries, including privatization of what previously had been publicly owned companies. The Uruguay Round of multilateral trade negotiations was then completed in 1994. And in January 1995, the General Agreement on Tariffs and Trade (GATT) turned into the World Trade Organization (WTO). Subsequently, China joined the WTO in 2001. This was a rise of global capitalism, hence accelerating international trade.

The second source of global transformation was the advances in technology. Developments and improvements in container ships and high-volume air freight were significant. Improvements in information and communications technology—notably computerization and the internet—were of far greater significance. These significant developments have significantly changed production structure across the world. That in turn created the opportunity for the fast development of export-oriented manufacturing, mainly from China, and export-oriented information technology services, mainly from India.

The third source of transformation is the relocation of production from developed countries to low-cost producing countries. This was accompanied by a shift in saving behavior of emerging economies, which pursued savings- and export-surplus growth strategies. China quickly became the largest manufacture-producing and exporting country. This was the first time since the industrial revolution that a still relatively poor developing economy had played such a huge role in world production and trade. This was mainly the result of the globalized and integrated production structure in the world generated by liberalization and information technologies. And this has mainly been maintained by systematically undervalued currencies; relatively low wage growth and thus low wage share in the national income; and financial repression that created low interest rates to provide cheap credits to real firms.

In the 2000s, distinct factors were largely influential on saving and investment behavior in emerging countries. Immediately after the Asian financial crisis of 1997–1998, crisis-hit countries changed their investment and saving behavior. These countries—such as Indonesia, South Korea, Malaysia, the Philippines, and Thailand—reduced their investment by about 10% of gross domestic product. However, particularly in Germany and the oil-exporting countries, this was more of a savings glut. In Germany, investment was weak, while profits and household savings were high. In the oil-exporting countries, income from higher oil prices, which were mainly generated by higher demand from China, led to a rise in saving. In China, there was an immense rise both in investment and saving in the 2000s. The Chinese economist Justin Lin (2013) argues that the structure of China's economy explains the extraordinarily high national savings rate, which far exceeded 50% of GDP in 2008. Government and corporate savings account for some 60% of these savings, with households making up the rest. Corporations, in particular, accounted for some 40% of gross national savings. This is because of policies and structural features of the economy that shift income from households to corporations.

Here we can ask why these countries ended up with high savings surpluses and hence substantial current-account surpluses. It is hard to answer this development clearly because there are several interdependent and coexisting factors. It may be that they put greater weight on production than on consumption. It may be that they see a need to reduce risks by becoming net creditors, as has also been true of China. It may be that they see success in export markets as a triumph in the form of peaceful economic warfare. It may be that export-driven growth after the Second World War shaped their subsequent economic structures. Overall, the outcome has probably been shaped by all these things.

8.2.3 Imbalances within the Euro area

The Eurozone is a large multinational economy—the second biggest economy in the world after the US. In 2016, for example, Eurozone GDP, at market prices, was a little short of 80% of that of the US. Similar to the fact that there are trade imbalances between the US and emerging Asia, there have been trade imbalances within the EU. Countries in the north such as Germany, Belgium, and Denmark have trade surpluses with countries in the south such Italy, Spain, Portugal, and Greece.

Figure 8.5 shows current-account developments of the peripheral EU countries (this term is used for Italy, Portugal, Ireland, Spain, and Greece)

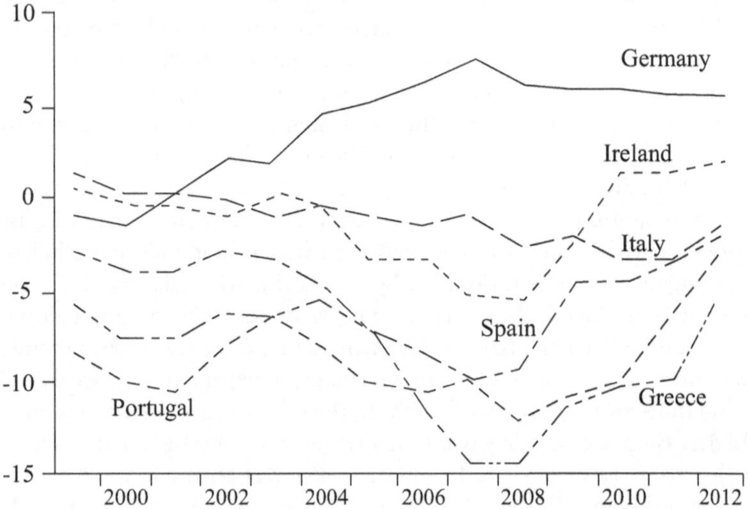

Figure 8.5 Current accounts for peripheral European countries and Germany (% of GDP).
Source: IMF (2012).

and Germany. It shows that with the introduction of the euro in 2002, current-account imbalances started to emerge in the EU. While the current-account deficits of the peripheral EU countries increased, the current-account surplus of Germany (the largest surplus-showing country in the EU) increased. This continued until the global financial crisis of 2007–2008. During this process, countries such as Greece and Portugal had more serious current-account deficits, while other peripheral countries like Italy and Ireland were not so seriously affected.

The Eurozone imbalances, in comparison with other previous imbalances in the world, had a different feature. With the other imbalances, the deficit-exhibiting countries used another currency as a reserve currency, which was in general the dollar. However, in the case of the Eurozone, the countries badly affected by imbalances used the same currency as the center of their currency area—Germany—which ran a surplus with these countries. That is, despite having a center, the currency area is constructed in a symmetrical way. There is an independent central bank—the European Central Bank (ECB)—which follows monetary policy in the euro area. Thus none of the EU countries is able to conduct their monetary policy for their own national purposes. In this sense, the euro crisis was different from the other current-account crises because the deficit countries in the EU were indebted in their own domestic currency, which they could not fully control; that is, they could not just monetize their debt.

The imbalances within the Eurozone resemble global current-account imbalances; that is, the imbalance between the East Asian countries and the US. However, these imbalances are not as severe as the global imbalances between the US and China. Moreover the euro area's external current account was approximately balanced in the years before the crisis in 2007–2008, as shown in Figure 8.6. Hence the contribution of the EU to global imbalances was not large. But this does not mean that the effect of global imbalances on the EU's intra-imbalances was not significant.

The increasing importance of China, along with its membership of the WTO in 2001, influenced the trade structure of the EU countries in different ways. The presence of China affected Germany positively because China imported more from Germany, especially machinery. However, since China competed with the peripheral countries in low-technological products, they were hit severely. This implies an asymmetric trade shock to the EU countries. That is, while Germany's exports to non-EU countries increased two times between 2000 and 2008, the peripheral countries' exports to these countries did not change at all. German exports to China and the so-called BRIC countries (Brazil, Russia, India, China) in particular more than tripled during that period (Dettmann, 2014).

During the period 2001–2008, the euro appreciated against the important currencies such as the dollar and the yen. However this did not affect Germany's export performance even while the other peripheral countries were badly affected by this development. This probably arises from the fact that while price

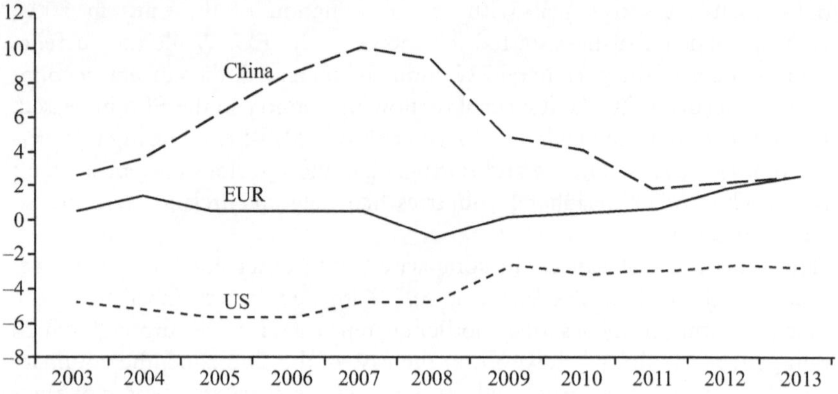

Figure 8.6 Current account positions (% of GDP).
Source: OECD Stat.

elasticity of Germany's medium- to high-tech goods was low, price elasticity for low-technology peripheral goods was relatively high.

Until now we have focused only on the current-account side, namely the trade side, of the problem. However, imbalances in capital markets in the euro area were also widespread. During the 2000s, the Fed followed a low interest-rate policy. The ECB feared that this policy could let the euro appreciate. Therefore, taking this into account, the ECB applied an interest policy which was regarded as low by the peripheral countries and high by the central countries. This led to an increasing capital flow from north to south, that is, to the peripheral countries. Capital flows in the euro area caused asset prices to increase hugely in these countries. In this way, the European banks accelerated housing bubbles in the euro peripheral countries such as Spain and Ireland, where the annual average increase in house prices was hovering around 8–12% during the bubble, much higher than the increase in the US, which was around 4.6% before the crisis (Lin and Treichel, 2012).

Capital movements in the euro area, in fact, were more complicated than it appeared. This is because the countries outside the EU that had trade surpluses invested their money in the core countries in the EU, which in turn lent to the peripheral countries. Hence more capital flowed to the peripheral countries than their trade deficit with the core countries in the EU. It was as if the banks in the core countries intermediated capital flows from outside the EU. Germany for example, recorded current-account surpluses of roughly the same size with the EU and the rest of the world, but had much larger surpluses on its financial account with the EU.

It seems that the flow of funds within Europe is a part of the broader circulation of funds throughout the world economy. If we focus on intra-European flows, it is clear that Germany, despite its export prowess, did not dominate the European financial system. Germany was not the largest net lender. Its status was like that of China in relation to the US economy. But financial flows within Europe did not map onto trade any more than they did in the world economy. That is, even though Germany was the greatest exporter of cars and machinery, other countries in Europe prevailed in banking and finance. Particularly the UK, France, and Ireland became the center of financial activities. The City of London, home to banks from around the world, stands out as the major financial partner for every Eurozone member. France and the Benelux were especially important because they served as channels through which funds flowed into the Eurozone from outside. American and other lenders from the rest of the world clearly preferred to do business with well-known French, Dutch and Belgian counterparts, who then channeled the funds to the European periphery.

Before 2007 the net financial flow from Asia to the US could reasonably be construed as the financial counterpart to the US's trade deficit with Asia. Capital flowed one way, from Asia to the US, roughly as much as trade deficit between the two. But the financial flows between Europe and the US were quite independent of the trade connections between the two. During this period the trade between the EU and the US was relatively balanced. Capital flowed both ways; from the US to the EU and from the EU to the US. The size of flows was much more than the trade between the two, which was almost balanced. The European banks purchased so-called toxic securities from the US in large amounts. In contrast, China preferred not to buy these securities and instead it bought US treasury bonds roughly as much as trade deficit. The scale of capital flows between the US and the EU is revealed if we look not at the net flow of capital in and out of the US (inflows minus outflows), but at the gross flows, which record how many assets were bought and sold in each direction. As the gross inflow data show, by far the largest purchasers of US assets, by far the largest foreign lenders to the US prior to the crisis, were not Asian but European. Indeed, in 2007, roughly twice as much money flowed from the UK to the US as from China (Tooze, 2018).

Finally we have to answer the question of what led to imbalances within the Eurozone. It seems mainly that three important developments occurred. The first of these was an immense shift by Germany towards external imbalance, in the form of a current-account surplus. During the 1990s, after reunification, Germany ran high fiscal deficits. By the end of the decade, the desire to tighten government finances had become strong as post-unification infrastructure spending in the old East Germany came to an end. Moreover, for much of this decade, Germany even ran a modest current-account deficit. Germany changed this over time. First, it ran a current-account surplus, that is, excess of private savings over investment. Second, it improved competitiveness: keeping the rise in wages down so that real wages grew more slowly than productivity. This would, over time, make Germany's traditionally strong manufacturing export sector even more competitive.

Furthermore, reforms of the labor market in Germany were introduced under the government in the early 2000s. The wages of German employees were constrained, and thereby domestic consumption was restrained. This in turn led manufacturing industry to increase export. This occurred at the expense of other manufacturing countries. Therefore, the race to the bottom was won by German capitalists who succeeded in constraining wages and containing the dominance of labor unions. The diverging paths of unit labor costs show the gains in competitiveness made by Germany compared to the peripheral countries. Here it is important to stress that German competitiveness has been overwhelmingly due to keeping the cost of labor low because productivity growth in Germany throughout this period has been poor, and in fact weaker than in the peripheral countries, with the exception of Spain.

The second development was financial integration. In the mid-1990s spreads between yields on Italian and Spanish government bonds and those on German bonds were around five or six percentage points. These spreads disappeared quite soon after the introduction of the euro until the crisis in 2010. That is, investors ceased to apply any notion of country risk. People in these countries enjoyed the resulting borrowing opportunities. With the exception of Greece, those who took advantage of these opportunities were overwhelmingly in the private sector. Low interest rates allowed banks to obtain euro-denominated liquidity cheaply in the interbank market. Given the availability of cheap funding due to low interest rates, banks in the peripheral countries increased their lending excessively, particularly after 2005. In short, peripheral banks incurred debt externally which they proceeded to transform into domestic lending; they also took the opportunity to expand their activities internationally.

The peripheral countries varied from each other in the way they used capital inflows to their countries. While Greece and Portugal used capital inflows, namely debt, for their current consumption purposes, Ireland and Spain channeled this inflowing capital to investments in mostly the construction sector. Hence increasing consumption and investment pushed up growth in these countries. However, this inflowing money did not go to more productive investments, that is, tradable sectors.

The financialization of peripheral countries in this context has thus entailed an enormous accumulation of debt domestically as well as internationally. As the international competitiveness of the peripheral countries declined, resulting in current-account deficits, the peripheral countries boosted domestic credit on the basis of low European Central Bank (ECB) interest rates, the bulk of which went to households and real estate investment; domestic saving, meanwhile, remained on a downward path. Important aspects of the US bubble were thus reproduced in the periphery of the Eurozone. The heaviest growth of indebtedness in the periphery has been due to private debt, for Spain, Portugal, and Greece, respectively. As peripheral sovereign debt began to escalate, bond markets came to realize that the debt of peripheral states was not of the same quality as the debt of core states. Even worse, in late 2009 it became clear that core Eurozone countries were not prepared to honor peripheral public debt. Consequently, the states of Greece, Ireland, and Portugal were progressively shut out of international bond markets in 2010–2011. Furthermore, the states of both Spain and Italy were placed in an increasingly precarious position. So the crisis of financialization had become a crisis of sovereign debt primarily because peripheral states had borrowed in a currency—the euro—which appeared to be domestic but was in effect foreign.

The third development was that the ECB followed a monetary policy designed to stabilize the rate of inflation in the Eurozone as a whole. Declining domestic demand in Germany could be solved only by expanding demand elsewhere. That occurred in countries where the exceptionally low interest rates granted by euro entry would drive a huge credit boom.

The increasing surplus of production over demand in "creditor Eurozone" (surplus countries, mainly Germany) was perfectly matched by the increasing surplus of demand over production in "debtor Eurozone" (deficit countries, namely the peripheral countries). The increasing surplus of tradable goods, relative to domestic demand, in creditor Eurozone was matched by an increasing deficiency of tradable goods, relative to demand, in debtor Eurozone (Wolf, 2014). This in turn resulted in the fact that the boom in investment in debtor Eurozone took the form of investment in non-tradable goods and services, notably property-related investments, because the most competitive suppliers of tradable goods in the domestic market were those in creditor Eurozone.

8.3 Global imbalances: some theoretical explanations

Global imbalances are probably one of the most complex macroeconomic issues facing economists and policy makers. They arise from many factors, from saving to investment to portfolio decisions, in many countries. As Blanchard and Milesi-Ferretti (2009) state:

> These cross-country differences in saving patterns, investment patterns, and portfolio choices are in part "good"—a natural reflection of differences in levels of development, demographic patterns, and other underlying economic fundamentals. But they are also in part "bad", reflecting distortions, externalities, and risks, at the national and international level.

There are several hypotheses that try to explain global imbalances. These hypotheses are mainly; the twin deficit, saving shortage, saving glut, asset shortage, and reserve currency. We will now briefly debate them in turn below.

The twin deficit hypothesis

The twin deficit hypothesis became prominent in the 1980s. It mainly proposes that there is a strong causal link between a country's government budget balance and its current-account balance.

From macroeconomic accounting definition, we know the following relationship $(S-I)+(T-G)=NX$, where S represents saving, I is investment, T is tax receipts, G is government spending and $NX=X-M$ stands for net exports. Rearranging the above equation yields $(G - T) = S - I - NX$. This means

Budget deficit = *Saving* – *Investment* – *NetExport*

This equation implies that if the budget deficit goes up and saving does not change at a given income level, either investment (*I*) or net export (*NX*) has to decline. The decline in net export means an increase in trade deficit. Therefore as a result, the budget deficit leads to trade deficit. This is the case of twin deficit. However, this does not happen automatically. It mostly follows a mechanism such as this: Along with increasing government spending, domestic interest rates rise in comparison to foreign interest rates. This in turn leads to capital inflows and thereby appreciation of domestic currency. In the end, the current-account deficit widens. This view was compatible with what was observed during the Reagan administration in the US. During that time, the twin hypothesis seemed valid because there was both budget deficit and trade deficit in the US. It was believed that high budget deficits caused trade deficit in the 1980s. However, this hypothesis is not compatible with budget surpluses and high trade deficits at the same time, as during the Bill Clinton period in the 1990s (Figure 8.7). Another case that contradicts the hypothesis was Germany and Japan in the 1990s. They had large trade surpluses but at the same time had persistent large budget deficits.

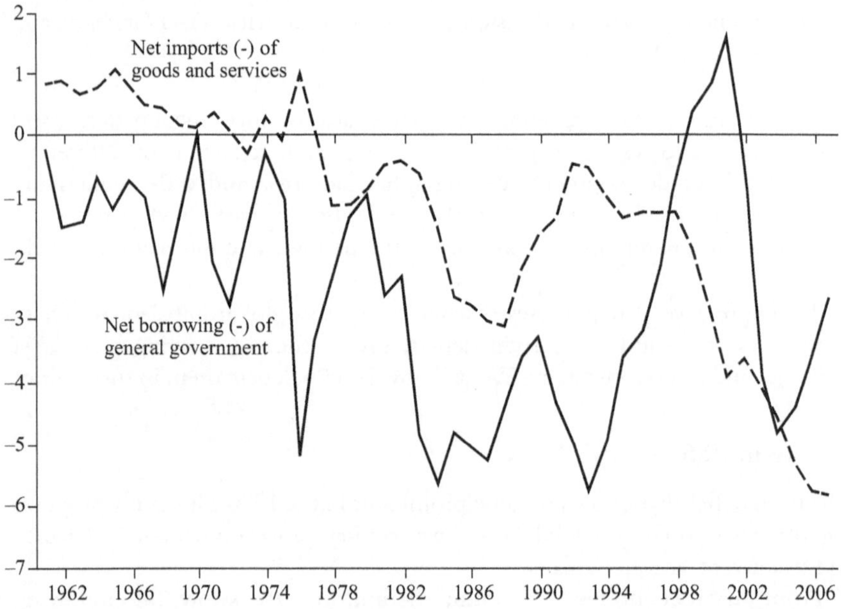

Figure 8.7 Twin deficit in the USA as % of GDP.
Source: AMECO database.

The saving shortage hypothesis

Another hypothesis that tries to explain global imbalances is the saving shortage hypothesis. This hypothesis came to the fore in the 1990s and dominated the twin deficit hypothesis. The main argument of this hypothesis is the existence of a low saving rate in the US (and thus excessive consumption). The personal saving rate in the US declined from about 5% of disposable income to about 2% in the mid-2000s (Gruber and Kamin, 2005).

Declining interest rates induced excessive borrowing. Along with excessive borrowing, consumption was maintained in the US for a long period. Personal consumption reached a level of 70% of GDP in 2007, which was twice that in China. In 2007, just before the crisis, household debt in the US (US $13.8 trillion) was roughly equal to the US GDP. If other categories of debt are added, thus including government and private business debt, its total value reached US $47.9 trillion—equal to 3.5 times the US GDP in 2007 (Huang et al., 2009). This implies mainly that the US economy generally changed from an overproduction economy to an overconsumption economy over time. The unbalanced structure of the US economy that could be maintained for so long was partially related to another type of structural imbalance in China. Overconsumption in the US was widely maintained via imported products from China. This increased the trade balance between two countries immensely.

The global saving glut hypothesis

The global saving glut hypothesis mainly argues that excess saving from the Asian emerging countries and the oil-exporting countries flowed primarily to the US. Increasing savings and falling investment in the emerging Asian countries including China, especially after the Asian financial crisis in the late 1990s, caused excess saving in these countries. Similarly, increased oil prices generated excess saving in oil-exporting countries such as the Gulf countries and Russia. The accumulated savings in these two regions financed the current deficits of the US.

In particular China's increasing foreign reserves due to trade surpluses as a result of its export-led growth strategy returned to the US because China purchased US financial assets, particularly government bonds. This reduced interest rates in the US. In other words, China provided subsidized borrowed resources for US growth. However, this was not a problem-free process because use of inflowing money was critical, and thus the allocation of credit by financial markets was problematic. This was used to finance mortgages, rather than in productive areas. Thus China financed overconsumption in the US.

If there were no overconsumption in the US, China would not absorb its production due to its low domestic demand. In China, the share of consumption in GDP has been falling for 50 years. As pointed out by Garnaut et al. (2011), while the share of final consumption fell from 62% to 49%, the share of household consumption also declined from 46% to 35% during the period 2000–2007. This is one of lowest shares in the world. And even though investment expanded sharply, it lagged behind growth in savings. This encouraged Chinese firms to sell abroad more rather than sell in domestic markets. This has created a symbiotic relationship between the US and China.

However, the analysis given by the saving glut hypothesis has been criticized by some scholars. For example, Palley (2015) discusses some shortcomings of the hypothesis. One of these is that it tries to explain trade deficits by benefiting from the loanable funds approach. But this is problematic because changes in short-term interest rates are determined by the monetary policies of central banks rather than the quantity of money in the market as asserted by loanable fund theory. This approach asserts that China financed the US trade deficit by buying US securities and this in turn increased the money supply sharply preceding the global crisis, leading to a fall in interest rates in the US. However, Palley says that the interest rate was mainly determined by monetary policies of the Fed, rather than by increased money supply due to the result of the trade deficit of the US with China.

A second shortcoming of the hypothesis is that it does not sufficiently elaborate the characteristics of the trade surplus run by China. It defines this merely as an excessive saving problem. This misunderstands the microeconomic perspective of global production. It is known that an important part of China's export capacity was generated by multinational companies that maintained their production in China. Palley (2015) shows that more than 50% of Chinese exports were produced by 100% foreign-owned companies and over 76% of China's exports are produced by foreign-owned companies or joint-venture companies (Palley, 2015). The saving glut hypothesis disregards this character of global production. It does not look at trends in trade and globalization in a critical way. Furthermore the saving glut hypothesis points out that the US actually benefited from these subsidized Chinese savings. This would be true only if these cheap funds were allocated to productive areas. But this mostly did not happen, as we know.

The asset shortage hypothesis

Another hypothesis to explain global imbalances is the asset shortage hypothesis. According to the hypothesis, demand for high-quality financial assets has been increasing in the world. The US provides such high-quality financial assets to investors around the world due to its deep financial markets and diverse financial products. This is why emerging markets keep their reserves in US treasury bonds or other private securities denominated in dollars. The lack of safe and liquid asset markets in their domestic markets forces these countries to invest in the US and also the UK. In particular their problems in the domain of macroeconomic stability, political uncertainties, weak institutions and rule of law intensify this process. As a result of a combination of these reasons, these countries cannot supply liquid and safe financial products. This is why there is a capital flow from these countries to countries that have more advanced financial markets.

Therefore, global imbalances in trade were simply related to global imbalances in providing safe financial products. In other words, developing countries run trade surpluses simply because they want to obtain safer and more liquid assets in comparison to their domestic financial assets. Some economists designate this asset-shortage case as the parking theory. They argue that the Chinese park their savings in the US, which is regarded as a safe haven until the domestic financial markets become efficient there. That is, until undeveloped property rights and financial markets improve, the capital flows keep going in the direction expressed.

However, as Palley (2015) mentions, there are also flaws with the asset shortage hypothesis. First, the hypothesis is not concerned with the structure of global production, which is sustained by multinational corporations. Second, the increase in demand for financial assets can be better explained by some other fundamental developments such as increasing income inequality and financialization.

The dollar reserve currency hypothesis

This hypothesis stresses that along with the Asian crisis in 1997 countries in the region began to hold more foreign reserves in their central banks by running trade surpluses. This implies that the international system forces emerging countries, which are unable to trade with their domestic currencies, to accumulate excessive foreign reserves in order to maintain the stability of their currencies in particular and of their economies in general. Holding dollars as reserve money gives countries the possibility of intervening in foreign exchange markets. In this way they are able to sustain the value of devalued currencies and preserve competitiveness of their products. This situation creates another externality for these emerging countries. Since emerging market countries invest their trade surpluses mostly into dollar-denominated assets, this causes the value of the dollar to rise, thus overvaluing. This in turn makes their products more competitive, allowing them to export more.

It is a fact that the US dollar became a reserve currency after the Second World War due to its rising economic and political power. This gave an asymmetric power to the US economy. It has benefited from its seigniorage power and financed its trade deficit just by issuing its domestic currency, which is a reserve currency for the world[1]. The dollar's power of being a reserve currency imposes a kind of complacency on the US in its trade policies and makes it less concerned with immense trade deficits.

8.4 Global imbalances and two growth model approach

The global economic system after the Second World War, as Palley (2012) points out, saw three main economic regimes that describe the main characteristics

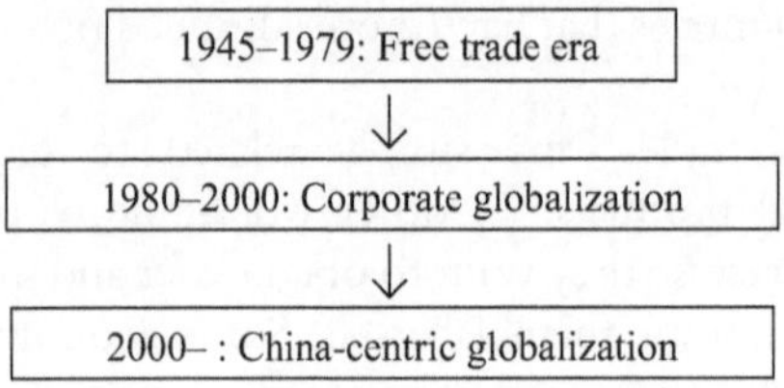

Figure 8.8 Main global economic regimes.

of the global economy. These are seen in Figure 8.8. During the period 1945–1979, a free-trade regime existed and tariffs were declining. In the following period 1980–2000, a neoliberal globalization regime emerged. And then this trade regime turned into the current China-centric globalization regime.

Trade was roughly balanced during the period 1945–1979 because policymakers were averse to large deficits for macroeconomic reasons. But during the neoliberal period, policymakers had no interest in constraining trade deficits and large companies benefited from this development. For emerging-market economies, there are several reasons why they adopted the new system. First, along with new arrangements, they obtained more access to developed countries' markets. Second, foreign direct investments in emerging-market economies by developed countries expanded and improved their production potential. Third, in the 1980s and early 1990s international institutions such as the IMF and the World Bank imposed neoliberal policy reforms in emerging market economies in order to avoid the problems that broke out in the 1980s debt crisis. These countries were encouraged to abandon strategic trade protection policies. Fourth, emerging-market economies obtained large trade surpluses by following export-led growth based on FDI and persistent depreciation policies. Trade surpluses mitigated the financial pressure on their growth. As a result, neoliberal globalization produced a global economic mechanism that ended up with a serious global imbalance problem. Furthermore, along with the liberalization of capital flows, international capital flows has loosened external trade constraints of emerging economies. This allowed them to maintain their trade imbalances for a long time.

Along with the intensifying globalization of the neoliberal period, the manufacturing base of the production in the US weakened, thus deindustrialization of the US economy accelerated. Furthermore manufacturing production was relocated to emerging-market economies. This development damaged the foreign tradable goods of the US. This led to the expansion of the US trade deficit. This is the supply-side explanation of increasing trade deficit in the US, arising from globalization. But there is also a demand side of this development. This is mainly the increasing consumption demand within the US. Along with this, developing countries did not increase their domestic consumption and based their growth on export-led strategy.

In order to explain the global imbalance problem, we also need to explain why policymakers permitted it. Thus the way policymakers view global imbalances is also critical. During the period before 1980, policymakers had generally Keynesian views, and hence they did not support trade deficits. However, starting in the 1980s, with the development of new classical views and the weakening of Keynesian views, policymakers focused on the issue of inflation rather than unemployment. This means that they did not care about trade deficits because trade was reducing inflation. Moreover, large international companies also benefited from reductions in trade constraints in the 1980s. They regarded this as a way to contain the power of labor unions and thereby wage payments. Starting in the 1990s, international firms in the US could obtain cheaper inputs or shifted their production to emerging markets and exported back to the USA. Therefore both policymakers and business came to see trade through the lens of costs and wages. For policymakers, trade openness also became a means of constraining inflation.

These overall developments mentioned above in fact have provided countries with opportunities to follow distinct growth models. While some countries applied a debt-led growth model, others applied an export-led growth model. In this context, Table 8.3 categorizes some important countries. According to this categorization, diverse core and peripheral countries in the world economy applied debt-led and export-led growth models. While core countries the US and UK used a debt-led growth model, peripheral countries such as Greece, Ireland, Portugal, and Spain also applied a similar growth policy. Export-led growth strategy was also followed by both core and peripheral countries. While Germany, Austria, and Japan followed this strategy, China, regarded as a peripheral country in this sense, had also been growing with the same strategy.

There are diverse reasons for the choices of growth model by the countries in Table 8.3. The export–growth strategy in Germany emerged after unification and the introduction of the euro. The debt-led structure of the European peripheral countries mainly originated from the financial liberalization that came along with European integration. The export-led growth in the Southern Asian countries was a response to the crisis in 1997. They emphasized accumulating foreign currency reserves because of the problems they had experienced during the crisis. China's export-led growth strategy is also related to its desire for accumulation of foreign reserves.

Table 8.3 Debt-led and export-led growth models

	Growth model	
	Debt-led	*Export-led*
Core	USA, UK	Germany, Austria, Japan
Periphery	Greece, Ireland, Portugal, Spain	China

It is also noticeable that while the countries following debt-led growth strategies experienced a higher consumption share of their national income, the reverse was valid in export-led economies and thus their share of consumption got lower. In countries where the consumption share increased, household debt also increased drastically. While household debt declined in Germany from 2000 to 2008 by 11 percentage points of GDP, household debt rose by 26 percentage points in the US and by 28 percentage points in the UK. In peripheral Europe the increases were even sharper (though levels in Mediterranean Europe were usually low). In Ireland it rose by 61, in Spain by 33 percentage points (Stockhammer, 2012).

Countries with current-account deficits are also those with higher increases in household debt. The US and the UK fit this well. This classification also is helpful in understanding developments in Greece, Portugal, Ireland, and Spain. But there are some other countries such as the Netherlands and Denmark which remain outside of this specification. Even though they have had sizable trade surplus for a long time, they have also had a large amount of household debt.

8.5 A debate on global imbalances and the global crisis in 2007–2008

All the concepts that we have used and the developments in the global system that we defined above can help us to find theoretical and empirical links between global imbalances and crises, particularly the global crisis of 2007–2008. Nevertheless, the links between the global imbalances and financial crises are very complicated to follow. This section discusses some of the factors underlying the global imbalances that led to the crisis of 2007–2008.

A country's current-account balance represents the difference between the savings and investment flows in that country. Non-zero current account balances are related to international capital flows—countries running current-account deficits (surpluses) experience capital inflows (outflows). Hence in recent years global current-account imbalances have been associated with substantial capital flows from high-saving emerging economies and commodity producers to lower-saving western countries.

The past decade was characterized by rapid growth in credit in deficit countries (Figure 8.9). Excess savings in emerging Asian countries and commodity exporters may have contributed to this. Bernanke (2005) pointed out that the credit boom in low-saving countries with trade deficits was the result of capital flows from the surplus countries' savings (the saving glut hypothesis).

In the late 1990s, domestic demand in the US and UK grew faster than their national productions. This was probably associated with appreciations of their currencies and the entry of China into the global markets by producing low-cost products. Along with increased domestic consumption and investment in deficit countries like the US and UK, demand for loans also expanded significantly, underpinning the global credit boom. Many loans in the US and UK were used to purchase houses and financial assets, rather than in productive areas. Hence

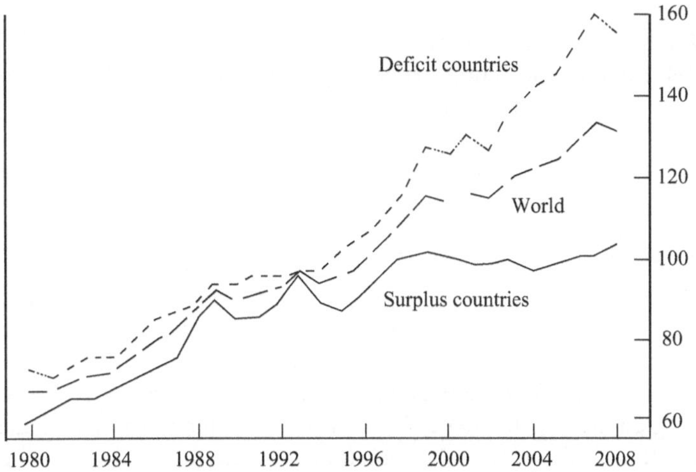

Figure 8.9 Private sector loans (% of GDP).
Source: Astley et al. (2009).

even though capital flows contributed to the growth of credit, they do not seem large enough to take the lion's share of the blame.

In contrast to the growing domestic demand in deficit countries, this remained low in the surplus countries for a long time. Domestic demand in these countries was mainly repressed through stagnant wage policies despite workers' increased productivity; thus wages in these countries lagged behind productivity. In fact this also happened in the US, as in the surplus countries. But in contrast to the US, the surplus countries did not encourage households to increase consumption by borrowing. Instead they were reliant on foreign demand to avoid insufficient domestic demand, and thus exporting their products. Hence the US current account deficit could not be understood only via developments in the US. Even increased loans in deficit countries such as the US or the UK were related to how surplus countries used their surpluses. As Bernanke mentioned, they invested their surpluses and savings in financial markets in advanced countries, especially the US in the 1990s and 2000s, rather than in the productive domestic investment.

In addition to their interaction with macroeconomic factors, capital flows did not only swell credits in the deficit countries. They induced the motivation of financial market participants for "search for yield". Although some of the capital flows were used to fund loans to households and firms directly, the majority were used to purchase existing safe assets, such as government bonds, which caused real long-term interest rates to fall. The low interest rates in turn further motivated financial actors to seek high but risky returns. This led to the development of new complicated financial products and methods that use high leveraged financing. The high returns created a positive environment where everything goes well. This was compatible with perceptions regarding long-standing macroeconomic stability and declining volatilities in financial markets. When this macroeconomic stability perception combined with low inflation environment, the central banks, especially the Fed, followed a loose monetary policy after the dot.com crisis in 2001. In this sense, the confidence to stabilize the power of monetary policy increased and this further spread the perception of stability. The role of capital flows related to global imbalances in this development was significant.

There is considerable evidence linking booms in credit availability to a heightened probability of future financial crisis. However, as Hume and Sentance (2009) point out, several large emerging markets have experienced credit booms without net inflows of capital. For example, there was a trade surplus in Japan in the late 1980s but it experienced a boom–bust cycle in these years. Despite such counterexamples, there is some evidence (stronger for developing countries) that net inflows of private capital may help generate credit booms and, in the presence of potentially fragile financial systems, raise the probability of a crash. This was more evident in emerging countries in the 1990s such as Mexico, Argentina, Turkey and several Asian countries. Along with their fragile financial systems, the credit expansion and appreciation of their currencies generated several crises during this period. For example, Ostry et al. (2011) studied an emerging-market sample from the period 1995–2008, and reached the conclusion that *"one half of credit booms are associated with a capital inflow surge, and of those that ended in a crisis, about 60% are associated with an inflow surge"* (p. 21). Similarly Reinhart and Reinhart (2009) evidence that there is a high connection between trade deficits and crises in developing countries.

Here we should state that large and persistent current-account deficits, while sometimes benign and sustainable, require careful scrutiny. Trade deficits may not be the true source of a problem. This is because there can be capital flows to a country even if it does not have current account deficits. Jorda et al. (2011), studying a large sample of advanced countries over a long time, reached such a conclusion: *"The current account deteriorates in the run-up to normal crises, but the evidence is inconclusive in global crises, possibly because both surplus and deficit countries get embroiled in the crisis"* (p. 372). Therefore the empirical studies are inconclusive on the effects of current-account deficits on crises. That is, trade deficits may not be the real source of a problem. For example, analyzing the case of the Eurozone, we see that current-account imbalances after the introduction of the euro in 1999 were signs of unsustainable trends in countries such as Greece (high governmental deficits), Spain, and Ireland (in both housing bubbles) and Portugal (excessive private borrowing). These countries were mainly financed by the other European countries. These increasing sovereign debts created problems for debtor and creditor countries later.

Therefore, a broader perspective on global financial flows can give us sounder evaluations about the validity of the saving glut hypothesis. There are several respects in which these patterns are not consistent with the view that global current-account imbalances played a critical role in the crisis. First, although global capital flows have increased tremendously since the 1990s—from around

10% of world GDP in 1998 to about 30% in 2007—those have been among the developed countries themselves. Even if the trade share of the developed countries in total world trade declined, the capital flows among them increased drastically (Lane and Milesi-Ferretti, 2008). In comparison, flows between, or from, emerging economies were much smaller. However, the saving glut view sees emerging-market countries as the main drivers of global financial conditions.

Second, it is striking that capital flows to the US mainly originated from European countries rather than emerging countries. About 50% of total capital flows to the US came from Europe in 2007. More strikingly, the UK, which is a trade deficit running country, is the source of more than half of this capital inflow. Furthermore roughly one third of capital inflows to the US came from the Eurozone, which itself had approximately balanced trade. This amount was larger than the capital inflows coming from China and Japan—countries running a large surplus. Therefore the role of these two countries and oil producing countries in financing trade deficits and credit boom in the US are not as significant as mentioned. Furthermore, European investors took on riskier investments in the US financial markets. They invested in toxic securities in addition to government bonds. However, Asian investors were more cautious with their investments. They preferred to purchase mostly government securities despite their lower returns, instead of risky securities presented by the shadow banking system in the US.

Third, current accounts did not play a dominant role in determining financial flows into the United States before the global crisis. It is evident that gross capital flows into and out of the US expanded independently of current-account balances from the early 1990s. The increase in net claims in the US, which mainly indicates the current-account deficit, was about three times smaller than the change in gross claims. Thus global capital flows exceeded movements in capital account balances. Thus, even if there were no trade deficits in the US during the 1990s and 2000s, there would be large foreign inflows into US financial markets.

Fourth, gross capital flows have a more critical role than net capital flows. Thus, net capital flows do not capture the degree of damage in the case where there is disruption in capital flows. The fall in gross capital flows become much more than net capital flows during crises. When the global crisis started in 2008, even though net capital flow declined marginally, the gross capital fell tremendously. This mainly stemmed from the fall in flows between advanced economies. For example, while in 2008 net capital inflows fell only marginally in the US—just about $20 billion—gross inflows fell roughly $1.6 trillion, a decline of approximately 75% from their 2007 level. This decline mainly occurred in the US and Europe, and reversed abruptly in both directions. However, the gross inflows from China and Japan continued. Therefore it seems that capital flows from Asia were a stabilizing force during the crisis (Borio and Disyatat, 2011).

8.6 Concluding remarks

Historically, there has always been an accumulation of current-account surpluses for countries that have been technologically advanced or had valuable commodities. This is regarded as normal or a good imbalance. However, in recent years, the gap between surplus and deficit countries has been widening sizably and becoming detrimental to the world economy.

It is clear that excessive global imbalances can turn into a global threat. However, the solution is hard to find due to the threat's asymmetric character; this arises from the different incentives in current-account deficit and current-account surplus countries. Since there are no self-correction mechanisms to truncate these tendencies, we need global economic policy coordination. This is not just related to trade policies but also associated with immense capital flows. That is, in order to understand the probable detrimental effects of global imbalances, developments in balance payments at global scale should be followed up in terms of both savings–investment perspectives and financial–capital perspectives.

In the short-run, we can propose various measures to overcome current global imbalances. These policy suggestions aim to induce surplus and deficit countries to act in a way to reduce global imbalances. For example, it is advised that the two major surplus countries, China and Germany, need more consumption and investment, respectively. Particularly in China, the saving–consumption imbalance has to be corrected through fundamental changes. And it is suggested that the major deficit economies, including the US, need to boost national savings. For other deficit economies, structural reforms are necessary to improve their competitive power.

In the long-run, there must a sounder and more resilient international monetary system. This requires international cooperation. This is because no country can avoid negative externalities that spread around the world. Making progress requires the adoption of analytical frameworks that stress the externalities involved. That is, no individual country can be safe unless the world as a whole is safe. Such a shift in perspective would be similar to the one that has already occurred in regulation and supervision, from a micro- to a macro-prudential orientation: No individual financial institution can be safe unless the financial system as a whole is safe. Hence to achieve this we can start by constraining risky capital flows. The most desirable and productive forms of capital flow, which are mainly foreign direct investments, should be encouraged. The obstacles to such flows need to be identified and overcome.

Note

1 The US dollar is currently the world's major currency, with approximately two thirds of world official foreign exchange holdings being dollars. But since 2001, the level of foreign exchange reserves held in dollars has been declining; this is mainly because the euro is used more now. Nevertheless, the US dollar is still by far the most important reserve currency in the world. Most of the current-account surpluses and foreign exchange reserves are held by Asian countries. According to Lim (2008), 10 Asian countries hold \$3.4 trillion or 59% of the world's foreign reserves.

Bibliography

Acemoglu, D. (2009). Thoughts on Inequality and the Financial Crisis. *World Bank/IMF Conference on Financial Regulation*. May 2009.

Akerlof, G. and Shiller, R. (2009). *Animal Spirits: How Human Psychology Drives the Economy and Why It Matters for Global Capitalism* (2nd ed.). New Jersey: Princeton University Press.

Argitis, G. and Pitelis, C. (2008). Global Finance and Systemic Instability. *Contributions to Political Economy* 27(1): 1–11.

Astley, M., Giese, J., Hume, M. and Kubelec, C. (2009). Global Imbalances and the Financial Crisis. *Bank of England Quarterly Bulletin* 2009 Q3.

Atkinson, A. B. and Morelli, S. (2015). Inequality and Crises Revisited. *Economia Politica* 32(1): 31–51.

Atkinson, A. B., Piketty, T. and Saez, E. (2011). Top Incomes in the Long Run of History. *Journal of Economic Literature* 49(1): 3–71.

Baran, P. A. and Sweezy, P. M. (1966). *Monopoly Capital: An Essay on American Economic and Social Order*. New York: Monthly Review Press.

Barba, A. and Pivetti, M. (2009). Rising Household Debt: Its Causes and Macroeconomic Implications—A Long-Period Analysis. *Cambridge Journal of Economics* 33(1): 113–137.

Barberis, N. (2011). Psychology and the Financial Crisis of 2007–2008, *SSRN Electronic Journal*.

Barrios, S., Langedijk, S. and Pench, L. (2010). EU Fiscal Consolidation After the Financial Crisis: Lessons from Past Experiences. *VOX, CEPR Policy Portal*. 2 October 2010.

Bello, W. (2006). The Capitalist Conjuncture: Over-Accumulation, Financial Crises, and the Retreat from Globalisation. *Third World Quarterly* 27(8): 1345–1367.

Bellofiore, R. and Halevi, J. (2009). A Minsky Moment? The Subprime Crisis and the New Capitalism. In C. Gnos and L.-P. Rochon (Eds.), *Credit, Money, and Macroeconomic Policy: A Post-Keynesian Approach*. Cheltenham: Edward Elgar: 13–32.

Berger, B. and Wolff, G. (2017). *The Global Decline in the Labour Income Share: Is Capital the Answer to Germany's Current Account Surplus?* Policy Contribution No. 12.

Bernanke, B. S. (2004). Remarks. Meetings of the Eastern Economic Association, Washington, D. C., 20 February 2004.

Bernanke, B. S. (2005). The Global Saving Glut and the US Current Account Deficit. Speech 77, Board of Governors of the Federal Reserve System (US).

Bibow, J. (2010). Financialization of the US Household Sector: The "Subprime Mortgage Crisis" in the US and Global Perspective. Düsseldorf: Macroeconomic Policy Institute.

Blanchard, O. and Milesi-Ferretti, G. M. (2009). Global Imbalances: In Midstream?. IMF State Position Note SPN/09/29. Washington: International Monetary Fund.

Blecker, R. (2011). Global Imbalances and the US Trade Deficit. In Barry Z. Cynamon, Steven M. Fazzari, and Mark Setterfield (Eds.), *After the Great Recession: The Struggle for Economic Recovery and Growth*, Chapter 8. New York: Cambridge University Press: 187–217.

Borio, C. and Disyatat, P. (2011) Global Imbalances and the Financial Crisis: Link or No Link? BIS Working Paper No. 346. Bank for International Settlements.

Bowles, S. Gordon, D. M. and Weisskopf, T. (1984). *Beyond the Waste Land: A Democratic Alternative to Economic Decline.* New York: Doubleday.

Bracke, T., Bussiere, M., Fidora, M. and Straub, R. (2008). A Framework for Assessing Global Imbalances. Occasional Paper Series No. 78. European Central Bank.

Brenner, R. (2006). *The Economics of Global Turbulence.* London: Verso.

Broda, C. (2004). Terms of Trade and Exchange Rate Regimes in Developing Countries. *Journal of International Economics* 63(1): 31–58.

Buiter, W. H. and Rahbari, E. (2012). Debt, Financial Crisis and Economic Growth. Paper presented at the Conference on Monetary Policy and the Challenge of Economic Growth at the South Africa Reserve Bank. Pretoria, South Africa. November 1–2, 2012.

Callinicos, A. (2010). *Bonfire of Illusions: The Twin Crises of the Liberal World.* Cambridge: Polity Press.

Camara, S. (2009). Construction of Series for the Long-Run Analysis of the US Economy: Profitability, Technology of Production and Income Distribution. Reporte de Investigación No. SAEC012. Departamento de Economía, División de Ciencias Sociales y Humanidades, Universidad Autónoma Metropolitana Azcapotzalco, Mexico.

Campbell, J. Y., Giglio, S. and Pathak, P. (2011). Forced Sales and House Prices. *American Economic Review* 101(5): 2108–2131.

Damen, F. (2012). *The Tendency for the Rate of Profit to Fall, the Crisis and Its "Detractors".* Revolutionary Perspectives.

De Antoni, E. (2006). Minsky on Financial Instability. In P. Arestis and M. Sawyer (Eds.), *A Handbook of Alternative Monetary Economics.* Cheltenham: Edward Elgar: 154–171

Dettmann, G. (2014). Global Imbalances, Fractures in the World Monetary System. Doctorate Thesis, University of Verona.

Detzer, D. and Herr, H. (2014). Theories of Financial Crises: An Overview. Working Paper No. 32/2014. Berlin: Institute for International Political Economy.

Diamond, W. D. and Dybvig, P.H. (1983). Bank Runs, Deposit Insurance, and Liquidity. *Journal of Political Economy* 91(3): 401–419.

Dodd, R. (2007). Subprime: Tentacles of a Crisis. *Finance and Development,* 44(4).

Domhoff, G. W. (2006). Wealth, Income and Power. http://sociology.uscs.edu/whorulesamerica/power.html.

Duménil, G. and Lévy, D. (2011). *The Crisis of Neoliberalism,* Cambridge, MA: Harvard University Press.

Duménil, G. and Lévy, D. (2014). The Crisis of the Early 21st Century: Marxian perspectives. In R. Bellofiore and G. Vertova (Eds.), *The Great Recession and the*

Contradictions of Contemporary Capitalism, Chapter 2: 26–49. Aldershot: Edward Elgar Publishing: 26–49.

Dünhaupt, P. (2016). Financialization and the Crises of Capitalism. Working Paper No. 67/2016. Berlin School of Economics and Law and Institute for International Political Economy.

Eggertsson, G. and Krugman, P. (2012). Debt, Deleveraging, and the Liquidity Trap: A Fisher–Minsky–Koo Approach. *The Quarterly Journal of Economics* 127(3): 1469–1513.

Engels, F. (1878). *Anti-Dühring; Herr Eugen Dühring's Revolution in Science.* Moscow: Progress Publishers, 1947.

Epstein, G. (2005). *Financialization and the World Economy.* Cheltenham and Northampton: Edward Elgar.

European Commisison (2009) Commission Staff Working Document, Brussels, SEC(2009) 580.

Federal Reserve of Minneapolis (2007). Interview with Eugene Fama. www.minneapolisfed.org/publications/the–region/interview–with– eugene–fama.

Federal Reserve of St. Louis, https://fred.stlouisfed.org/series.

Fisher, I. (1933). The Debt–Deflation Theory of Great Depressions. *Econometrica* 1(4): 337–357.

Fitoussi, J-P. and Saraceno, F. (2010). Inequality and Macroeconomic Performance. OFCE—Centre de recherche en économie de Sciences Po.

Fitoussi, J-P. and Stiglitz, J. E. (2009). The Ways Out of the Crisis and the Building of a More Cohesive World. Document de Travail. OFCE 2009 (17): 471–482.

Flanders, M. (2015). It's Not a Minsky Moment, It's a Minsky Era, Or: Inevitable Instability. *Econ Journal Watch* 12(1): 84–105.

Fligstein, N. and Goldstein, A. (2010) The Anatomy of the Mortgage Securitization Crisis. In M. Lounsbury and P. Hirsch (Eds.), *Markets on Trial.* Bingley: Emerald Group Publishing: 29–70.

Foster, J. B. and Magdoff, F. (2009). *The Great Financial Crisis: Causes and Consequences.* New York: Monthly Review Press.

Galbraith, J. K. (2012). *Inequality and Instability: A Study of the World Economy Just Before the Great Crisis.* Oxford University Press.

Garling, T., Kirchler, E., Lewis, A. and Van Raaij, F. (2009). Psychology, Financial Decision Making, and Financial Crises. *Psychological Science in the Public Interest* 10(1): 1–47.

Garnaut, R., Ligang S. L. and Woo, T. W. (2011). *China's New Place in a World in Crisis: Economic, Geopolitical and Environmental Dimensions*. ANU E Press.

Goda, T., Onaran, Ö. and Stockhammer, E. (2014). A Case for Redistribution? Income Inequality and Wealth Concentration in the Recent Crisis. Greenwich Political Economy Research Centre Working Paper No. GPERC05.

Graham, B. (2006). *Intelligent Investor: The Definitive Book on Value Investing. A Book of Practical Counsel (Revised Edition).* New York: Harper Business Essentials.

Greenwood, R. and Hanson, S. (2010). Issuer Quality and Corporate Bond Returns. *Review of Financial Studies* 26(6): 1483–1525.

Gruber, J. W. and Kamin, S. B. (2005). Explaining the Global Pattern of Current Account. International Finance Discussion Paper No. 846. Board of Governors of the Federal Reserve System.

Hall, R. E. (1978). Stochastic Implications of the Life Cycle-Permanent Income Hypothesis: Theory and Evidence. *Journal of Political Economy* 86(6): 971–987.

Hall, R. E. (2011). The Long Slump. *American Economic Review* 101(2): 431–469.

Harman, C. (2010). *Zombie Capitalism: Global Crisis and the Relevance of Marx*. London: Haymarket Books.
Harvey, D. (2005). *A Brief History of Neoliberalism*. Oxford: Oxford University Press.
Harvey, D. (2015). Crisis Theory and the Falling Rate of Profit. In Turan Subasat and John Weeks (Eds.), *The Great Meltdown of 2008: Systemic, Conjunctural or Policy-created?* Edward Elgar Publishing Limited: 1–30.
Hayek, F. A. (1931). *Prices and Production*. London: Routledge.
Hayek, F. A. (1941). *The Pure Theory of Capital*. Chicago: University of Chicago Press.
Hilferding, R. (1910). *Finance Capital: A Study of the Latest Phase of Capitalist Development*. London: Routledge & Kegan Paul.
Hobson, J. A. (1896). *The Problem of the Unemployed*. London: Methuen & Co.
Hobson, J. A. (1969). *The Industrial System*. New York: Kelley.
Huang, Y., Peng, K. and Shen, M. (2009). Macroeconomic Performance Amid Global Crisis. In Ross Garnaut, Ligang Song and Wing Thye Woo (Eds.), *China's New Place in a World in Crisis*. ANU E-Press: 121–136
Hume, M. and Sentance, A. (2009). The Global Credit Boom: Challenges for Macroeconomics and Policy. *Journal of International Money and Finance* 28(8): 1426–1461.
ILO (2010). Global Wage Report 2010/11: Wage Policies in Times of Crisis. Geneva: International Labour Organisation.
ILO (2015). Income Inequality and Labour Income Share in G20 Countries: Trends, Impacts and Causes. Geneva: International Labour Organisation.
IMF (2010). World Economic Outlook, Recovery, Risk, and Rebalancing, Washington: International Monetary Fund.
IMF (2012). Dealing with Household Debt. In Growth Resuming, Dangers Remain. World Economic Outlook. Washington: International Monetary Fund.
Inside Mortgage Finance (2009). Mortgage Market Statistical Annual.
Johnson, S. (2011). Did the Poor Cause the Crisis? Project–Syndicate. www.projectsyndicate.org/commentary/johnson16/English. Accessed 20 March 2016.
Jones, C. (2015). Pareto and Piketty: The Macroeconomics of Top Income and Wealth Inequality. *Journal of Economic Perspectives* 29(1): 29–46.
Jorda, O., Schularick, M. and Taylor, A. M. (2011). Financial Crises, Credit Booms, and External Imbalances: 140 Years of Lessons. *IMF Economic Review* 59(2): 340–378.
Jorda, O., Schularick, M. and Taylor, A. M. (2013), Sovereigns versus Banks: Crises, Causes and Consequences. CEPR Discussion Paper 9678.
Kahneman, D. (2003). A Perspective on Judgment and Choice Mapping Bounded Rationality. *American Psychologist* 58: 697–720.
Kahneman, D. and Tversky, A. (1979). Prospect Theory: An Analysis of Decision Under Risk. *Econometrica* 47(2): 263–291.
Kahneman, D. and Tversky, A. (2000). *Choices, Values and Frames*. New York: Cambridge University Press.
Kamalodin, S. (2011). Asset Bubbles, Financial Crises and the Role of Human Behaviour. Rabobank Economic Research Department.
Karabarbounis, L. and Neiman, B. (2013). The Global Decline of the Labor Share. NBER Working Paper No. 19136. National Bureau of Economic Research.
Kennickell, A. B. (2009). Ponds and Streams: Wealth and Income in the US, 1989 to 2007. Finance and Economics Discussion Series 2009–2013. Board of Governors of the Federal Reserve System.

Keynes, J. M. (1936). *The General Theory of Employment, Interest, and Money.* London: Macmillan.

Keynes, J. M. (1937). The General Theory. *Quarterly Journal of Economics*. 51: 209–223.

Kindleberger, C. P. and Aliber, R. Z. (2011). *Manias, Panics, and Crashes: A History of Financial Crises.* London: Palgrave Macmillan.

Kotz, D. M. (2009). The Financial and Economic Crisis of 2008: A Systemic Crisis of Neoliberal Capitalism. *Review of Radical Political Economics* 41(3): 305–317.

Kotz, D. M. (2011). Financialization and Neoliberalism. In G. Teeple and S. McBride (Eds.), *Relations of Global Power: Neoliberal Order and Disorder.* Toronto: University of Toronto Press: 1–18.

Kotz, D. M. (2013). Social Structures of Accumulation, the Rate of Profit and Economic Crises. In Jeannette Wicks-Lim and Robert Pollin (Eds.), *Capitalism on Trial: Explorations in the Tradition of Thomas E. Weisskopf.* Cheltenham: Edward Elgar Publications: 335–349.

Kotz, D. M. (2016). The Roots of the Current Economic Crisis: Capitalism, Forms of Capitalism, Policies and Contingent Events. In Turan Subasat (Ed.), *The Great Financial Meltdown Systemic, Conjunctural or Policy Created?* New Directions in Modern Economics Series.

Kotz, D. M. and McDonough, T. (2010). Global Neoliberalism and the Contemporary Social Structure of Accumulation. In Terrence McDonough, Michael Reich, and David M. Kotz (Eds.), *Contemporary Capitalism and Its Crises: Social Structure of Accumulation Theory for the Twenty First Century.* Cambridge: Cambridge University Press: 93–120.

Kregel, J. (2008). Minsky's Cushions of Safety: Systemic Risk and the Crisis in the US Subprime Mortgage Market. Public Policy Brief No. 93. Annandale-on-Hudson, New York: The Levy Economics Institute of Bard College.

Krippner, G. R. (2005). The Financialization of the American Economy. *Socio-Economic Review* 3(2): 173–208.

Krugman, P. (2009). How Did Economists Get It So Wrong? Column in the New York Times Magazine. www.nytimes.com/2009/09/06/magazine/06Economic–t.html.

Krugman, P. (2012). *End This Depression Now.* New York: W. W. Norton.

Kumhof, M. and Rancière, R. (2010). Inequality, Leverage and Crises. IMF Working Paper No. 268. International Monetary Fund.

Laeven, T. (2013). Financial Innovation and Shadow Banking. In V. V. Acharya, T. Beck, D. D. Evanoff, G. G. Kaufman and R. Portes (Eds.), *The Social Value of the Financial Sector: Too Big to Fail or just Too Big?* World Scientific: 229–235.

Lane, P. and Milesi-Ferretti, G. M. (2008). The Drivers of Financial Globalization. *American Economic Review: Papers and Proceedings* 98(2): 327–332.

Lapavitsas, C. (2011). Theorizing Financialization. *Work, Employment and Society* 25(4): 611–626.

Lim, M. (2008) Old Wine in A New Bottle: Subprime Mortgage Crisis—Causes and Consequences. Working paper No.532. Levy Institute of Bard College.

Lin, J. Y. (2013). *Against the Consensus: Reflections on the Great Recession.* Cambridge: Cambridge University Press.

Lin, J. Y. and Treichel, V. (2012). The Crisis in the Eurozone: Did the Euro Contribute to the Evolution of the Crisis?. World Bank Policy Research Working Paper No. 6127.

Llewellyn, D. T. (2009). Financial Innovation and the Economics of Banking and the Financial System. In L. Anderloni, D. T. Llewellyn and R. H. Schmidt (Eds.), *Financial Innovation in Retail and Corporate Banking*. Cheltenham: Edward Elgar: 1–38.

Lowenstein, R. (2000). *When Genius Failed: The Rise and Fall of Long-Term Capital Management*. New York: Random House.

Luxemburg, R. (1913). *The Accumulation of Capital*. London: Routledge and Kegan Paul.

Lysandrou, P. (2011). Global Inequality as one of the Root Causes of the Financial Crisis: A Suggested Explanation. *Economy and Society* 40(3): 323–344.

Magdoff, F. and Foster, J. B. (2014). Stagnation and Financialization: The Nature of the Contradiction. *Monthly Review* 66(1).

Magdoff, H and Sweezy, P. (1987). *Stagnation and the Financial Explotion*. New York: Monthly Review Press.

Malthus, T. (1798). *An Essay on the Principle of Population*. London: Electronic Scholarly Publishing Project.

Marx, K. (1857). *Grundrisse: Foundations of the Critique of Political Economy*. London: Penguin Classics.

Marx, K. (1867), *Capital : A Critique of Political Economy Vol. 1*. London: Penguin Classics.

Marx, K. (1885) *Capital : A Critique of Political Economy Vol. 2*. London: Penguin Classics.

Marx, K. (1894). *Capital: A Critique of Political Economy, Vol. 3*. London: Penguin Classics.

McDonough, T., Reich, M. and Kotz, D. (2010). *Introduction: Social Structure of Accumulation Theory for the 21st Century*. New York: Cambridge University Press.

McKinsey (2010). *Equity Analysts: Still too Bullish*. McKinsey.

Milanovic, B. (2010). *The Haves and the Have–nots: A Brief and Idiosyncratic History of Global Inequality*. New York, Basic Books.

Minsky, H. P. (1975). *John Maynard Keynes*. New York: Columbia University Press.

Minsky, H. P. (1977). The Financial Instability Hypothesis: An Interpretation of Keynes and an Alternative to "Standard" Theory. *Nebraska Journal of Economics and Business* 16(1): 5–16.

Minsky, H. P. (1982). *Can It Happen Again? Essays on Instability and Finance*. New York: M. E. Sharpe.

Minsky, H. P. (1985). The Financial Instability Hypothesis: A Restatement. In P. Arestis, T. Skouras (Eds.), *Post-Keynesian Economic Theory: A Challenge to Neoclassical Economics*, 24–55. Brighton: Wheatsheaf Books.

Minsky, H. P. (1986). *Stabilizing and Unstable Economy*. New Haven: Yale University Press.

Minsky, H. P. (1992). The Capital Development of the Economy and The Structure of Financial Institutions. Working Paper No. 72. Annandale–on–Hudson, New York: Levy Economics Institute of Bard College.

Minsky, H. P. (1993). Schumpeter and Finance. In Salvatore Biasco, Alessandro Roncaglia and Michele Salvati (Eds.), *Market and Institutions in Economic Development: Essays in Honor of Paulo Sylos Labini*. New York: St. Martin's Press: 103–115.

Minsky, H. P. (1996). Uncertainty and the Institutional Structure of Capitalist Economies. Working Paper No. 155. Annandale–on–Hudson, NY: Levy Economics Institute of Bard College.

Minsky H. P. (2008). Securitization. Jerome Levy Economics Institute Policy Note No. 2.

Montgomery, H. (1997). Naturalistic Decision Making. Proceedings of the Subjective Probability, Utility and Decision Making Conference 20–23 June 2017.

Montgomery, H. (2011). The Financial Crisis—Lessons for Europe from Psychology. Swedish Institute for European Policy Studies Report No:1, Stockholm.

Moseley, F. (1999). The Decline of the Rate of Profit in the Post-War United States: Due to Increased Competition or Increased Unproductive Labour? Historical Materialism 4.

Mummery, A. F. and Hobson, J. A. (1889). *The Physiology of Industry: Being an Exposure of Certain Fallacies in Existing Theories of Economics.* London: John Murray.

New Economics Foundation (2014). *Financialization and Inequality: A Dangerous Mix.* London: New Economics Foundation.

Noah, T. (2012). *The Great Divergence: America's Growing Inequality Crisis and What We Can Do About It.* New York: Bloomsbury.

Obstfeld, M. and Rogoff, K. (2010). Global Imbalances and the Financial Crisis: Products of Common Causes. Federal Reserve Bank of San Francisco, Asia Economic Policy Conference 18–20 October 2009: 131–172.

OECD (2011). Divided We Stand. Paris: Organisation for Economic Co-operation and Development.

OECD (2012). Employment Outlook 2012. Paris: Organisation for Economic Co-operation and Development.

Okishio, N. (1961). Technical Changes and the Rate of Profit. *Kobe University Economic Review* 7: 85–99.

Ostry, J. D., Ghosh, A. R., Habermeier, K., Laeven, L., Chamon, M., Qureshi, M. S. and Kokenyne, A. (2011). Managing Capital Inflows: What Tools to Use? IMF Staff Discussion Note, April. Washington: International Monetary Fund.

Palley, T. I. (2002). Economic Contradictions Coming Home to Roost? Does the US Economy Face Long-Term Aggregate Demand Generation Problem? *Journal of Post Keynesian Economics* 25(1): 9–32.

Palley, T. (2009). A Theory of Minsky Super-Cycles and Financial Crises. IMK Working Paper No. 5/2009.

Palley, T. I. (2010a). America's Exhausted Paradigm: Macroeconomic Causes of the Financial Crisis and Great Recession. *New School Economic Review* 4(1): 15–43.

Palley, T. I. (2010b). The Limits of Minsky's Financial Instability Hypothesis as an Explanation of the Crisis. *Monthly Review* 61(11).

Palley, T. I. (2012). *From Financial Crisis to Stagnation: The Destruction of Shared Prosperity and the Role of Economics.* Cambridge: Cambridge University Press.

Palley, T. (2015). Theory of Global Imbalances: Mainstream Economics vs. Structural Keynesianism. *Review of Keynesian Economics* 3(1): 45–62.

Phillips, K. (2002). Too Much Wealth, Too Little Democracy. *Challenge* 45: 6–20.

Pigou, A. C. (1943). The Classical Stationary State. *Economic* 53(212): 343–351.

Piketty, T. (2014). *Capital in the 21st Century.* Cambridge: Harvard University Press.

Piketty, T. and Saez, E. (2006). The Evolution of Top Incomes: A Historical and International Perspective. *American Economic Review* 96(2): 200–205.

Piketty, T. and Saez, E. (2013). Top Incomes and the Great Recession: Recent Evolutions and Policy Implications. *IMF Economic Review* 61(3): 456–478.

Rajan, R. G. (2005). Global Imbalances—An assessment. International Monetary Fund website. 25 October 2005. www.imf.org/en/News/Articles/2015/09/28/04/53/sp102505. Accessed 4 January 2016.

Rajan, R. G. (2010). *Fault Lines: How Hidden Fractures Still Threaten the World Economy.* Princeton: Princeton University Press.

Rapp, D. (2009). *Bubbles, Booms and Busts: The Rise and Fall of Financial Assets.* Copernicus Books.

Reed, H. and Himmelweit, J. M. (2012). Where Have All the Wages Gone? Lost Pay and Profits Outside Financial Services. TUC London. www.tuc.org.uk/sites/default/files/tucfiles/where_have_all_the_wages_gone_touchstone_extras_-2012.pdf. Accessed 14 April 2016.

Reich, R. (2010). *Aftershock: The Next Economy and America's Future.* New York: Knopf.

Reinhart, C. M. and Reinhart, V. R. (2009). Capital Flow Bonanzas: An Encompassing View of the Past and Present. In J. A. Frankel and C. Pissarides (Eds.), *International Seminar on Macroeconomics 2008.* Chicago: University of Chicago Press: 9–62.

Reinhart, C. M., Reinhart, V. R. and Rogoff, K. S. (2012). Debt Overhangs: Past and Present. Working Paper No. 18015. National Bureau of Economic Research.

Reinhart, C. M. and Rogoff, K. S. (2009). *This Time is Different: Eight Centuries of Financial Folly.* Princeton: Princeton University Press.

Reinhart, C. and Rogoff, K.S. (2010). Growth in a Time of Debt. *American Economic Review: Papers & Proceedings* 100: 573–578.

Reinhart, C. M. and Rogoff, K. S. (2011). From Financial Crash to Debt Crisis. *American Economic Review* 101(5): 1676–1706.

Reinhart, C. M., Rogoff, K. S. and Savastano, M. A. (2003). Debt Intolerance. Brookings Papers on Economic Activity 2003 No. 1.

Resnick, S. and Wolff, R. (2010). The Economic Crisis: A Marxian Interpretation. *A Journal of Economics, Culture & Society* 22(2): 170–186.

Rodbertus, J. K. (1898). *Overproduction and Crises*, translated by Julia Franklin, with an Introduction by J. B. Clark. New York: A. M. Kelley.

Romer, C. (2002). Back to the Future: Lessons from the Great Depression. IMF Survey, December 2002.

Roubini, N. (2011). The Instability of Inequality. Project–Syndicate. www.project–syndicate.org/commentary/the–instability–of–inequality.

Roubini, N. and Mihm, S. (2010). *Crisis Economics.* New York: The Penguin Press.

Saez, E. and Zucman, G. (2014). Who Benefits from Tax Expenditures on Capital? Evidence on Capital Income and Wealth Concentration. Working Paper Series, IRS Statistics of Income.

Shaikh, A. (1978). An Introduction to the History of Crisis Theories. The US Capitalism in Crisis. New York: URPE.

Shaikh, A. (1987). The Falling Rate of Profit and the Economic Crisis in the US. In R. Cherry et al. (Eds.), *The Imperiled Economy*, Book I, Union for Radical Political Economy: 115–126.

Shaikh A. (2011). The First Great Depression of the 21st Century. *Socialist Register* 47(47): 44–63.

Sherif, M. (1935). A Study of Some Social Factors in Perception. *Archives of Psychology*, 187.

Shiller, R. (2005). *Irrational Exuberance.* Princeton: Princeton University Press.

Shiller, R. (2008). *The Subprime Solution How Today's Global Financial Crisis Happened, and What to Do About It?* New Jersey: Princeton University Press.

Shiller, R. (2012). *Finance and the Good Society.* Princeton: Princeton University Press.

Simon, H. (1955). A Behavioral Model of Rational Choice. *Quarterly Journal of Economics* 69(1): 99–118.

Snowden, K. A. (2010). The Anatomy of a Residential Mortgage Crisis: A Look Back to the 1930s. NBER Working Paper No. 16244. National Bureau of Economic Research.

Stiglitz, J. E. (2009). The Global Crisis, Social Protection and Jobs. *International Labour Review* 148(1–2): 1–13.

Stockhammer, E. (2010). Financialization and the Global Economy. Working Paper No. 242. Political Economy Research Institute.

Stockhammer, E. (2012). Financialization, Income Distribution and the Crisis. Investigación Económica / Escuela Nacional de Economía, Universidad Nacional Autónoma de México 71(279): 39–70.

Sweezy, P. M. (1942). *Theory of Capitalist Development: Principles of Marxian Political Economy.* New York: Oxford University Press.

Sweezy, P. M. (1994). The Triumph of Financial Capital. Monthly Review. www.monthlyreview.org/940600sweezy.php.

Taleb, N. N. (2007). *The Black Swan: The Impact of the Highly Improbable.* New York: Random House.

The US Congress Joint Economic Committee (2010). Income Inequality and the Great Recession.

Tobin, J. (1980). *Asset Accumulation and Economic Activity: Reflections on Contemporary Macroeconomic Theory.* Oxford: Basil Blackwell.

Tomz, M. and Wright, M. L. J. (2007). Do Countries Default in "Bad Times"? *Journal of the European Economic Association* 5(2–3): 352–360.

Tooze, A. (2018). *Crashed: How a Decade of Financial Crises Changed the World.* London: Penguin Books.

Tridico, P. (2012). Financial Crisis and Global Imbalances: Its Labor Market Origins and the Aftermath. *Cambridge Journal of Economics* 36(1): 17–42.

Ueno, M. (2001). Personal Interview Through June to August. He has been working in the Japanese financial sector since 1990, and was Vice President, Controller Division at PT Bank LTCB Central Asia (A Japanese–Indonesian Bank in Indonesia) in 1997–1998.

Vandemoortele, M. (2009). Within-Country Inequality, Global Imbalances and Financial Instability. Desk Study for Netherlands Ministry of Foreign Affairs, Overseas Development Institute, London.

Van Den Hauwe, L. M. P. (2014). Understanding Financial Instability: Minsky Versus the Austrians. Working paper No. 61832.

Veblen, T. (1899). *Theory of the Leisure Class.* Oxford University Press.

Wallerstein, I. (2003). *The Decline of American Power: The US in a Chaotic World,* New York: The New Press.

Warren, E. and Warren T. A. (2004). *The Two-Income Trap.* New York: Basic Books.

Wisman, J. D. and Baker, B. (2011). Rising Inequality and the Financial Crises of 1929 and 2008. Working Paper No. 2011–01. American University, Department of Economics.

Wolf, M. (2014). *The Shifts and the Shocks: What We've Learned—and Have Still to Learn—from the Financial Crisis.* London: Penguin Books.

Wolff, E. N. (2010). Recent Trends in Household Wealth in the United States—Rising Debt and the Middle-Class Squeeze—an Update To 2007. Economics Working Paper No. 589. The Levy Economics Institute.

Wolfson, M. and Kotz, D. (2010). A Reconceptualization of Social Structure of Accumulation. In Terrence McDonough, Michael Reich and David M. Kotz (Eds.),

Contemporary Capitalism and Its Crises: Social Structure of Accumulation Theory for the 21st Century. New York: Cambridge University Press: 72–90.

World Bank (1993). *The East Asian Miracle: Economic Growth and Public Policy.* Oxford: Oxford University Press.

Wray, L. R. (2009). The Rise and Fall of Money Manager Capitalism: A Minskian Approach. *Cambridge Journal of Economics* 33(4): 807–828.

Index